SOPRINTENDENZA ARCHEOLOGICA DI ROMA

On the cover

Hall of Achilles at Skyros,
detail of the panel on the vault
depicting Achilles among the
daughters of the king Lykomedes

DOMVS AVREA

Irene Iacopi

ELECTA

Electa per i beni culturali
Scholarly co-ordination
by Rosanna Cappelli

Published by Electa, Milan
Elemond Editori Associati

TABLE OF CONTENTS

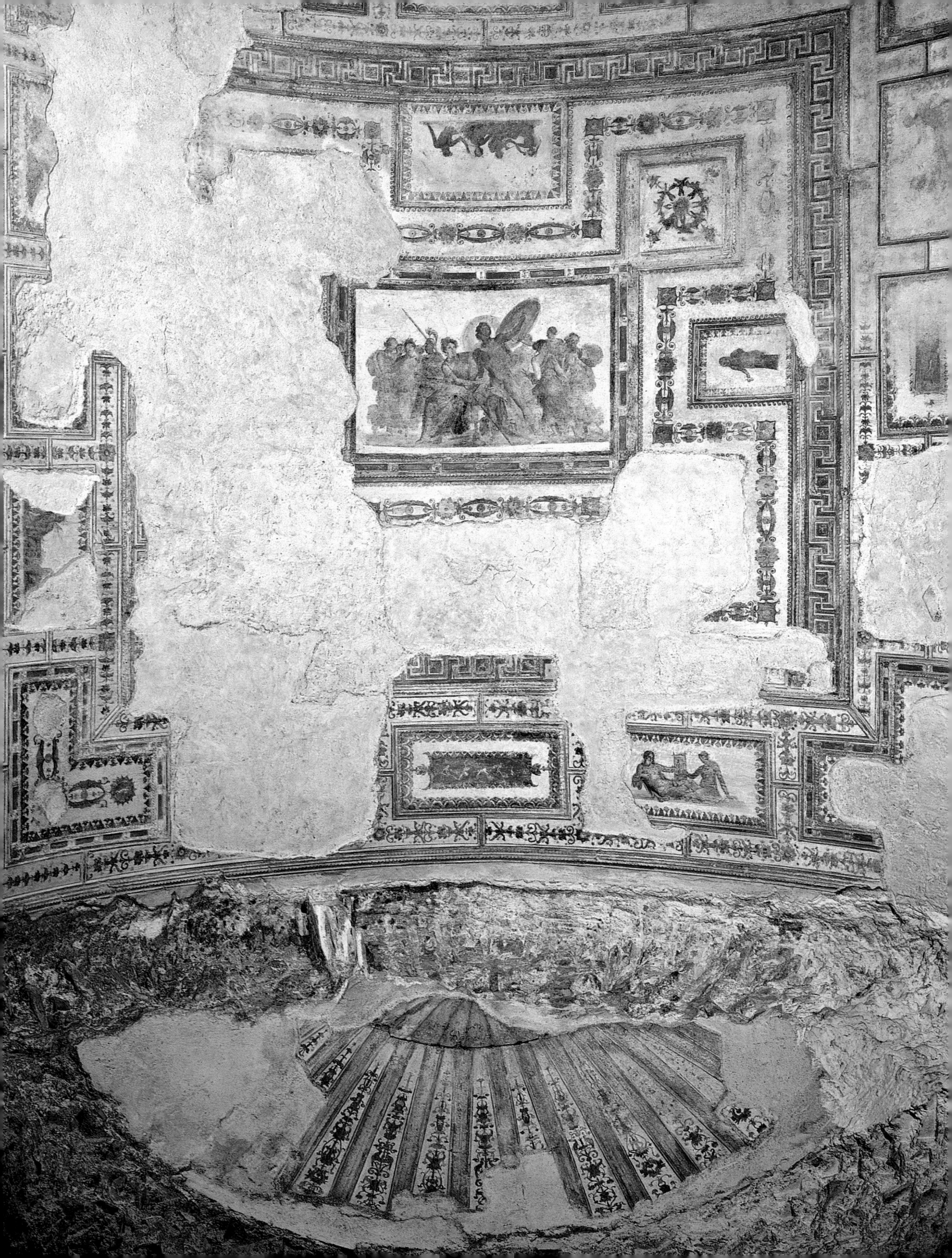

THE PALACE COMPLEX

The discovery towards the end of the 15th century of Nero's *Domus* on the Oppian hill can be seen as an event of great importance for the artistic culture of the Renaissance. Its decorative schemes full of fantastic, unreal images gave life to a new artistic style that was ornamental in character, and allowed it to flourish. From the beginning this new style consisted of ornate depictions of pilasters, pedestals, and billowing vaults, and through the course of the sixteenth century it became dominant, covering vaults and walls in their entirety.

Sculptors and painters made their way deep into the 'grottoes' and were fascinated by the fanciful paintings that densely adorned the vaults. From their raised positions in the earth-filled vaults, the artists were able to admire from close up the paintings' refined, miniaturistic quality. They found in them an inexhaustible source of inspiration for the decoration of papal palaces, chapels and aristocratic villas with new and distinctive artistic forms.

The buried frescoes stimulated Raphael and Giovanni da Udine, who brought the new artistic style to the peak of its perfection. Their interest is echoed in Vasari's comments: 'some underground rooms were discovered, all buried, and full of grotesque images, of small figures and narrative scenes, with ornamental elements of moulded plaster. Giovanni and Raphael went to see them, and they were both amazed at the freshness, beauty and quality of these works of art.... And so these *grotesques*.... entered, as it were, into the heart and head of Giovanni, who set himself to study them. He was not content to draw and to record just one vault or two.' Thus the decorative schemes that these men carried out in *Logge* (galleries), such as that in the Stufetta of Cardinal Bibbiena in the Vatican and in the Villa Madama, aimed at complete imitation of the ancient paintings. They recalled the composition of Nero's cryptoporticus and covered the entire surface of the architectural structure with grotesques.

These 'explorations' of the *Domus*, which the men of the late 15th century and the Renaissance carried out by torch-light, followed a route which would be retraced through the centuries. This can be seen by the many names left on its vaults by artists, architects and engravers, among them Ghirlandaio, Pinturicchio, Martin van Heemskerck, Polidoro da Caravaggio, Giovanni da Udine, Francesco di Giorgio Martini, 'Antonio da Feltro', Karol van Mander and Bartolomeo Spranger. Beyond these explorations, the

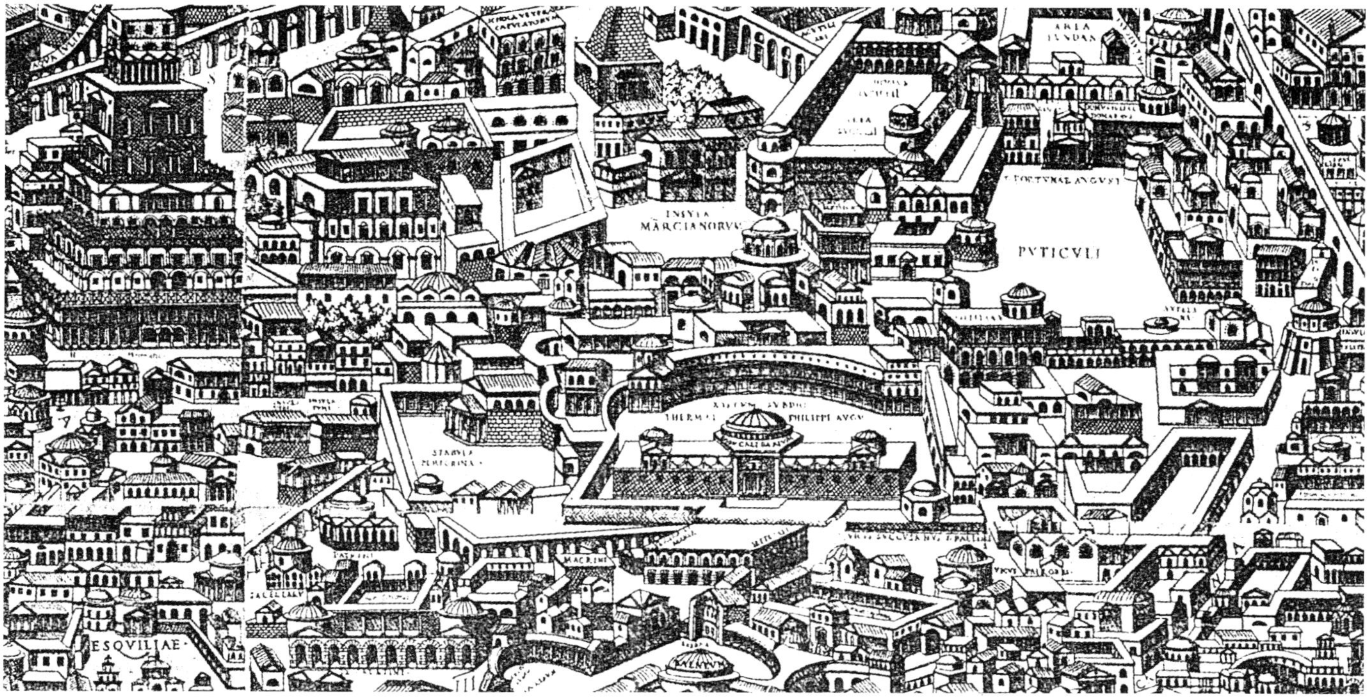

1. Hall of Achilles at Skyros, general view of the decoration of the vault and the apse

2. The Baths of Titus in the ancient map of Rome by Pirro Ligorio (1561)

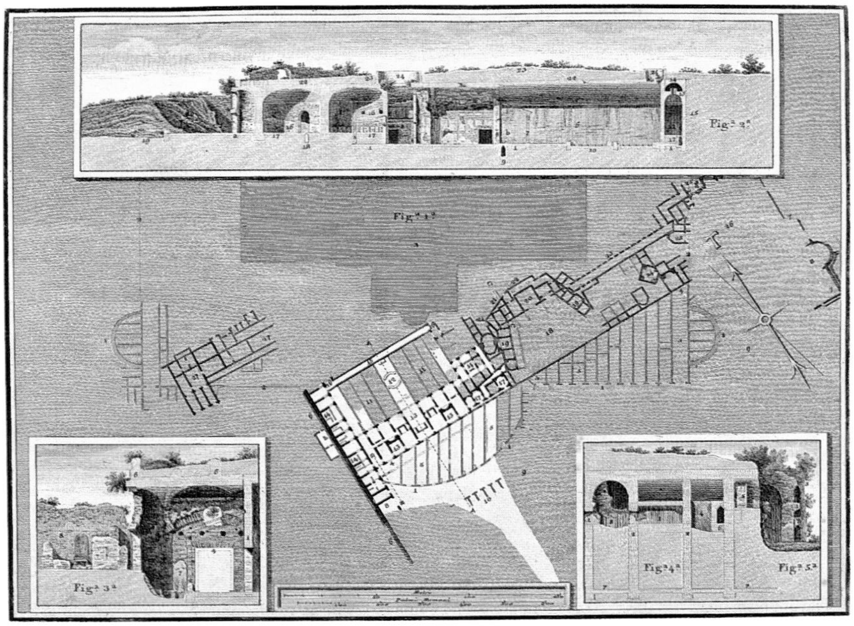

3. Plan and section of the pavilion on the Oppian hill after the excavations of De Romanis (1822)

first excavations to open up the 'Esquiline rooms' took place in the 18th century. Until that time the site was identified as that of the Baths of Titus, even though it had already been mentioned by its correct name as early as the 16th century, by Raphael and by painters like Francisco de Hollanda.
After the excavations which the architect Cameron conducted in 1758-1769, there followed in 1774 those of the antiquarian Ludovico Mirri. These revealed the plan of sixteen rooms in the west wing, and the abbott Giuseppe Carletti produced illustrations of the paintings which were discovered.
Still in the west wing, the explorations of the architect Antonio De Romanis in 1811-1814 added another fifty rooms to those which had been opened up by Mirri. De Romanis drew plans and wrote critical descriptions of the structures he found, and established a relative chronology for them. Just over a century later, in 1912-1914, Antonio Muñoz began excavations to reveal the east wing of the *Domus*, in particular parts of the building behind the great pentagonal court. F. Weege, oversaw the relevant archaeological publication, also had accurately drawn reproductions made of the decoration (of the great cryptoporticus), along with a plan showing the extent of the explorations.
The excavation of the east wing continued in the 1940s and 1950s. In this period the great cryptoporticus (92) and the *nymphaeum* of Polyphemus were uncovered. Excavations carried out in the 1970s in the north-east wing of the *Domus*, at the level of the gardens on the Oppian hill, led to the discovery of remains of *nymphaea* and peristyles relating to the upper floor of the building complex.
Although many areas of the palace remain buried, Nero's structure is known to us through the evidence of 150 rooms. It was never completed (nor was the painted decoration), and reveals the existence of multiple phases of construction chronologically close together. These cannot always be attributed to second thoughts and changes in the course of construction; it incorporated and often adapted structures pre-dating the great fire of AD 64, which led to the construction of the new palace complex.
It was this fire, more or less on the tenth anniversary of Nero's reign, which devastated the whole city of Rome, destroying ten thousand *insulae* (apartment buildings). It gave the emperor the chance to undertake, if only partially, the grandiose project of urban renewal in Rome, with its narrow city quarters, which he had already envisaged at the time of his accession to the throne.
The new Rome, *Neropolis* (Suetonius, *Nero* LV; Tacitus, *Annals* XV, XL, 3) was to be a monument to the glory and eternal memory of the name of Nero, brought into being through monumental architectural structures and regular urban planning with broad vistas. This urban planning took its form from the grandiose plan designed by Deinocrates for the royal city of Alexandria in Egypt. This, the 'first city of the world' had been founded by Alexander of Macedon, with whom Nero, 'the new Alexander' wished constantly to be compared. The 'new Rome' was to provide a proper setting for the real centre of political power in the Roman empire.
Nero's urban redevelopment was eventually limited, and was considered the product of the caprices and megalomania of a philhellene emperor. Nevertheless, the historians Tacitus and Suetonius attest the validity of the rational principles on which the *nova Urbs* ('new Rome') was to be founded, in contrast to the poorly constructed *vetus Urbs* ('old Rome').
The innovative project of a new city along the lines of the great metropolitan centres of the Hellenistic east encompassed the widening of streets and squares, the use of architectural forms such as lengthy porticoed facades and grid-planned avenues, and the rationalisation of domestic construction. This project necessarily required the adoption of broad spatiality and daring techniques of construction in order to do justice to the greatness of a *princeps* (emperor) who had now taken on the character of a Hellenistic king.
Like the rulers of Hellenistic cities, Nero took over a huge area of the centre of his city to build the *Domus Aurea*, a palace appropriate to the majesty of his imperial role. Nero had been aware of a need for such a structure when he first came to the throne and began to build a lavish residence, the *Domus Transitoria*. This first palace, which served as a 'passage-way' between the property of the Claudian family on the Palatine and imperial possessions on the Esquiline and which was destroyed by the fire, was itself innovative in its decorative schemes and architectural

forms, and at the same time splendid and refined. These characteristics can be seen on a greater scale in the *Domus Aurea*, and their presence enables us to see, in both palaces, the same individual creative spirit.

Ancient writers unanimously cite the new *Domus* as an expression of pomp and of the immoderate exercise of power. It was realised in accord with a grandiose plan which made this imperial residence a unique phenomenon unequalled in its day, not only because of the area of ground it covered (80 hectares) but also because of the originality of its conception.

Equalled only by Hadrian's villa at Tivoli, there is surely no comparison for the *Domus Aurea* even in the greatest *praedia* (rural estates) and suburban villas, luxurious retreats where Romans indulged in leisure activities such as hunting and fishing, and which often were provided with zoological gardens, atria, cryptoporticus and pools, with extensive meadows/lawns and pathways, vineyards and kitchen gardens.

Indeed, one feature of the *Domus Aurea*, its boundless parkland in an urban setting, can be compared only to the palaces of the Achaemenid Persian kings, the *paradeisoi*, the great gardens and royal quarters of Alexandria, which provided Nero with a model of luxury and of theocratic monarchy. From this derived Nero's conception of sun-king, by which he came to identify himself, as Alexander had already done, with Helios, the sun-god who ruled the universe.

The palace complex occupied the heart of the city, and, with deliberate ideological intent, one of its most sacred sites, namely that of the ancient *Septimontium*. It covered the area from the Palatine to the Esquiline and Caelian hills, the Velia (where the entrance hall of the palace was located, adorned with a triple portico 300 metres long and a colossal gilded bronze statue of Nero) and the Oppian hill. The palace lay in a setting of gardens, vineyards, woodland and even areas set aside for productive activities such as agriculture. As Suetonius (*Nero*, 31) recorded 'there were villas/farms with fields, vineyards and pastures, full of every kind of animal, domesticated and wild.'

A lake, "almost like a sea" was situated in the low-lying area or valley (where the massive Flavian amphitheatre was built subsequently), surrounded by the pavilions into which the complex was organised. These were located within a fantasy landscape, set between porticoes and peristyles in vistas akin to stage sets, such as those which can be seen in Pompeian second style paintings.

The visible archaeological evidence consists of the ample remains of structures from the public *Palatium* on the Palatine and of the *Domus* on the Oppian hill, and, in the valley bounded by the Palatine, Velia and Oppian, rectilinear porticoed streets, long axial boulevards, terraces and porticoes overlooking the lake, the remains of a large entrance hall to the *Domus*, porticoes leading uphill from the *Sacra Via* towards the Palatine, and the substructures of an impressive *nymphaeum* on the Caelian. These enable us to form an impression of the huge scale of the plan of the palace, in complete harmony with the absolutist ideology of the *princeps*. Distancing himself from the political stance of his predecessors, he did not hesitate to appropriate and privatise for exclusively imperial

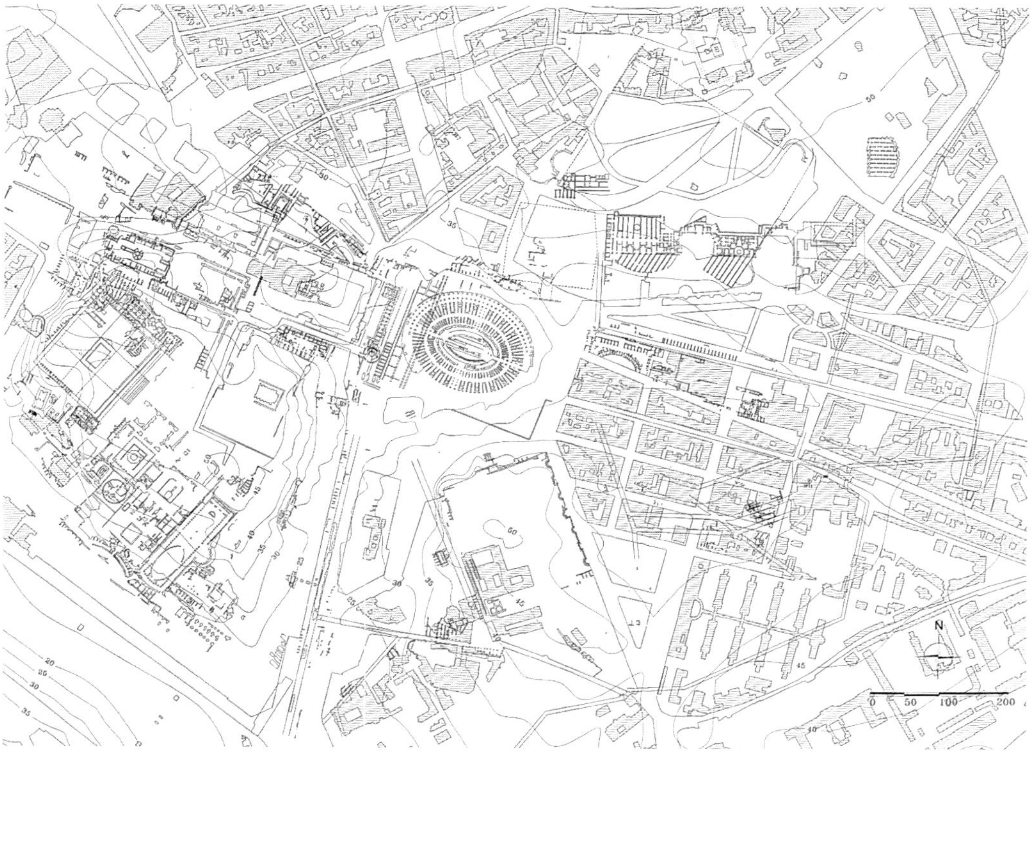

4. Plan of the relevant buildings of the palace complex of the Domus Aurea *(in red)*

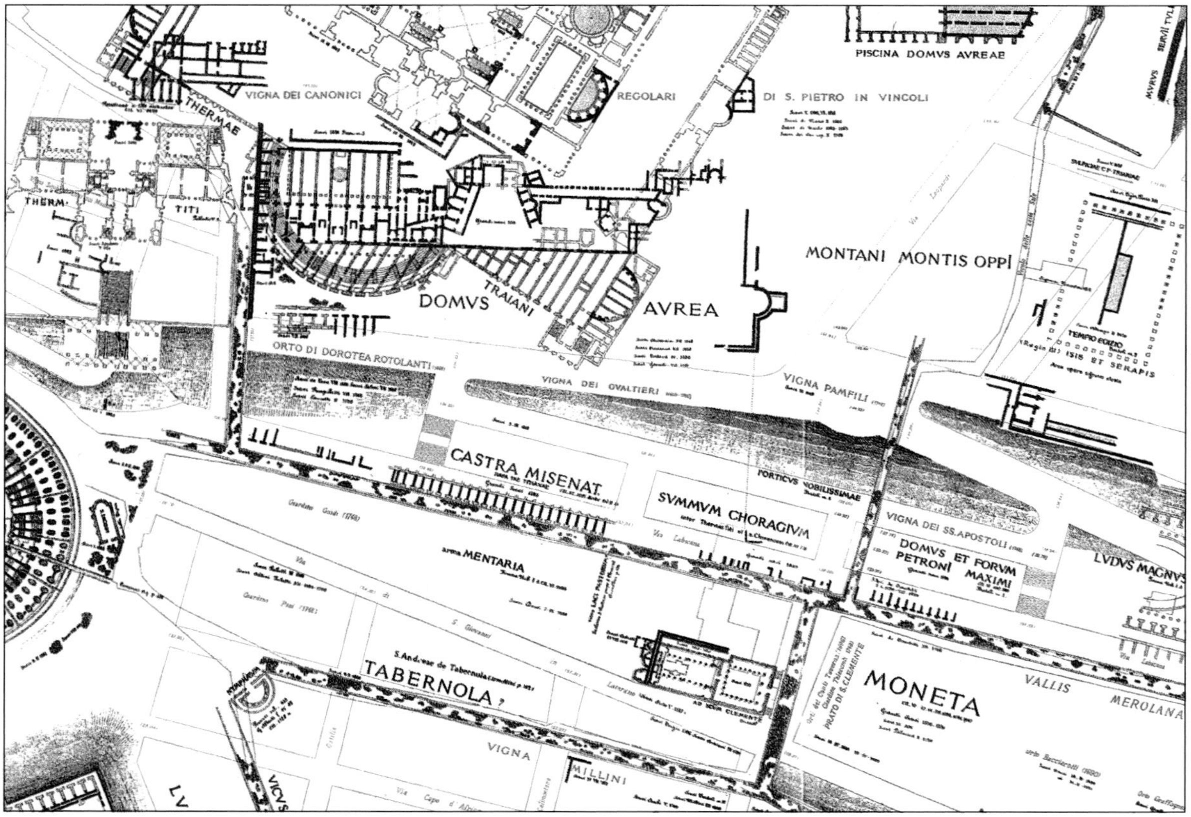
PISCINA DOMVS AVREAE
VIGNA DEI CANONICI
REGOLARI
DI S. PIETRO IN VINCOLI
THERMAE
THERM·
TITI
MONTANI MONTIS OPPI
DOMVS
TRAIANI
AVREA
ORTO DI DOROTEA ROTOLANTI
VIGNA DEI GVALTIERI
VIGNA PAMFILI
CASTRA MISENAT
SVMMVM CHORAGIVM
PORTICVS NOBILISSIMAE
VIGNA DEI SS. APOSTOLI
DOMVS ET FORVM
PETRONI MAXIMI
LVDVS MAGNVS
MENTARIA
TABERNOLA ?
MONETA
VALLIS
MEROLANA
VIGNA
MILLINI
ISIS ET SERAPIS

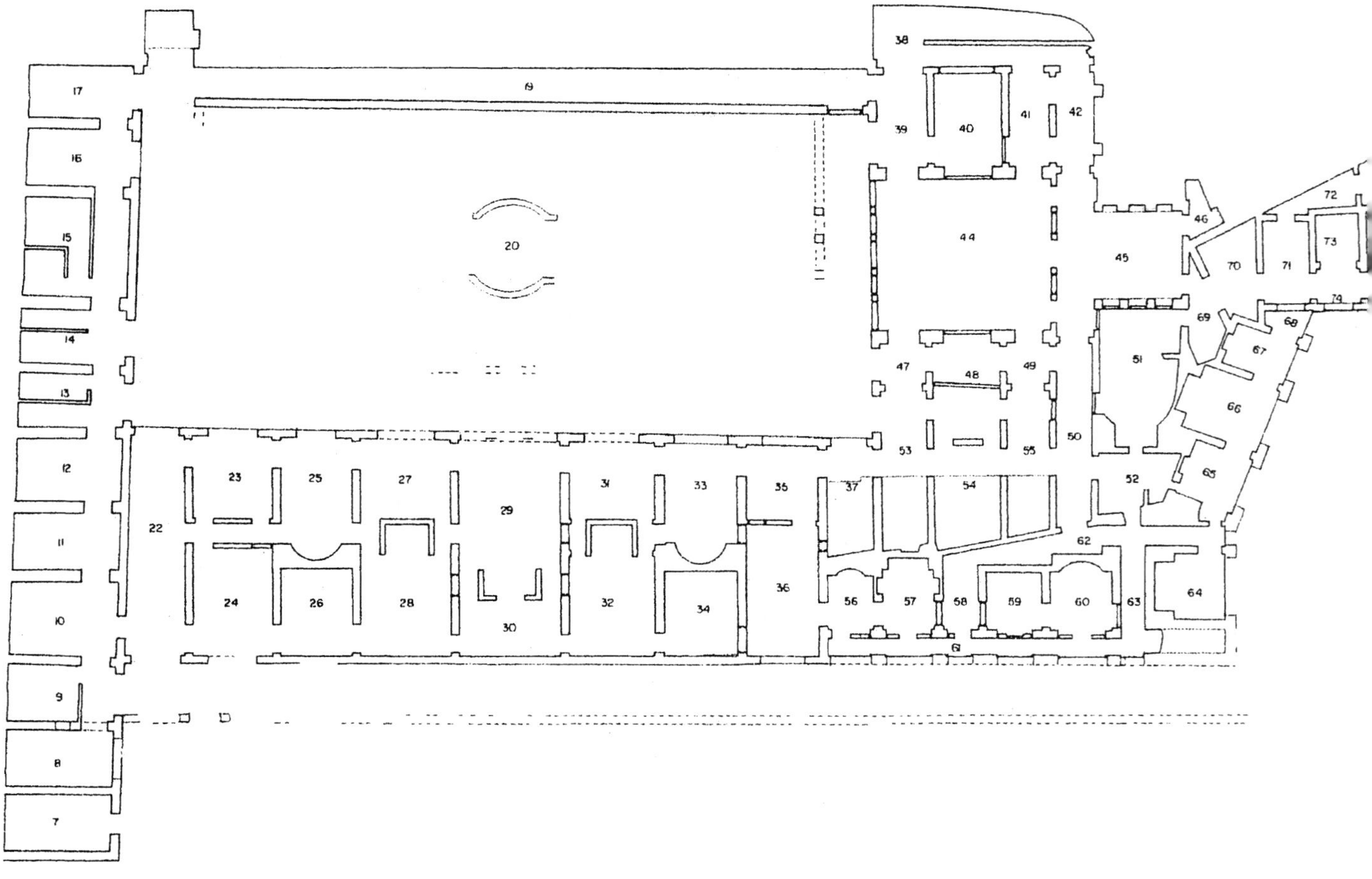
7
8
9
10
11
12
13
14
15
16
17
19
20
22
23
24
25
26
27
28
29
30
31
32
33
34
35
36
37
38
39
40
41
42
44
45
46
47
48
49
50
51
52
53
54
55
56
57
58
59
60
61
62
63
64
65
66
67
68
69
70
71
72
73
74

use these areas which as late as the end of the Republic retained a residential and public character. Nero's Flavian successors, in accord with their populist aspirations, eliminated from this area the buildings of the *'invisa domus'* (hated palace). In its place they built monumental structures designed for the pleasure of the populace which, according to the court poets of the time (such as Martial, 2, 11-12) praised Titus for 'having restored Rome to Rome itself'.

The Esquiline part of the *Domus* flanked the valley with a grandiose and varied backdrop on different alignments for a length of around 400 metres; it was articulated by the projection of the porticoes which fronted the rectilinear facades and by the recesses of the grand pentagonal exedras. The Esquiline pavilion was the part of the palace reserved for the *otium* (leisure) of the emperor, while historically his official seat remained on the Palatine.

The upper storey of this huge pavilion lay on the brow of the Oppian hill, in an area subsequently occupied by the Baths of Trajan. Remains of the layout of the pavilion, with gardens containing fountains, surrounded by porticoes, with lavishly decorated water basins, have been found under the level of the *xystus* of the bath building. The baths used as sub-structures the lower story of the Neronian palace, which consequently came to be completely buried. Before this, all the precious marble wall and floor decoration was taken away and the structure was reinforced by the construction inside it of long brick walls. These formed galleries lying parallel to one another, some of which were used in conjunction with the bath-building above. The varied elements that make up the complex surviving today on the Oppian hill have been interpreted in different ways. They have been considered as examples of traditional architectural schemes such as the Roman peristyle house (although in a version that was highly original in, for example, its unusual sources of light). They have been considered as innovative and particularly bold architectural creations, which allow one to consider Neronian architecture as a forerunner of later and more developed solutions, giving it a pre-eminent position in the development of Roman architecture.

The west wing of the surviving complex (with rooms set around three sides of a peristyle) and the east wing (architecturally much more sophisticated, with a complex system of rooms laid out radially, around a room of octagonal plan) are connected by a court of pentagonal form, dominated on its northern side by a large hall.

5. The pavilion on the Oppian hill, with the Baths of Trajan superimposed, in the Forma Urbis Romae *of R. Lanciani (1893-1901, fig. XXX)*

6. Plan of the pavilion on the Oppian hill

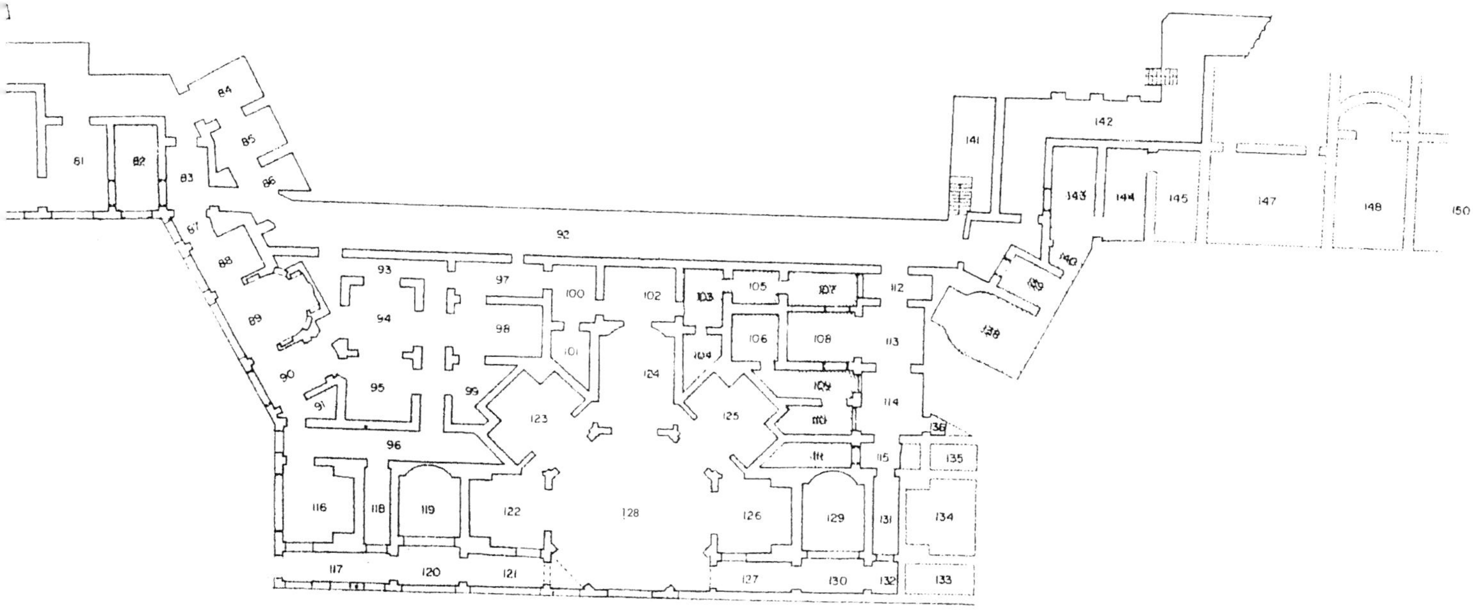

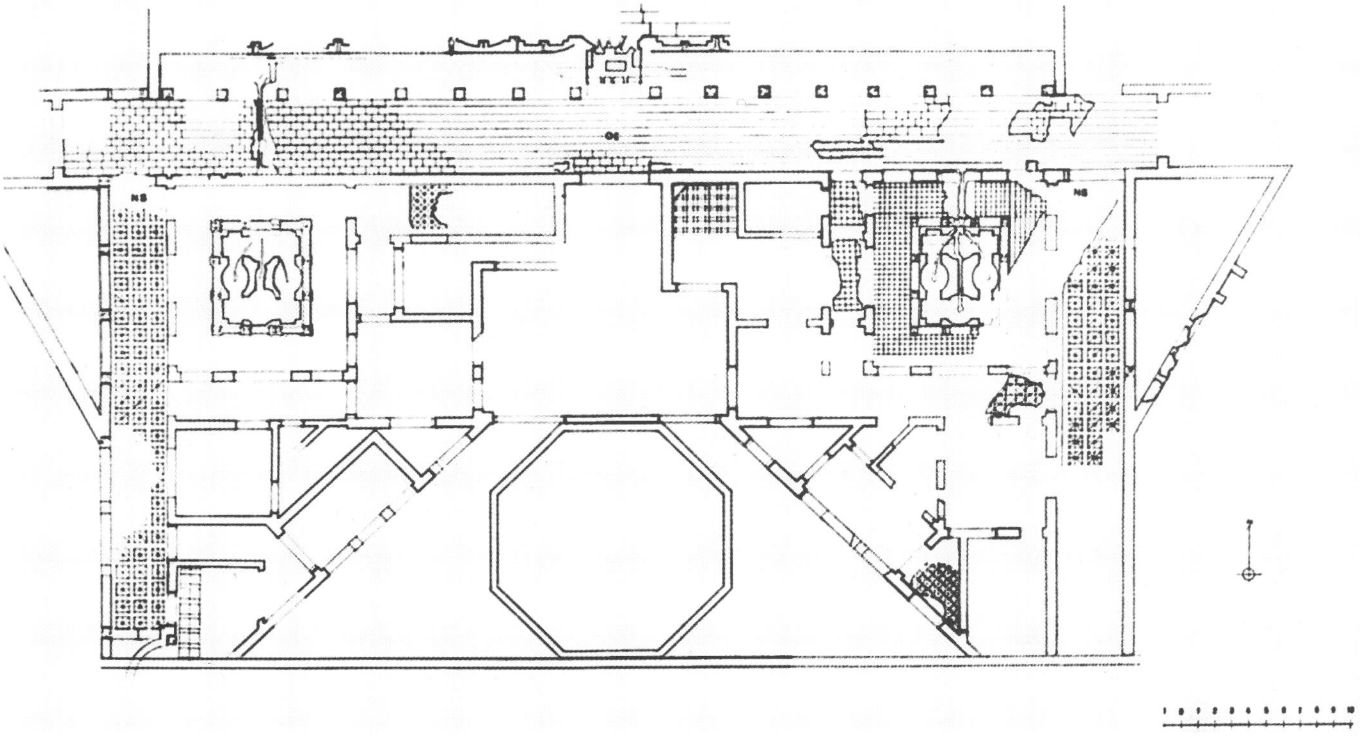

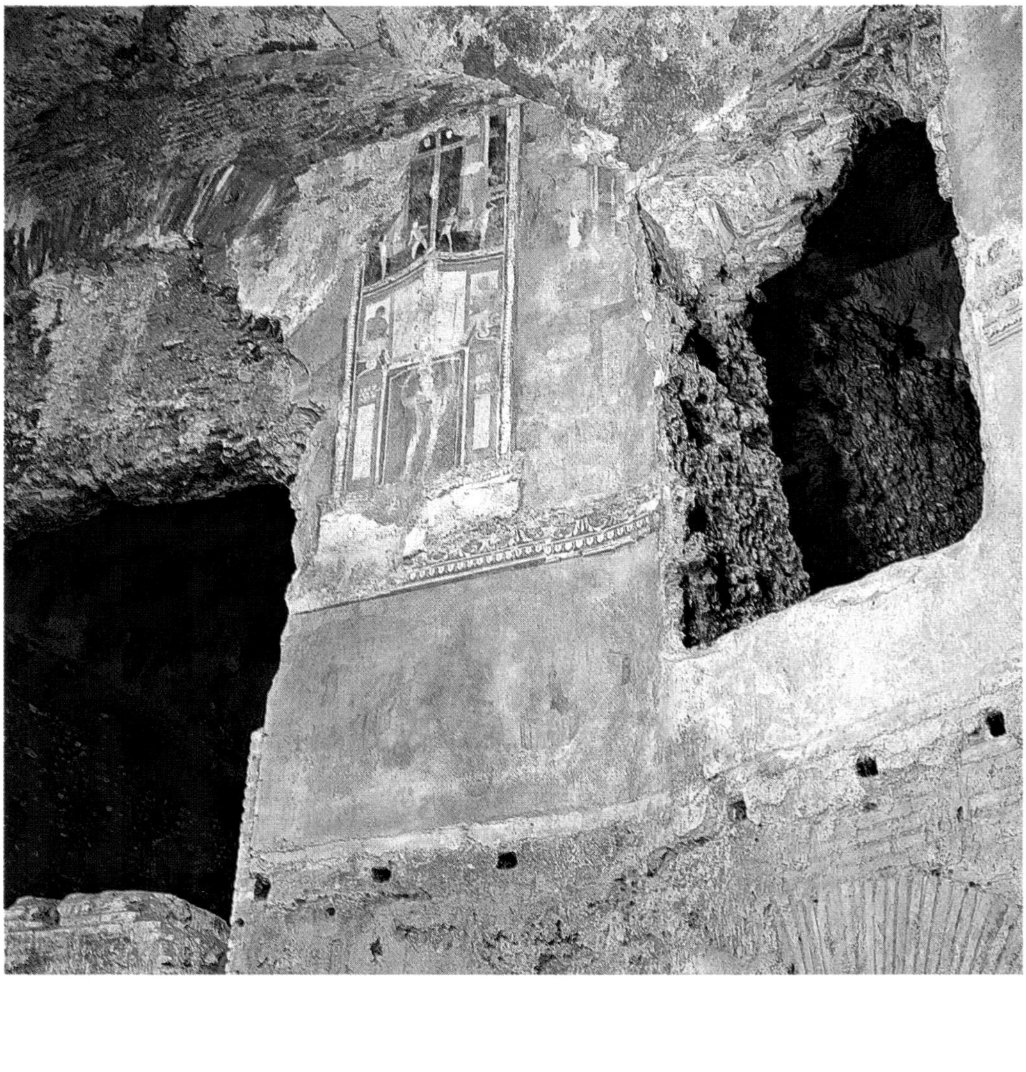

7. Plan of the upper floor in the area of the octagonal hall, with porticoes and fountains

8. Stucco and painted decoration in the pentagonal courtyard

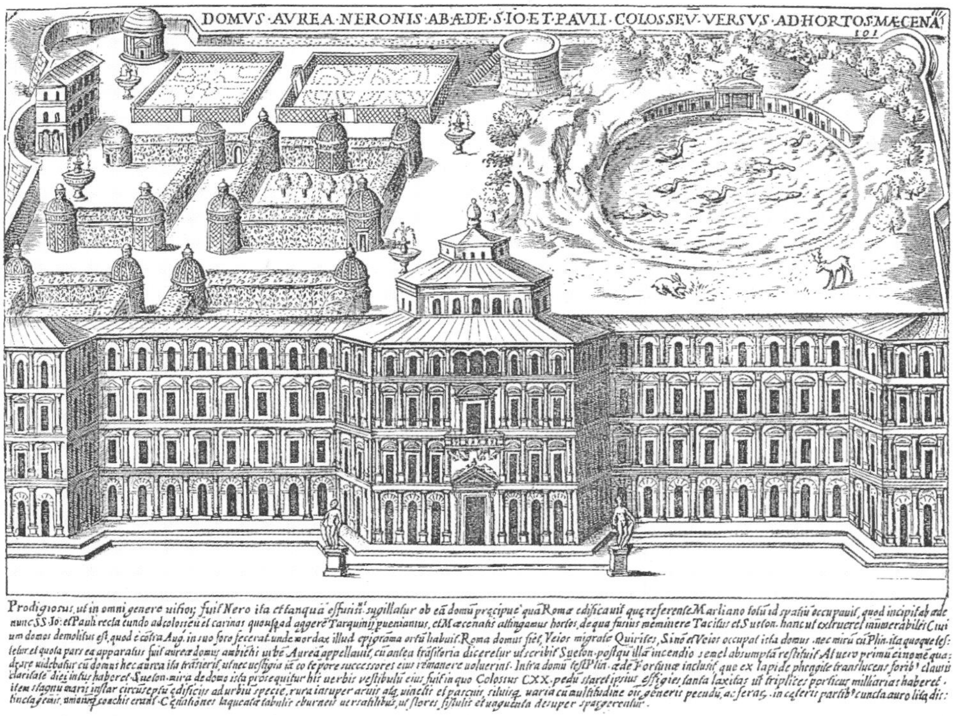

9. 'Domus Aurea Neronis…. Colosseus versus' *in the etching by G. Lauro (1637)*

In its original, organic composition the iconography of the Esquiline emphasised the centripetal positioning of the complex with the octagonal hall. This was connected on its east and the west sides via two large, five-sided courtyards to two more complexes, each in turn centred on large, traditional peristyles. It is amazing that even in the seventeenth century it was obvious that there must have been another pentagonal exedra east of the octagonal hall, even though its existence was only confirmed by recent investigations.
The diverse architectural concepts that characterise the complex have led scholars to identify in it either the work of two architects of different abilities (just as it can be argued that the decorative schemes of the two wings were produced by two distinct artistic personalities) or of two projects, separate also in chronological terms. Those who hold the latter view recognise in the western wing structures pertaining to the *Domus Aurea* constructed after the fire while, for some, the eastern wing constitutes a Flavian addition. It is implied in a note of Pliny, who saw the Laocoon sculptural group (found in 1506 in the vicinity of the Baths of Trajan) *in domo Titi*, that the Flavian emperors lived in part of the huge *domus*. But the more generally held opinion is that the character of the two wings was determined by two discrete functions/roles, private and public. The nature of the locations suggest that the pavilion on the Oppian hill was, in function set aside purely for pleasure, and conceived as a place for banqueting (Moormann), with views looking out over the valley and lakes. From this location beautiful panoramas could be viewed through a luxurious, sumptuous frame, accentuated by the profusion of expensive marbles and of valuable paintings and sculpture. In the view of many scholars (Moormann) the eastern wing, together with the pair of five-sided courtyards, appears to have preceded in construction the wing of traditional plan; other scholars (Fabbrini) believe that it may have been built before the fire, at least in part.
The western group of rooms, with a cryptoporticus to the north, designed to separate the building from the hill behind, was the location of the supposed imperial private apartments. These included the alcoved bedrooms with alcoves; the living rooms (24, 26-28, 32, 34-36) on the porticoed façade which looked out on the valley; and the dining-room complex made up of a large room (29) flanked by two lateral spaces (31, 27) facing the portico of the peristyle.
The monumental niche called the '*nymphaeum* of Polyphemus' (45), located on the eastern side of this peristyle, dominated this group of rooms. It gets its name from the scene in which Polyphemus receives a goblet of wine from Ulysses. This is reproduced in a medallion in the centre of the vault, made of mosaic with glass paste tesserae. Opposite the niche, on the same axis, is a vaulted corridor (44), perhaps a dining room for winter use, set on walls that were broken by broad passageways crowned by architraves. This allowed a view of the sumptuous *nymphaeum* from the peristyle, through the colonnades.
The arrangement of the rooms to the sides of the

pentagonal court both culminates at and centres on the "Hall of the Golden Vault" on the northern side. This is the largest and most sumptuous room of the whole complex, and it is possible to hypothesise that this was the throne room, the vestibule of the palace, or a dining room.

The group of rooms including the octagonal hall has recently been identified (Fabbrini) with the image on a Neronian *dupondius* coin of a circular structure covered by a cupola, flanked by double porticoes. The inscription on this coin traditionally has been read as *Mac*(cellum) *Aug*(usti), that is to say, a market of the emperor. This reading is still accepted by some scholars. However, it has been reinterpreted as *Mac*(china) *Aug*(usti), calling to mind the *machinatio* of Nero, a device designed by the famous *machinatores* Severus and Celer which, according to Suetonius (*Nero*, 31) circled day and night like the movement of the sky.

This evidence perhaps makes it possible to identify the octagonal room, the boldest architectural unit of the Esquiline palace, with the *praecipua cenationum rotunda quae perpetuo diebus ac noctibus, vice mundi circumageretur* ('extraordinary rotunda for banquets which continuously turns itself round by day and by night, just like the earth does').

Given Nero's astrological interests, the various tentative interpretations of Suetonius' text consider it to refer to a type of planetarium, a sphere which revolved according to the movement of the sun. Some scholars suppose that this was covered by an awning, others that it was transparent, but able to coincide with the movements of the planets, shown on the inside of the

10. West wing, large room at the centre of the peristyle called 'the vault of the owls'

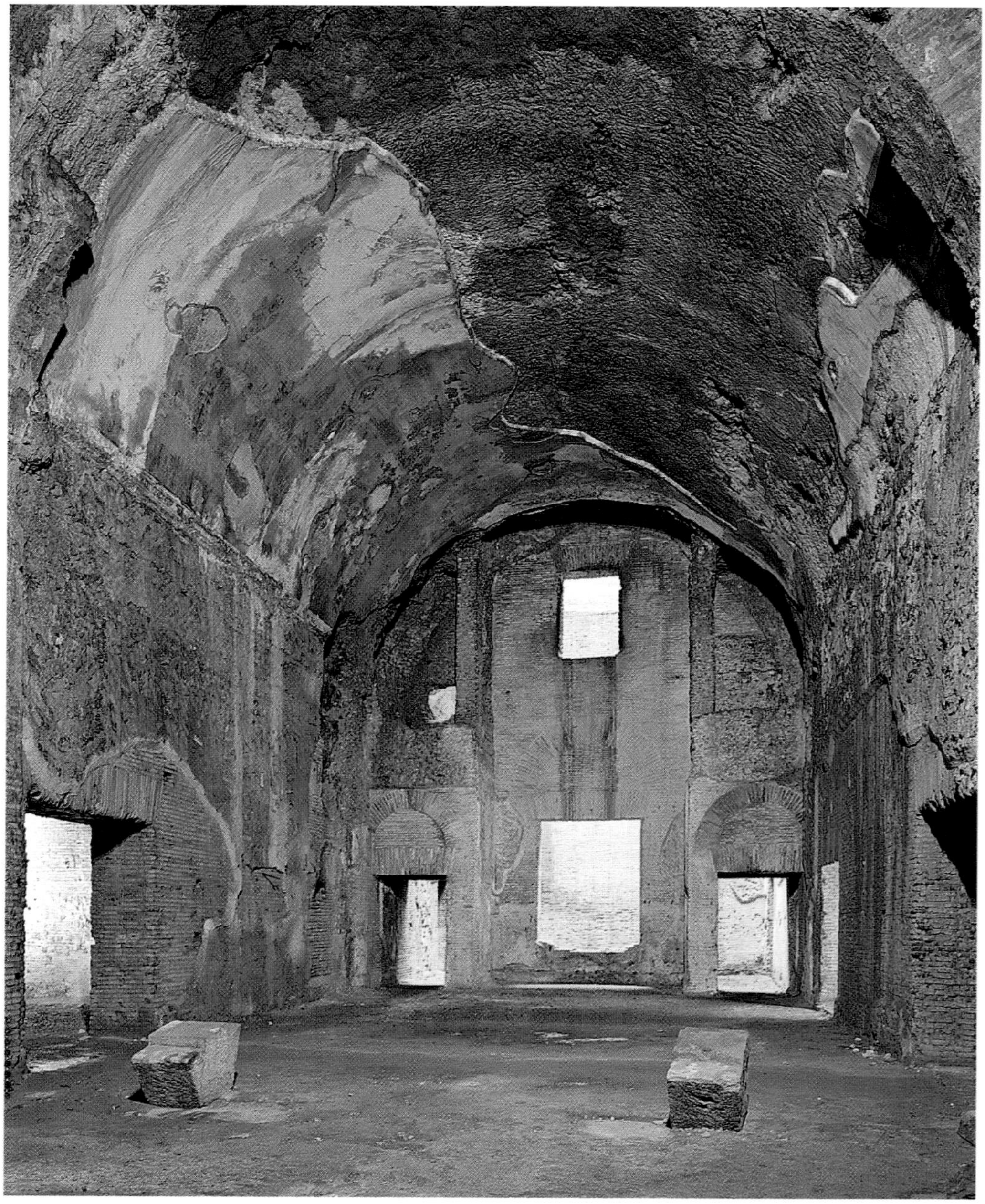

cupola of the hall. Others consider that this room also contained the throne on which Nero, assimilated to the sun god, would have been worshipped, revolving every twenty-four hours like an astral body (L'Orange). Interpretation of archaeological evidence has suggested that the furrows recorded on the *lumen* of the vault had performed the function of tracks in order to make a wooden structure set on the cupola rotate, moved by a hydraulic system (Pruckner, Storz).

Severus and Celer, the *magistri* and *machinatores* of Nero recorded by Tacitus (*Annals* 15, 42) were perhaps hydraulic engineers who also planned to connect lake Avernus to Ostia. They must have designed complex and bold mechanisms working on hydraulic principles to move this remarkable machinery for the writer the Annals to thus emphasise their *audacia* and *ingenium* (audacity and ingenuity).

The machinery could not have been must have been not too dissimilar to the hydraulic clock which Ctesibius created for Alexandria in the 3rd century BC. This projected the movement of the celestial sphere on an equatorial plane. Certainly Nero would not have overlooked this in his constant attempts to imitate the Alexandrian court. It is equally noteworthy that, after his victory over Darius, Alexander seated himself on a golden throne within a circular, vaulted tent, symbolising the celestial vault and the earth. This lay in the centre of a park or *paradeisos*, with woods and wild animals (Diodorus Siculus 17, 36, 5; Athenaeus 12, 537d).

Equipped with awnings and drapes (which would explain the absence of decoration on the cupola) and thus adaptable to the event, the room could be a vestibule, the atrium of the eastern wing (negating its function as a dining room), or the dining room described by Suetonius**.** The octagonal room, with its great nymphaeum (124) and with its nucleus of the alcove-spaces (123-125) arranged like in rows, constituted the focus of the Esquiline palace.

With this ingenious construction, whose bold system of buttressing and support of the broad vault supported by discontinuous walls, open on all sides with wide corridors, it surpassed in the brilliance of its conception the solutions of analogous type which the famous Rabirius achieved in the Palatine palace of the Flavian emperors. The Neronian architects anticipated an architectural form, the octagon, which from the imperial palaces on the Palatine imprinted itself on Roman architecture, finding in the reign of Hadrian its most complex and fantastic form.

In this context it is striking that the remains of the foundations of a circular structure have also been found in the Palatine part of the *Domus Aurea*, underlying the *cenatio* or dining-room of the Flavian palace. These remains emerge at the centre of a large rectangular pool. If one considers that the famous *cenationum rotunda* of the Neronian *domus* may have been completely round, like a *tholos*, then the buried remains on the Palatine are also suggestive of such a structure.

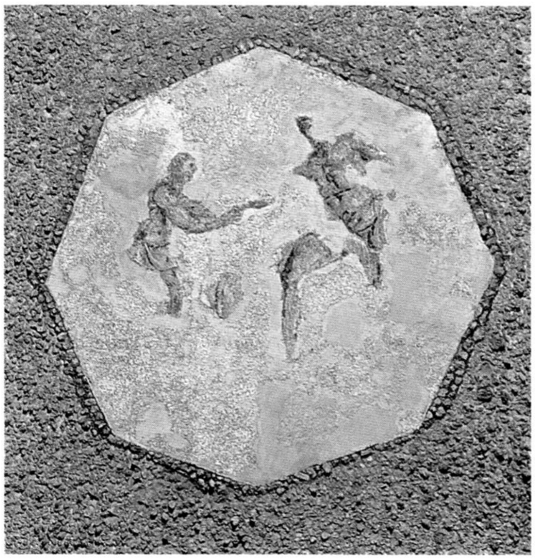

11. Nymphaeum of Polyphemus, vault, detail of the central medallion with the scene of Ulysses offering a wine cup to the Cyclops

12. Nymphaeum of Polyphemus

on the following pages:

13. Octagonal room with lumen *in the pavilion vault*

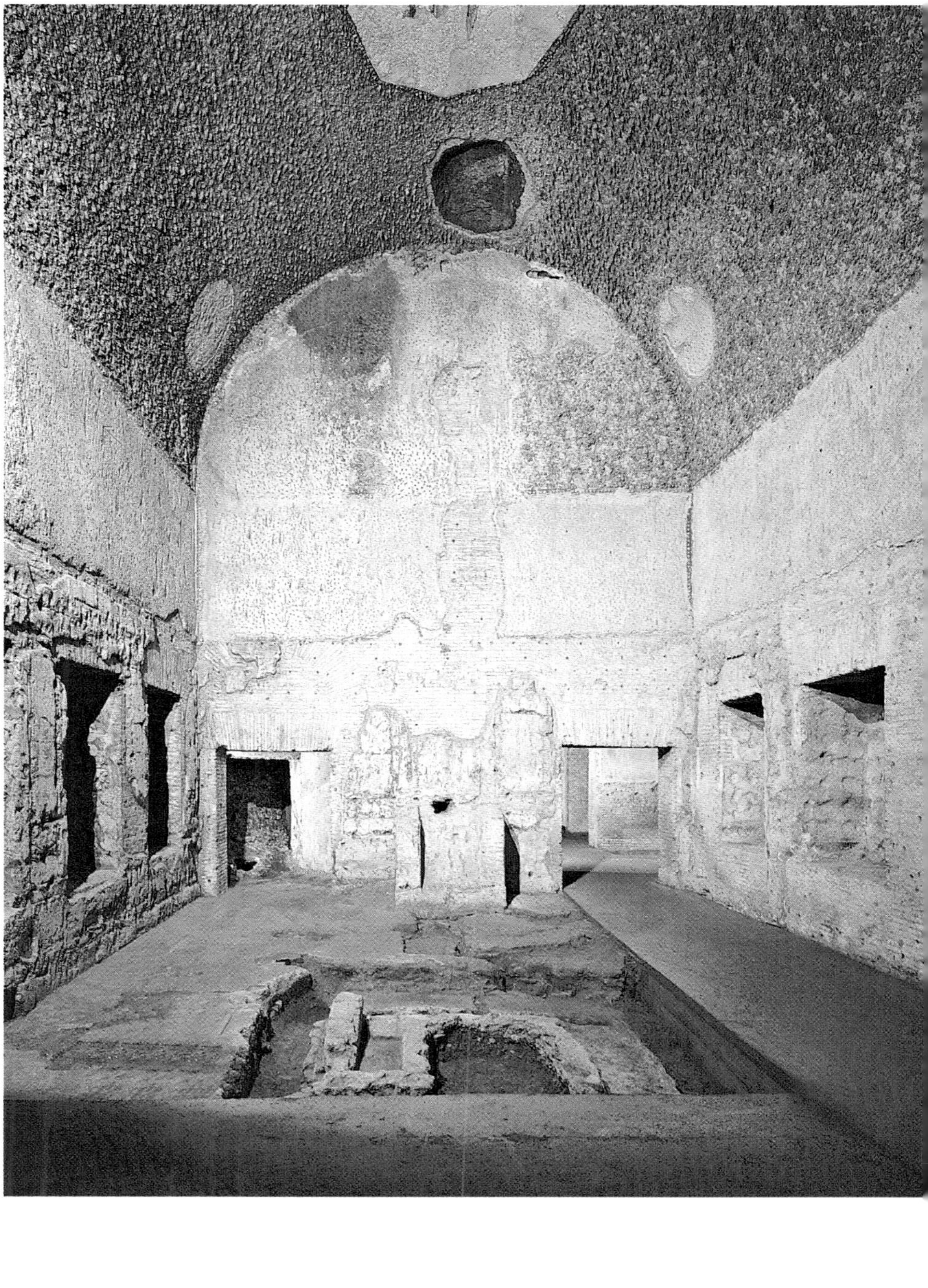

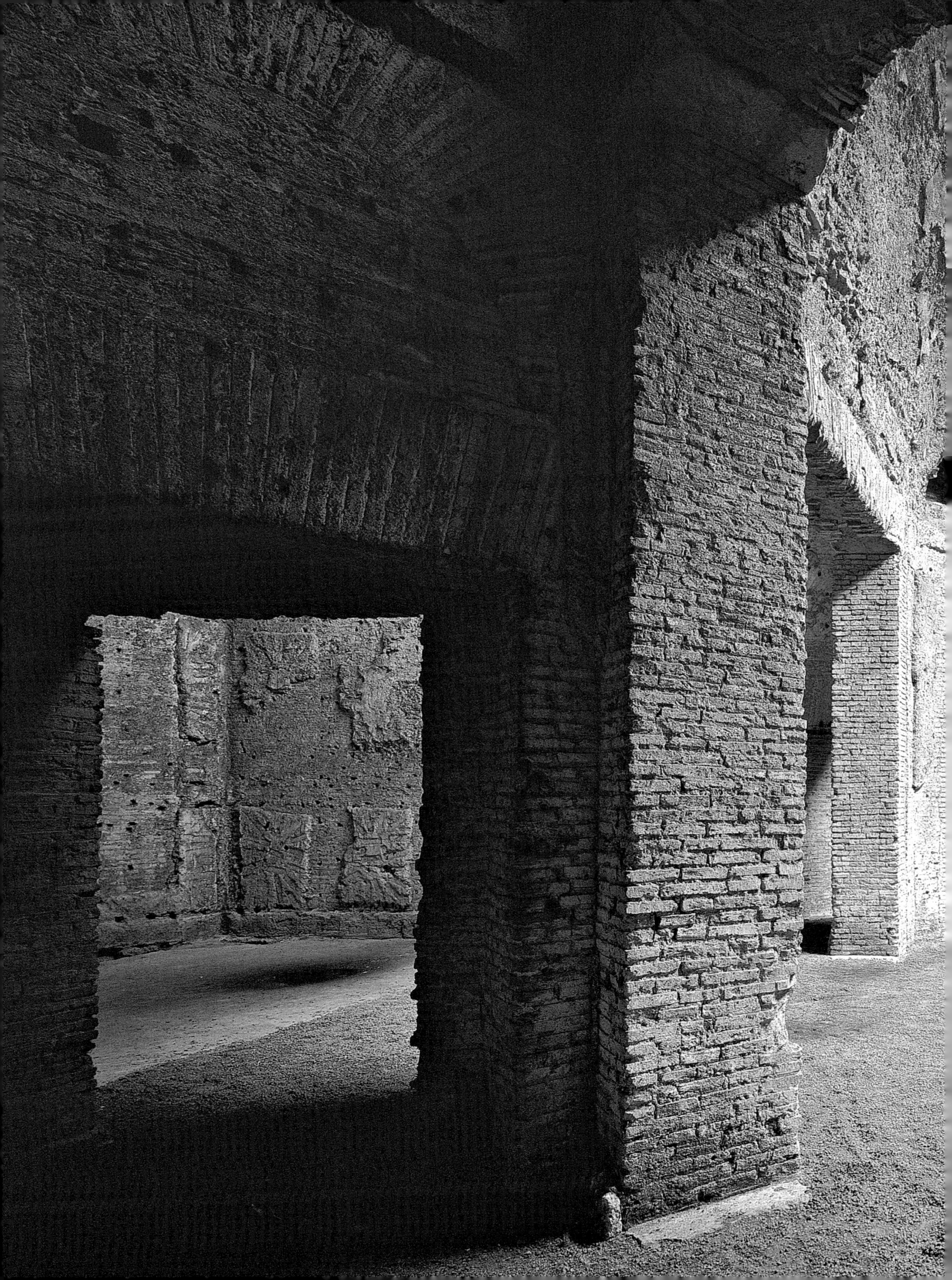

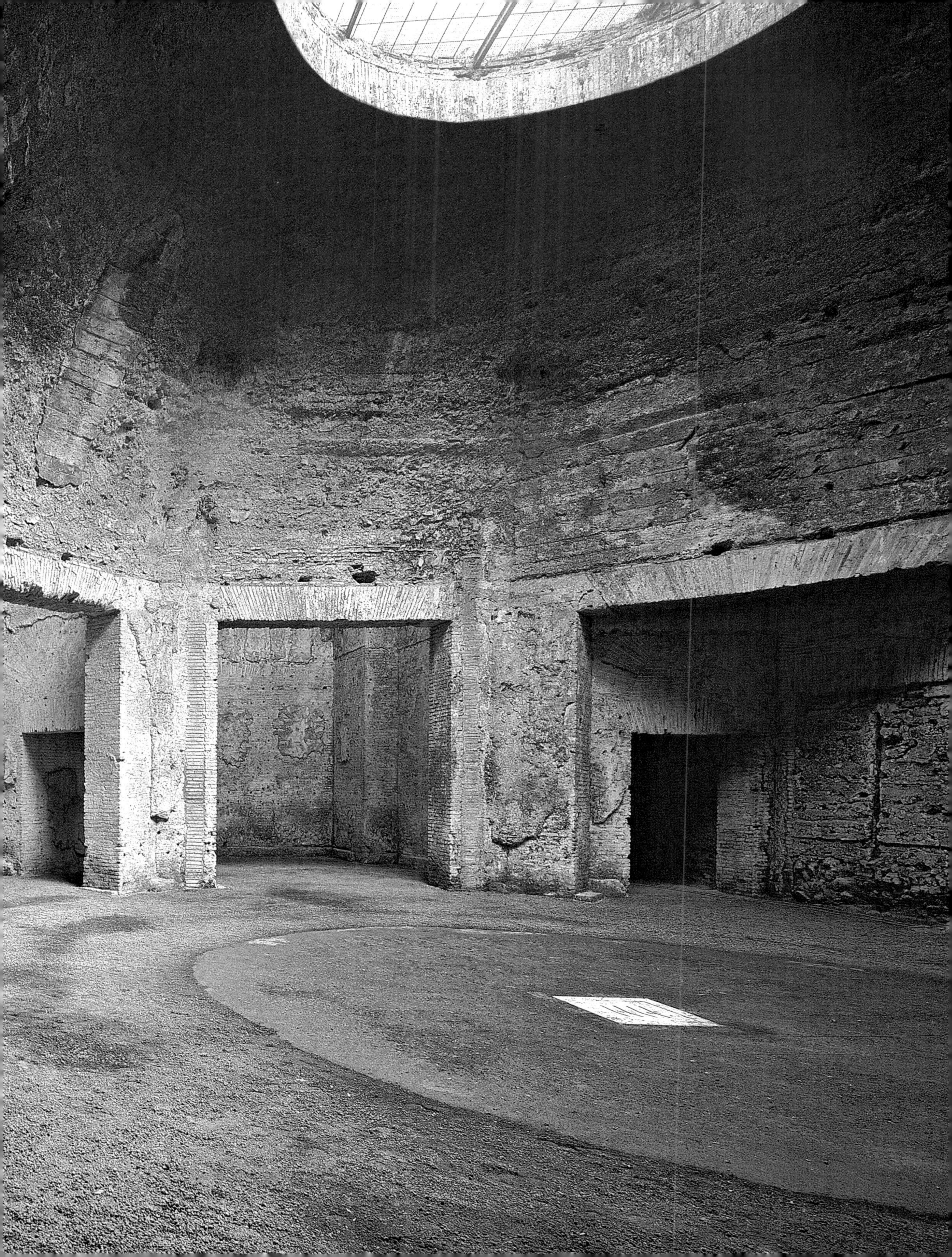

THE PAINTED DECORATION

The significant name that Nero wished to give to his royal residence (Suetonius, *Nero* 31) was designed to evoke the triumph of a new golden age. The guarantor of this golden age was the emperor, who identified himself with the sun god Helios. The golden age was equally brought to mind by the expense of the palace. This luxury derived from the use of innovative techniques, the most extravagant and remarkable of their era (Pliny, *Natural History* 35. 3, 37. 17; Tacitus, *Annals* 15. 42), from the valuable *opus sectile*, the polychrome marble, the pearls and glass paste, the gold veneers, to the lavish painted and gilded stucco décor.

The splendid grandeur of the whole complex, architecturally organised into airy spaces with wide views, was further increased by deliberate effects of lighting, which diffused from windows, colonnades and peristyles. This accentuated the luminous quality that the large-scale employment of gold leaf in the decoration gave to the palace's interior spaces. The appearance of the palace was further enhanced by the elaborate sculptural *ornamentum* and famous groups of statuary specially brought from Greece and Asia Minor. Among them, most likely, was the sculptural group depicting Laocoon by the Rhodian school, celebrated by Pliny who saw it in *domo Titi*. The Trojan priest is seen with his two sons being strangled in the coils of a serpent, because he had opposed the entry of the wooden horse into the city. Nero's tendency to collect, an interest shared, moreover, by all the other emperors, along with many important Roman patricians, made the imperial *domus* into a veritable gallery of the most famous sculptural works produced by Greek artists. In particular these included the works of Praxiteles, a sculptor who enjoyed particular popularity in the Roman world. But surely more in tune with the taste and spirit of Nero as *princeps*, since they were marked by an amazing baroque quality, were the 'Gallic votives', the Pergamene bronzes which commemorated the battles against the Gauls of Attalus I and Eumenes II. According to the writings of Pliny (*Natural History*, 34. 84) these were transferred to Rome 'by Nero by force, and exhibited in the halls of the *Domus Aurea*.'

The only indication of the ostentation which characterised the most extensive of the imperial residences that survives today is the painted decoration of the Esquiline pavilion; its original core, with its decoration made up of the most developed versions of the decorative phases of third and fourth style, can be dated between AD 64 (the date of the fire) and AD 68 (the date of the suicide of Nero). Later additions of painted decoration pertain to the post-neronian phases of the building's existence. In these phases it may have continued in imperial use, if, as Suetonius (*Otho*, 7) records, the emperor Otho spent 50 million sesterces for work on the palace.

When considered in terms of its technical aspects and stylistic characteristics, the painted craftsmanship of the Neronian phase of the palace is not homogeneous and cannot all be judged at the same level. Nor can it be considered the creation of a single artist. Amongst other things, it varies in quality according to the function and the degree of importance and prestige of the rooms. Nevertheless, it forms a pictorial cycle of Roman taste in decoration at that time (the transition from the Julio-Claudian to Flavian period) which was innovative and certainly not lacking in originality. But, above all, since this decoration belonged to the emperor's own residence, it constitutes the most elevated and solemn expression of that particular taste in painting, the so-called Pompeian fourth style, which dominated the reign of the last Julio-Claudian emperor. It can be defined as fantastic due to its excessive use of ornamental details, architectural depictions and fantastic fillings, and the way it stretches the vistas and glimpses of stage-sets in spatial illusion. It seems that this style could have been invented by the multi-faceted personality of Nero himself (Schefold). Nero was quite capable of stamping his views on the taste and fashion of the official art of the era, even if its characteristics, such as the incipient sense of the baroque, can already be perceived in the artistic direction taken by painting (and figurative art in general) in the reigns of Claudius and Caligula.

In the disagreements over its origins and composition, this decorative style is interpreted as a natural chronological and stylistic evolution of the so-called third style, with which it is assumed to be contemporary. In vogue at Rome between AD 15 and AD 40, the third style shows for the most part realistically enclosed walls, lacking expansive vistas and bounded by flat dividers or stretched drapery (but not drawn as fabric, as became the case in the fourth

14. Corridor no.50 'of the eagles', decorative motif of the vault with hippocamps alongside a floral candelabrum

15. Domus Transitoria, *detail of the 'grotesque' decoration with a harpy within floral scrolls*

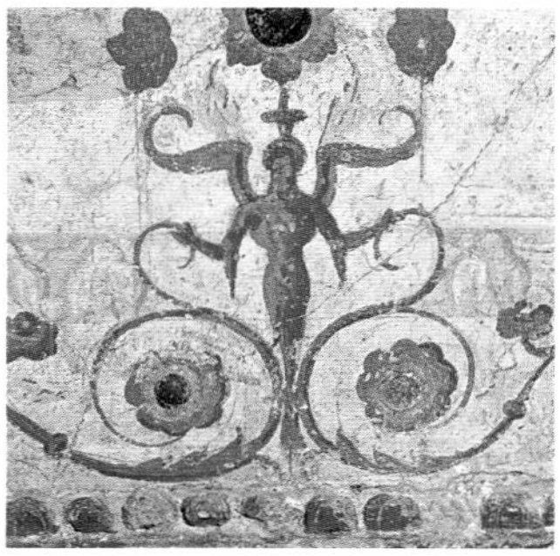

16. Domus Transitoria, *decoration of the vault with characters from the Homeric epics between extravagant 'grotesque' decorations*

style). Between them figures and painted frames appear as if floating in a void. Alternatively, it shows a simple revival of the last phases of the so-called second style, the elegant form of decoration dating to the second half of the 1st century BC, and in particular the Augustan period. By depicting openings in the wall looking out onto architectural backgrounds, this style tended to open up the interior space of a room. This style reached its maturity and the peak of its most free and fantastic expression during the principate of Nero, and in particular during the years in which artistic forms began to transform in a direction which was completely Roman, impressing its individuality even though it derived from Hellenistic tradition.

The *Domus Aurea* constitutes a true corner stone of this particular decorative style. The first clear manifestations of this style in Rome can be seen in the refined decoration of the *Domus Transitoria*, the first imperial palace built by Nero as soon as he became emperor and destroyed by the fire of AD 64. However, relevant examples also come from Pompei, on buildings rebuilt or restored after the earthquake, the date of which is given by historians as, alternatively, AD 63 (Seneca, *Quaestiones naturales* 6.1.2) or AD 62 (Tacitus, *Annals* 15.22). In this Campanian city the development of painting (which conforms to the stylistic phases which developed in sequence in Rome) is delimited by the earthquake and the deadly eruption of Vesuvius in AD 79. Here the fantastic style predominates, with rich evidence provided by many groups of private houses. The early phases of this style can be seen in the decorative scheme of the house of Marcus Lucretius Fronto, the triclinium of the house of the Vettii and the house of Epidius Sabinus. A more mature version, characterised by more markedly scenographic illusionism, with human figures set between the architectural elements, can be seen in the houses of Pinarius Cerialis, of P. Cornelius Tegetes, of the Dioscuri and, again, in the House of the Vettii.

This new taste in decorative painting achieved coloured effects of particular intensity by means of distinctive and vivid shading, of strong and contrasting tones. It is related to the impressionistic technique that was used to produce the figured and landscape panels in the Neronian palace.

This is an impressionistic technique, involving fast work and soft outlines, a technique essentially based on tones of light and shade. Aiming for an overall effect, it accentuated the characteristics of impressionistic painting (whose antecedents existed already in the work of painters in Greece in the 4th century BC). This had already been recorded and defined as

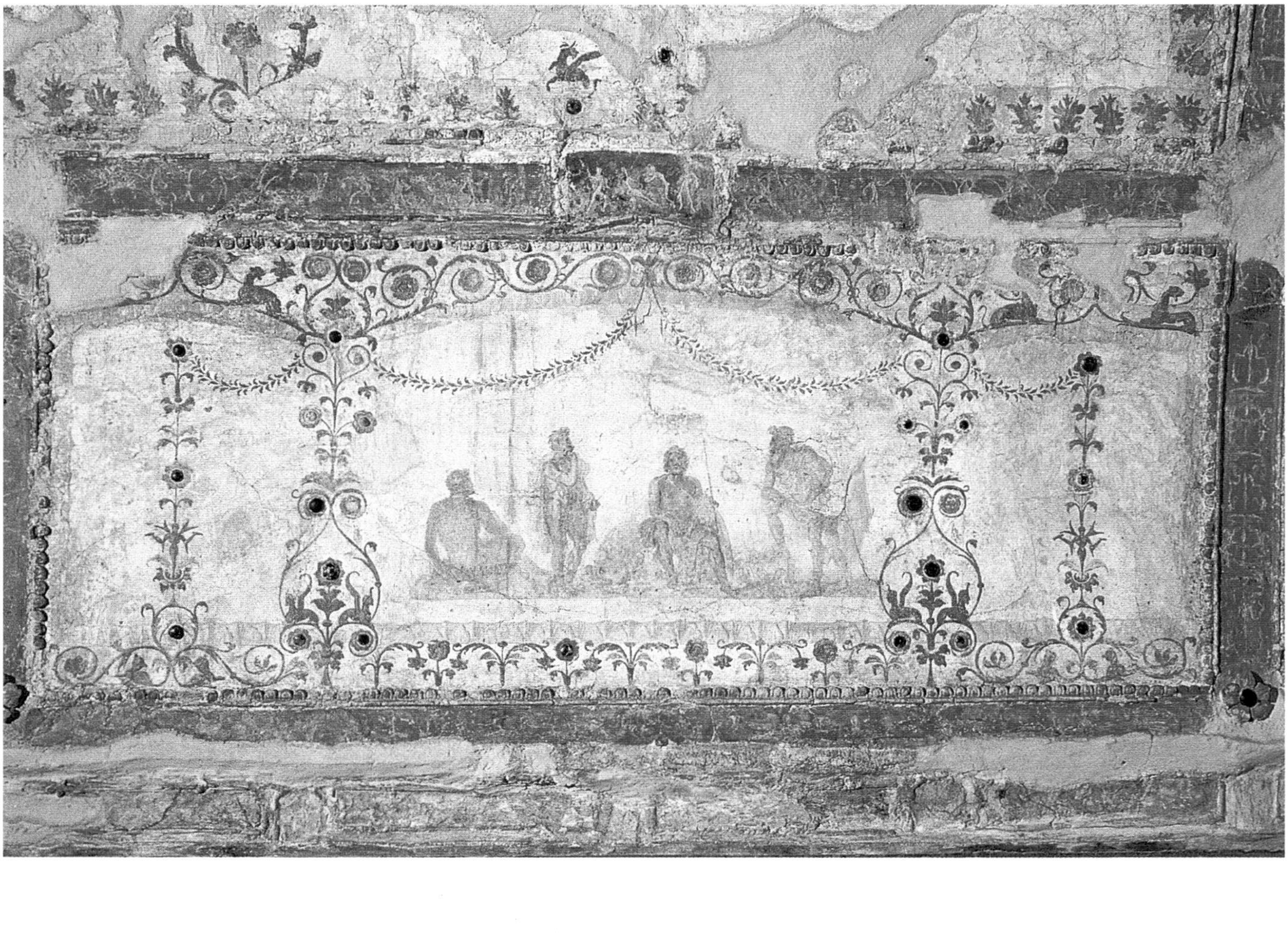

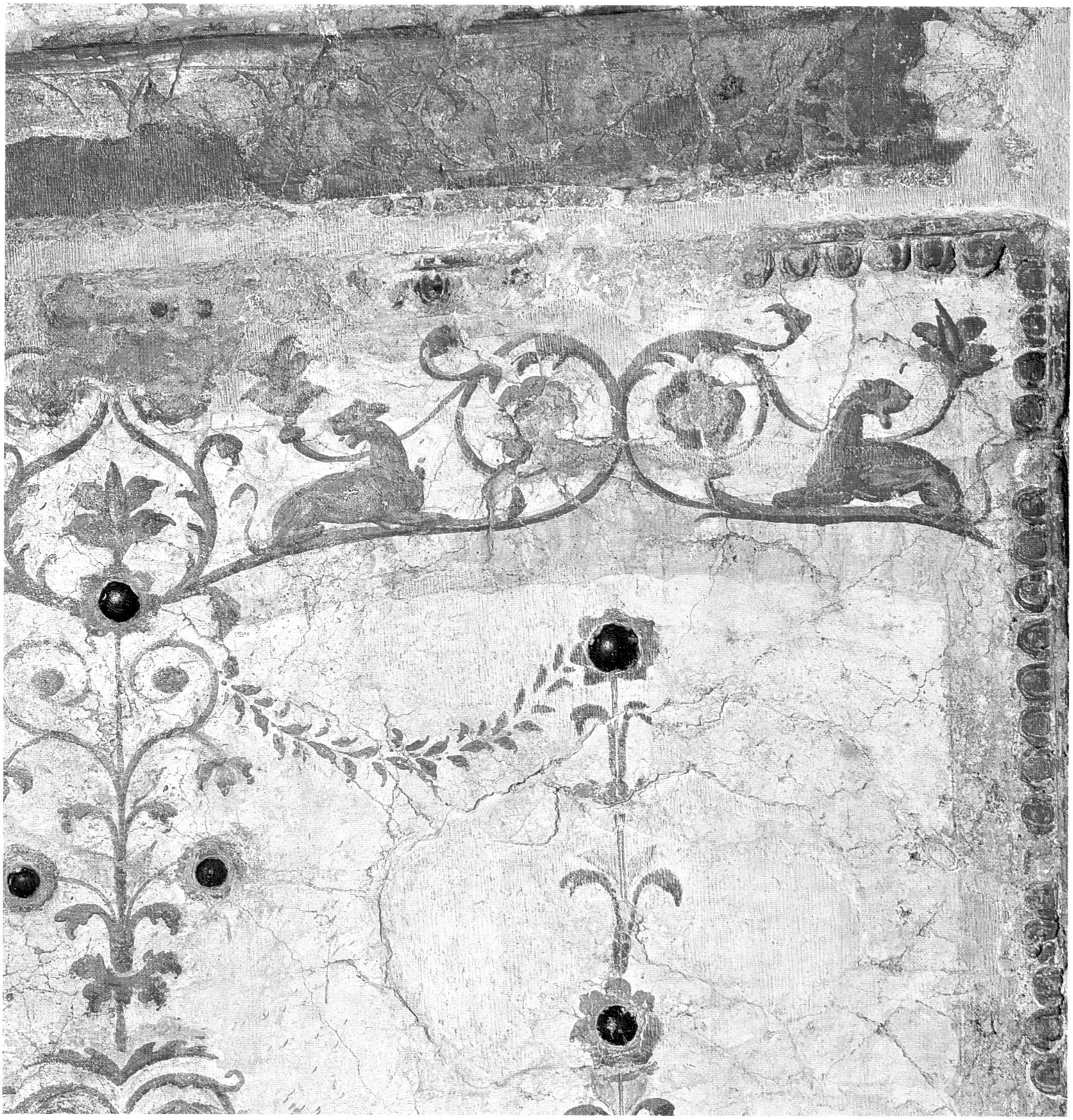

17. Domus Transitoria, *detail of the 'grotesque' decoration*

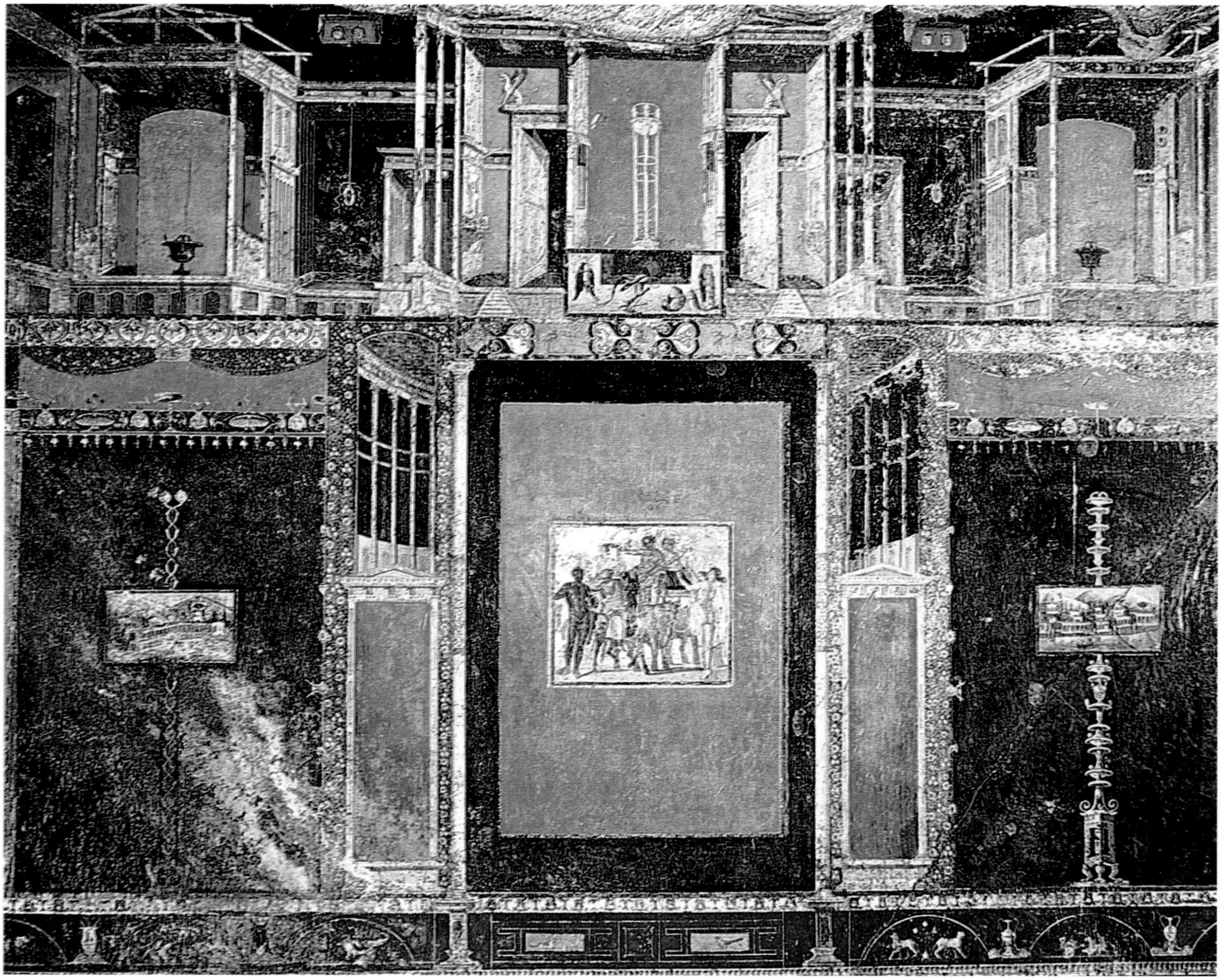

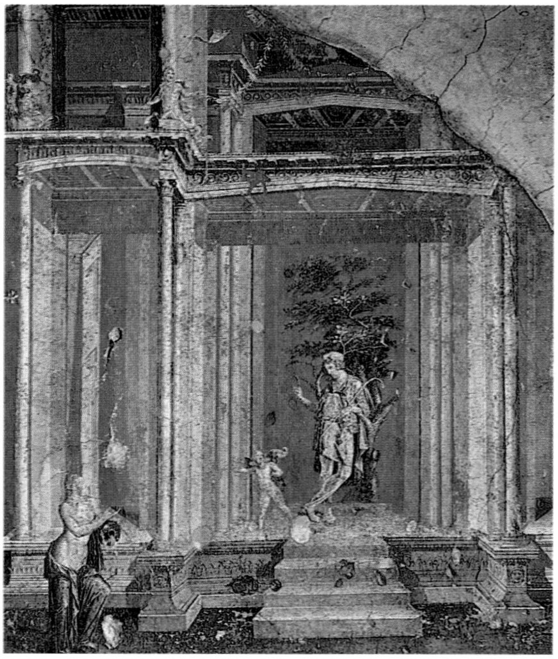

18. Pompei, House of Marcus Lucretius Fonto, tablinum, *example of late third style*

19. Pompei, House of Pinarius Cerialis, grandiose fourth style stage scene

20. Pompei, House of the Vettii, northern triclinium, example of advanced fourth style

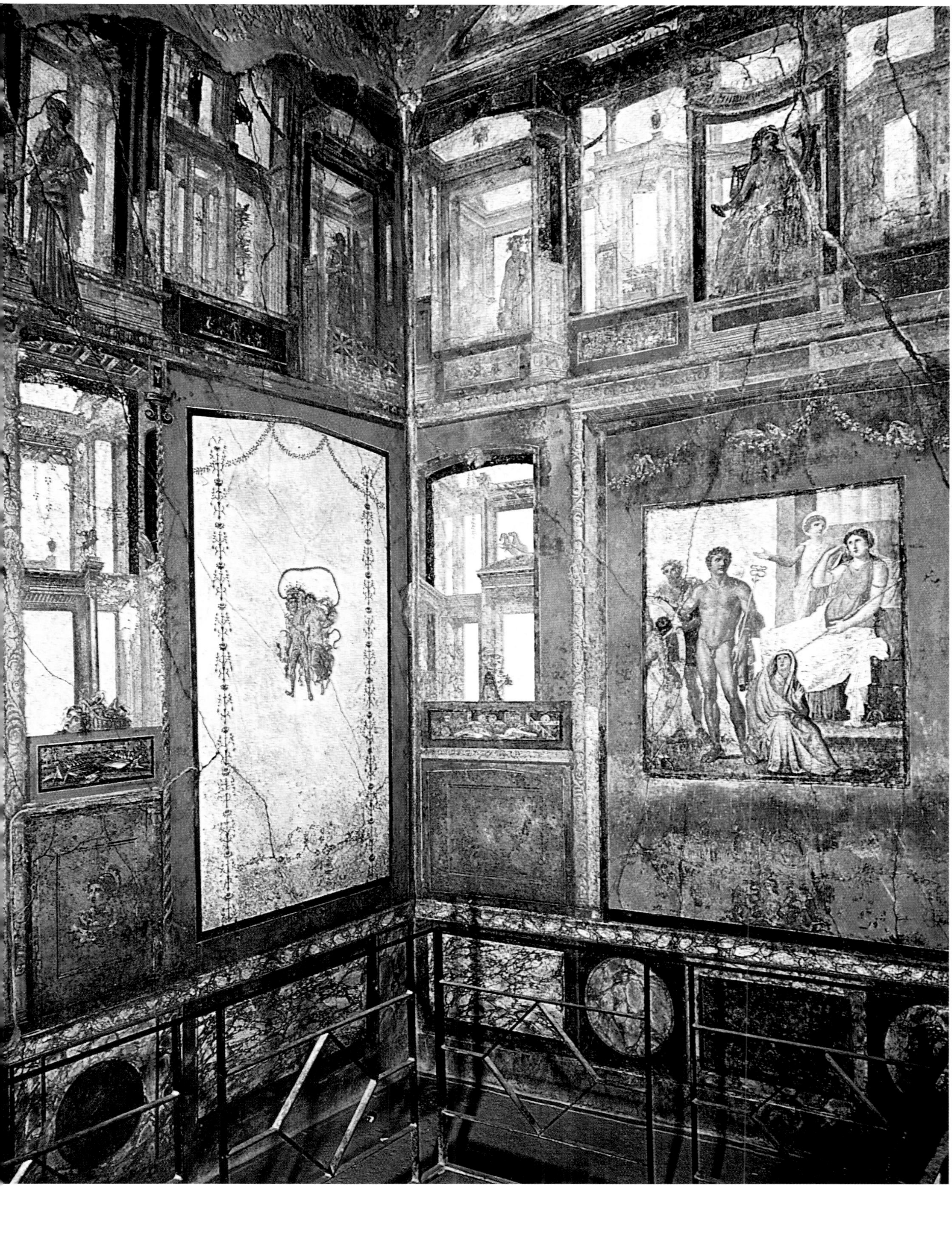

compendiaria by Roman writers such as Pliny (*Natural History* 35.110) and Petronius (2.2). An outstanding example can be seen in the 'monochrome room' of the House of Livia on the Palatine. The most notable characteristics of this style, and of the decoration of the Esquiline palace in particular, are the motifs employed in compositions which were extremely complex and displayed great skill. These motifs encompassed unreal and fantastic forms, oriental in their inspiration and appearance, and human and animal figures appearing out of plant-like columns and culminating in vines and floral garlands. It is clear from Vitruvius that such motifs were already present in the paintings of the second style (and disappeared in the naturalistic tendencies of the Antonine period); in his comments on the wall painting of his own time, he criticises them as *monstra,* senseless and unnatural, the product of *iniqui mores.*

It was this hybrid element, fantastic and bizarre, which the exuberant imagination of the ancient decorator spread lavishly over the vaults and walls of the palace. This fascinated painters already at the end of the 15th century, but particularly in the Renaissance. In the Neronian 'grottoes' (from which derived the term 'grotesque') they discovered new models to imitate and reproduce until they produced the characteristically ornamental style of that period, seen particularly in the work of Raphael and his school.

The decorative schemes painted on the walls in the palace for the most part can be defined as 'stage sets', as seen in the preserved remains and in the drawn reconstructions (mostly from the west wing) handed down to us by the great engravers of the 18th century. In addition to simpler schematic architectural depictions, they comprise scenic views clearly influenced by the *scaenarum frontes* of theatres. Architectural elements open onto backgrounds which are depicted as lying in the distance by strong spatial illusionism, and facades of palaces are articulated by niches and exedras and enlivened by frequent and isolated figures. Numerous panels in regular alignment, with various motifs spread over them, recall draperies, tapestries and embroidered hangings. These, along with closed frames containing depictions of shrines and *pinakes* and small panels with landscape views, decorate corridors and cryptoporticoes. But a baroque influence dominates the decorative composition of the vaults of the most

21. Palatine, House of Livia, right ala 'monochrome room', impressionistic scene

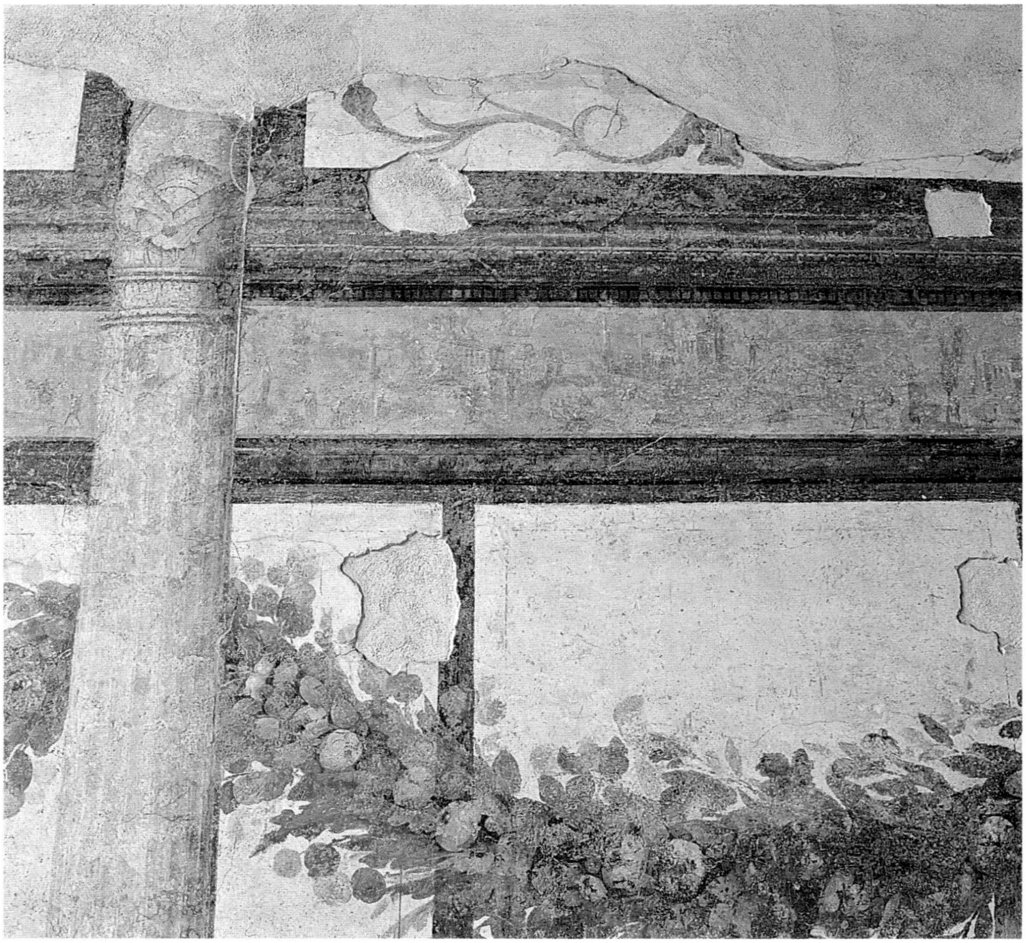

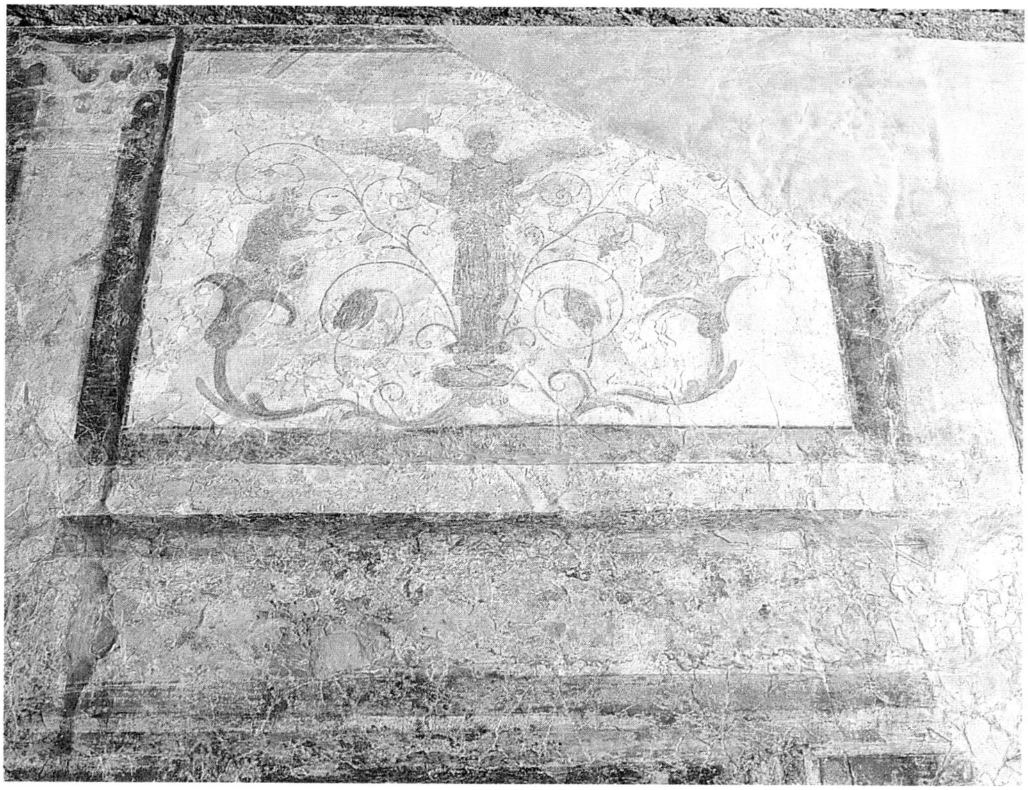

22. Palatine, House of Livia, left ala, winged figures in the wall panels

important rooms of the residence, where the paint is complemented by stucco. This stucco emphasises the partitions and fields into which the vault is subdivided by framing them, moulds the decorative figures of the friezes and gives shape to the architecture itself.

One element of the decoration can quite properly be termed geometric, and is marked out by subdivision of the vaults into a network of compartments, mostly of modest size. In these are set ornamental motifs or panels with figured scenes in them, *thiasoi*, processions or single figures. This kind of decoration is mostly found in the east wing. Alongside it, mostly in the west wing, are decorative schemes based on the free and fantastic combination of a number of elements which share the character of furnishings: these include depictions of tapestries, draperies, swags of foliage, candelabra, small figures hovering and flying, small panels with figured scenes, chains of human beings and fantasy animals. These are all woven into a fabric which is exuberant and baroque in character, but arranged with great skill. This ornate scheme, a prelude to the decorative formulations of the subsequent Flavian period, was enriched in its execution by the use of expensive gold leaf and a Bacchanalian polychromy based on *floridi colores* – vivid colours like *minium* (blood red), *purpurissum* (dark purple), *armenium* (intense blue), *indicum* (indigo) or *melinum* (a luminous white). It cannot but evoke in the viewer, even at first glance, an impression of luxurious sumptuousness and refined expense. This is true even despite the prevailing miniaturist character of the painting, which can only be fully appreciated by study at close quarters.

Nevertheless a different stylistic and formal tendency is encountered in the pictorial language employed in the private imperial apartments of the west wing. This contrasts with that seen in the great audience halls in the east wing. The former is more restrained, but also includes a greater degree of fantasy, and adheres to tradition and to the third style. The second is more innovative and free, derived from characteristics already typical of the so-called fourth style.

This distinction is still generally accepted (Dacos, Perrin), even if it has been observed recently (Meyboom, Moormann) that the painting of the west wing might be considered as 'an affected elaboration, a stage of evolution later than that of the east wing' and that in both wings two workshops worked at the same time, in an indistinguishable manner. The artist of the decoration of the public area knew how to express his art with originality even outside traditional schemes, and it is thought that it is possible (Dacos, Perrin) to recognise Nero's official painter Fabullus (or Famulus). Of Fabullus' artistic work (which included paintings on wooden panels, a rarity in the Roman period) we have only a few complementary comments handed down by Pliny (*Natural History* 35. 120), with which more recent critical literature does not seem to agree entirely.

The figured panels with mythological scenes or with individuals from the most significant episodes of the

23. Castel Sant' Angelo, papal apartment, 'grotesque' decoration

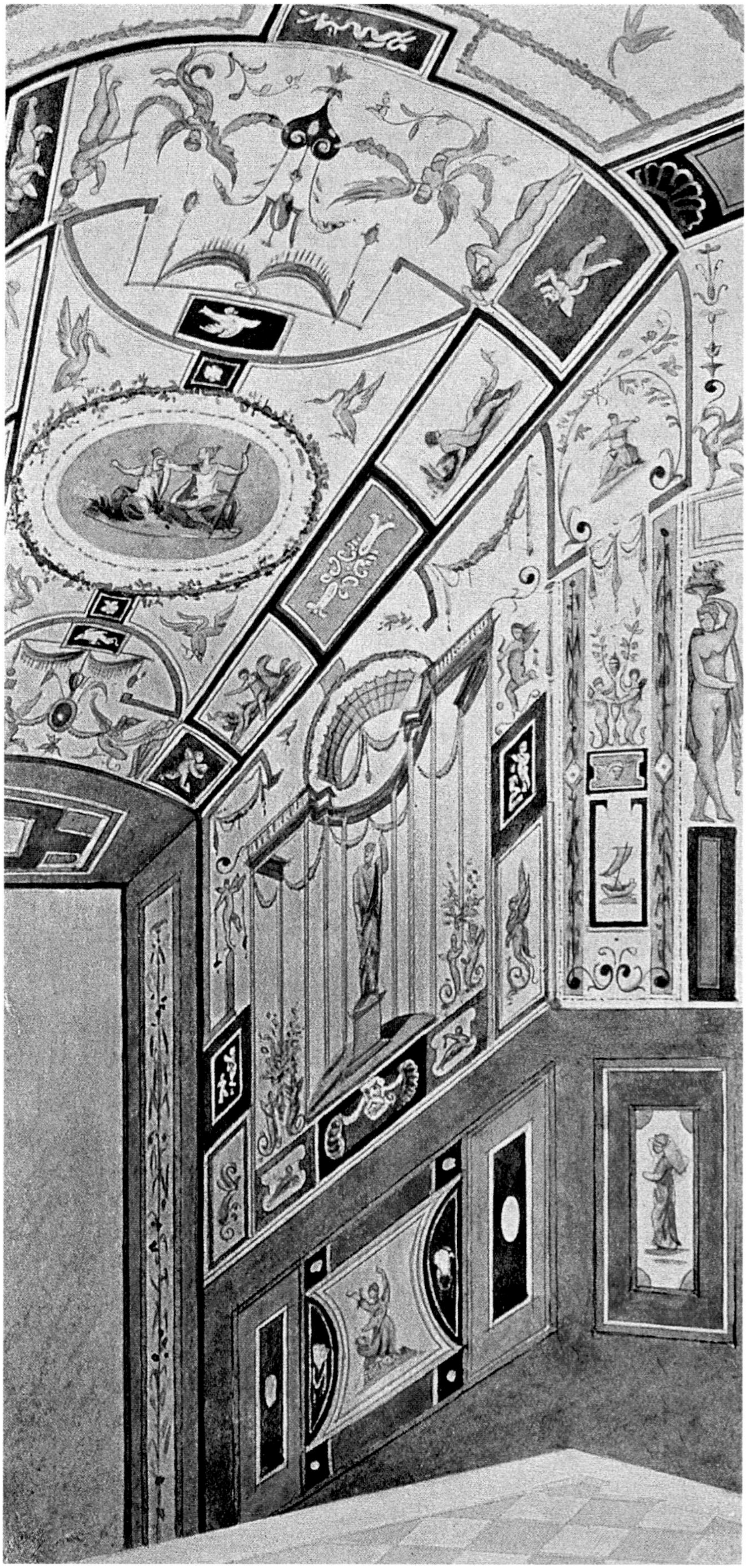

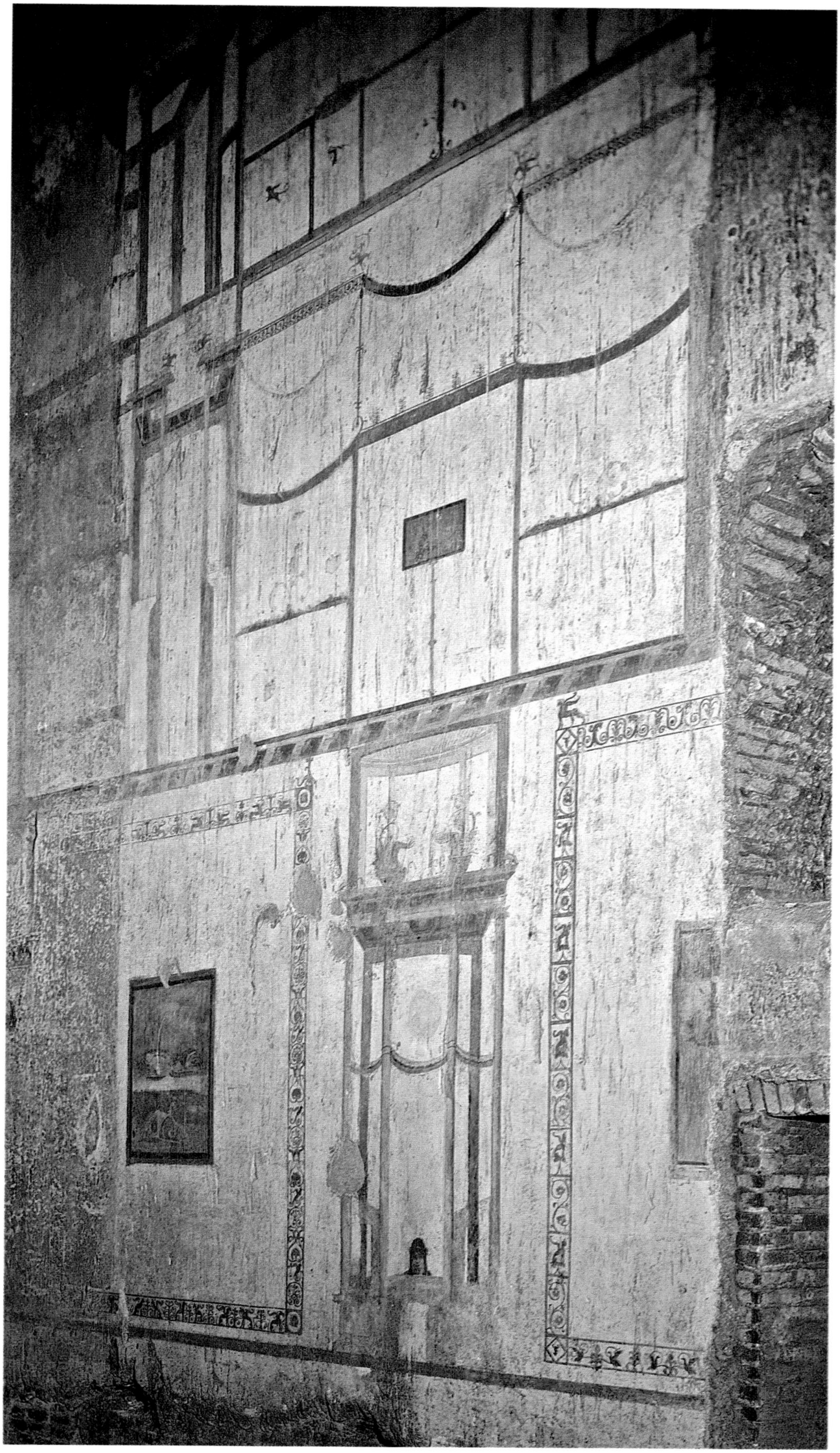

24. Domus Aurea, *corridor no. 79, wall decoration with linear architectural facades*

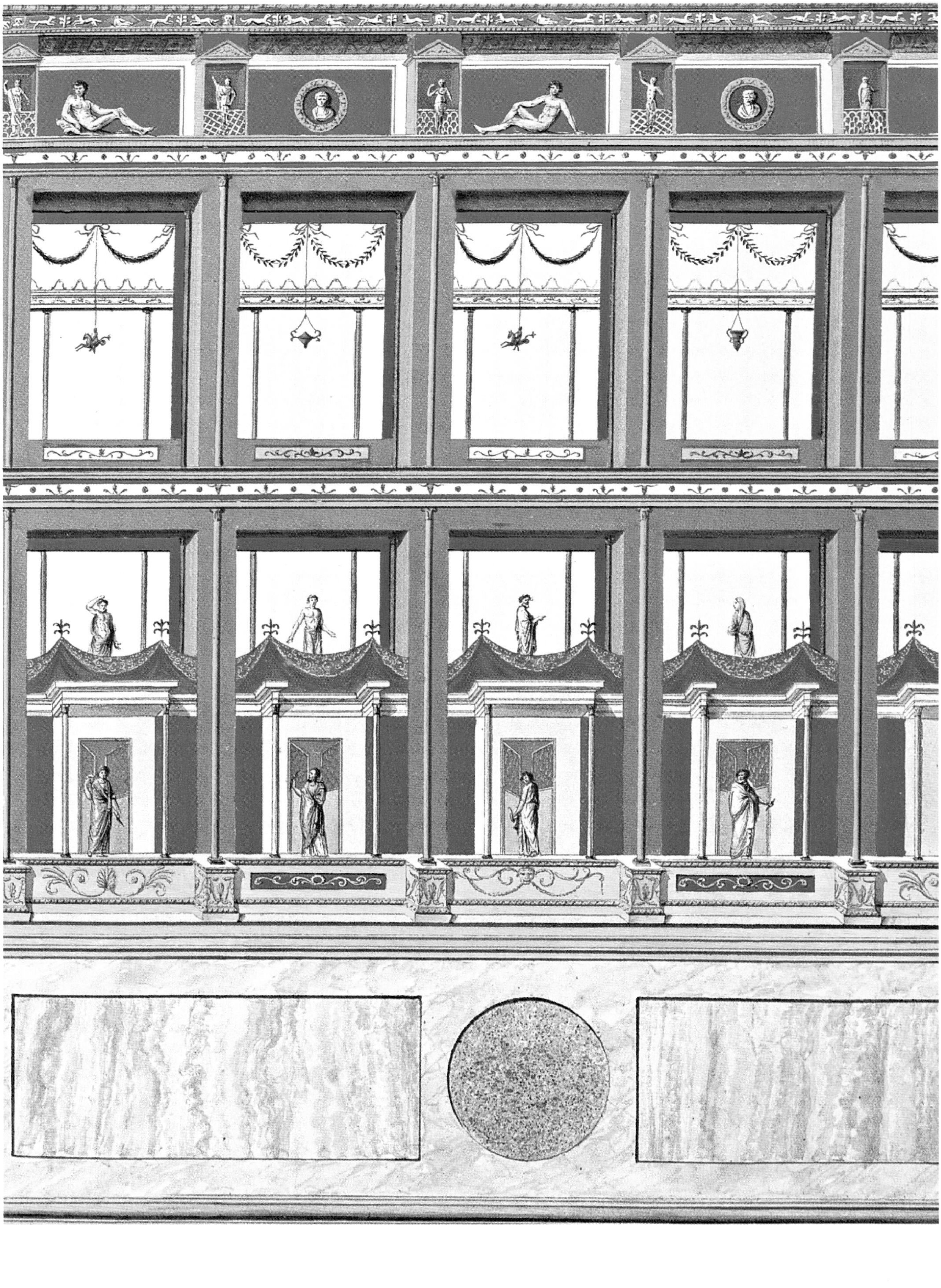

25. Domus Aurea, *stage scene from a room in the west wing (Mirri 1776)*

26. Domus Aurea, *room no. 87, architectural view of a stage-scene with elements depicted in sharp projection*

27. Domus Aurea, *room no. 131, wall decoration with open stage set on a background of dense and complex architecture*

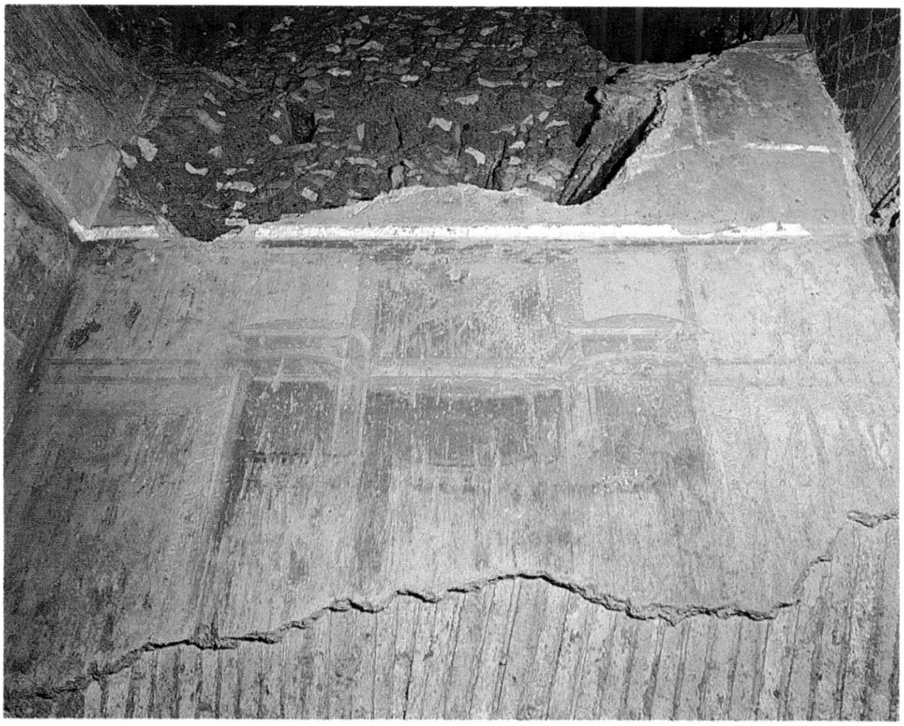

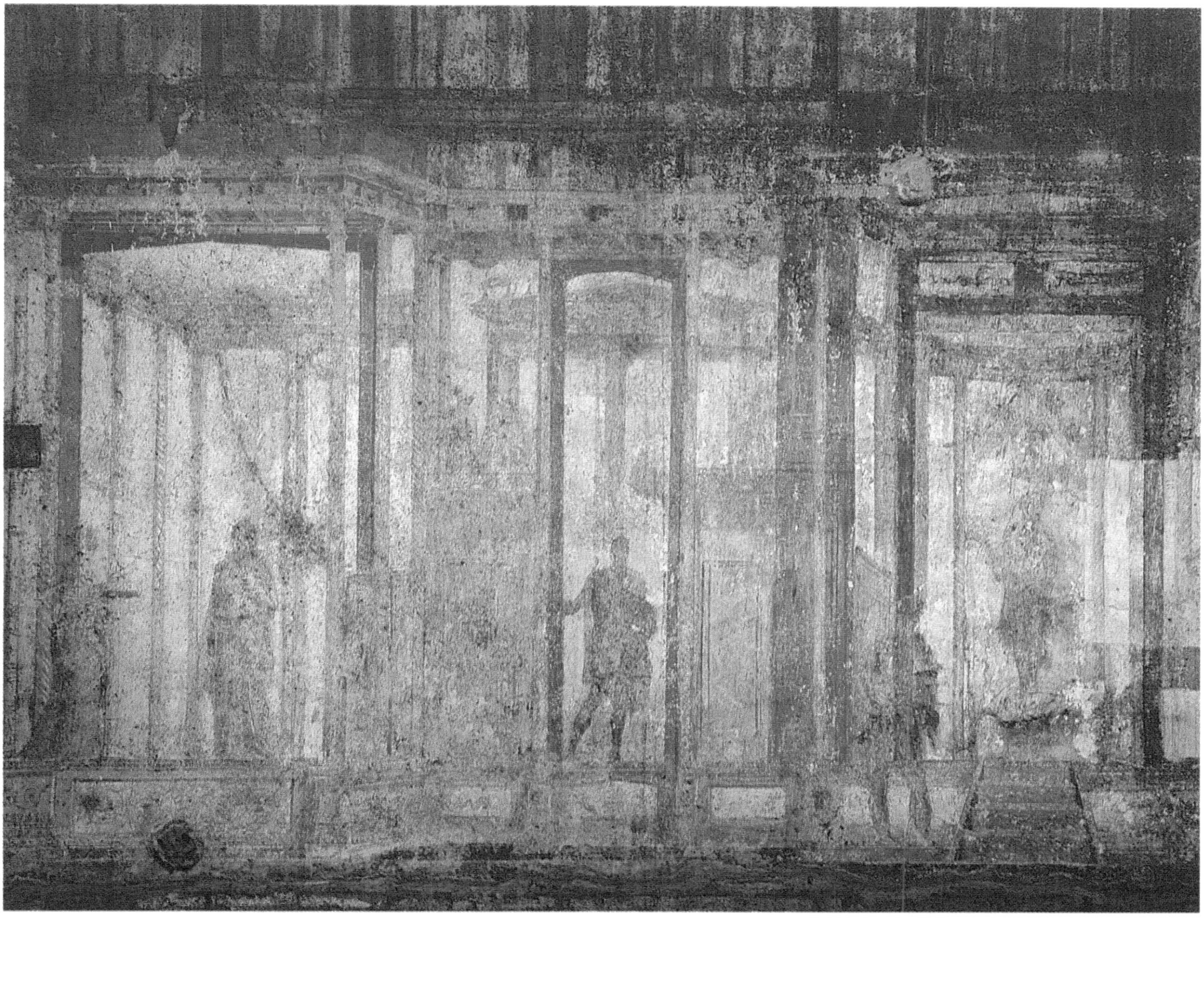

work of Homer (the judgement of Paris, Hector's farewell to Andromache, the meeting of Helen and Paris (?), Thetis carrying away Achilles' arms (?), Achilles at Skyros) are connected by a common concept and make up the most noteworthy theme in the decoration of the vaults of the palace's reception rooms. In these one perceives the imprint of an artist working in a style permeated with 'togate solemnity' and in a painting technique employing the new chromatic tones, soft and sharp. This is in line with the passage of Pliny describing the nature of painted decoration produced by Fabullus, who, *gravis ac severus idemque floridus ac umidus* expressed his art almost exclusively in the *Domus Aurea.* But corresponding equally to the literary tradition, according to others, is the character and the style of the refined decoration of the private apartments. Its noteworthy artistic level certainly does not exclude the possibility of attributing it to this dignified and magniloquent court painter, chosen to express Neronian ideology and aesthetics.

If, as is the case today, one is inclined to maintain (Schefold) that, besides serving purely ornamental aims, in every decorative scheme one can discern contents and significance relating to propaganda programmes, then the cycle of paintings in the Domus might be permeated by contents of the political stance of the *princeps*, such as a glorification of aesthetic-pacific-agonistic values.
Even if the themes of Homeric epic tend to support the idea of a glorification of *virtus bellica* and of heroic *pathos*, only the attraction of beauty and the idea of paradisiacal happiness, in contrast with the dominant aristocratic stoicism, make up the thread that leads through the painted decorative programme of the Neronian palace.
This conception is based on the glorification of physical youth as well as its poetic-theatrical and cosmological principles. Underlying this is the widespread presence of Dionysus, whose pre-eminence, in contrast to the total absence of Apollo-related

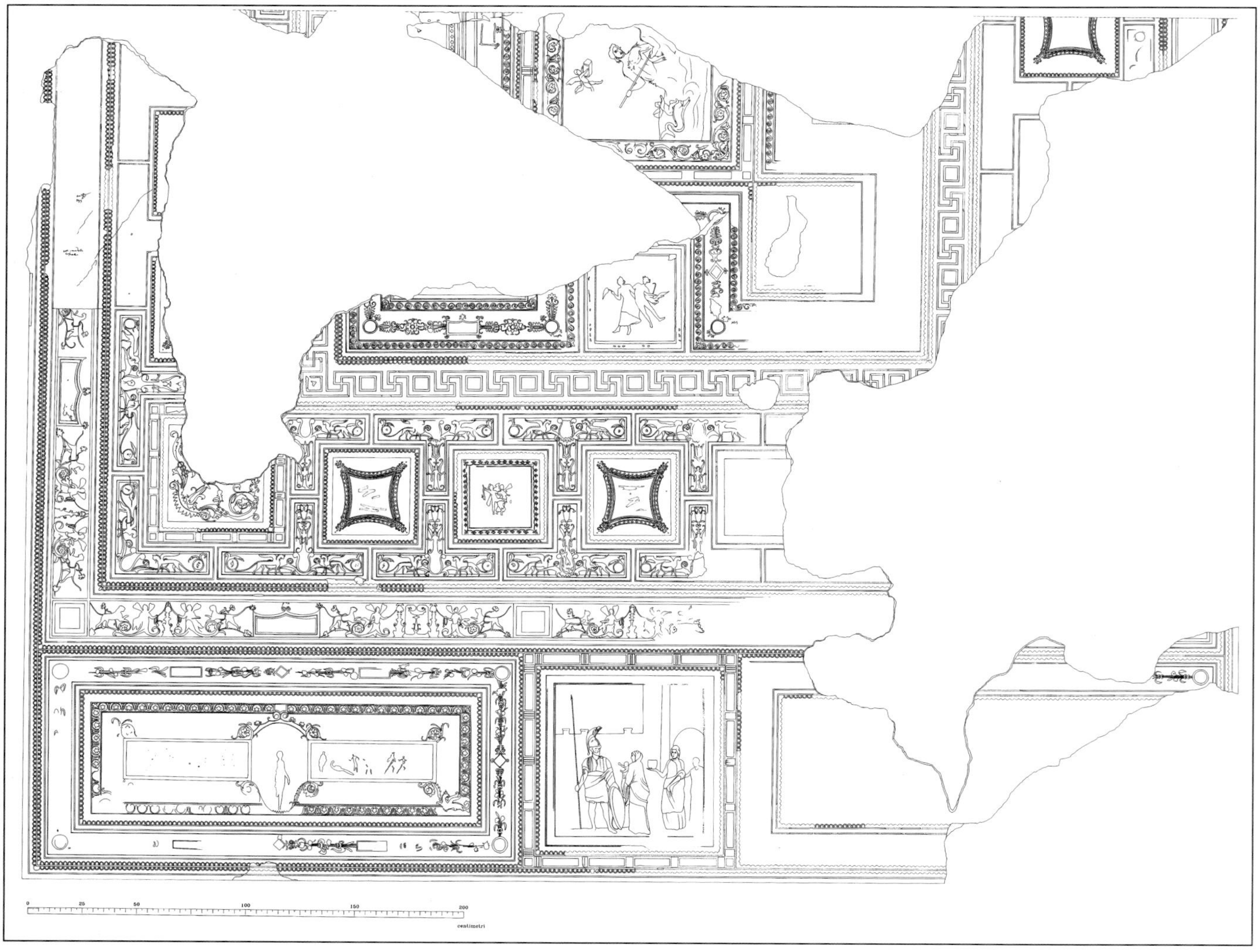

28. Hall of Hector and Andromache, geometric decorative composition of the vault, in stucco and paint (reconstructed drawing)

themes (Perrin), leads one to discuss the hypothesis of some scholars (L'Orange) who assign a solar character to the *Domus* of Nero, in line with the Neronian concept of sun-kingship derived from the east. Even if one cannot exclude the possibility that we are perhaps dealing with a Dionysus with a solar character, Apollo was certainly equated to the sun in the 5th century BC in Greece and subsequently in the Roman world.

Depictions of Bacchic themes symbolize the advent of *aurea saecula* (which Seneca predicted would begin at the moment of the ascent to the throne of the seventeenth disciple). Scenes of ritual and of sacrifice also take on a symbolic initiatory character when interpreted in mystic-Dionysiac terms. Also connected with initiation rituals are many of the ornamental motifs and the creatures who serve as accessories, such as griffons (in connection with Dionysus), centaurs and winged genies, whereas eagles, sphinxes and winged figures signify the relationship and connection between the human sphere and the ideal, the divine, of gods and of harmony.

The themes from the Trojan cycle, on the other hand, take up the concept of the destroyed city and glorify the builder-emperor of the Nova Urbs, even if one does not exclude entirely the possibility that these same themes may refer to the Trojan origins of Rome and the descent of the Julian family from the Trojans. These Homeric themes, along with the Dionysiac subjects, were already employed often in the decoration of the *Domus Transitoria*, before the fire of AD 64.

29. Domus Aurea, *hall no. 29, decoration of the 'vault of the owls' arranged in different ornamental friezes*

on the following pages:

30. Corridor no.50 'of the eagles', wall and vault decoration

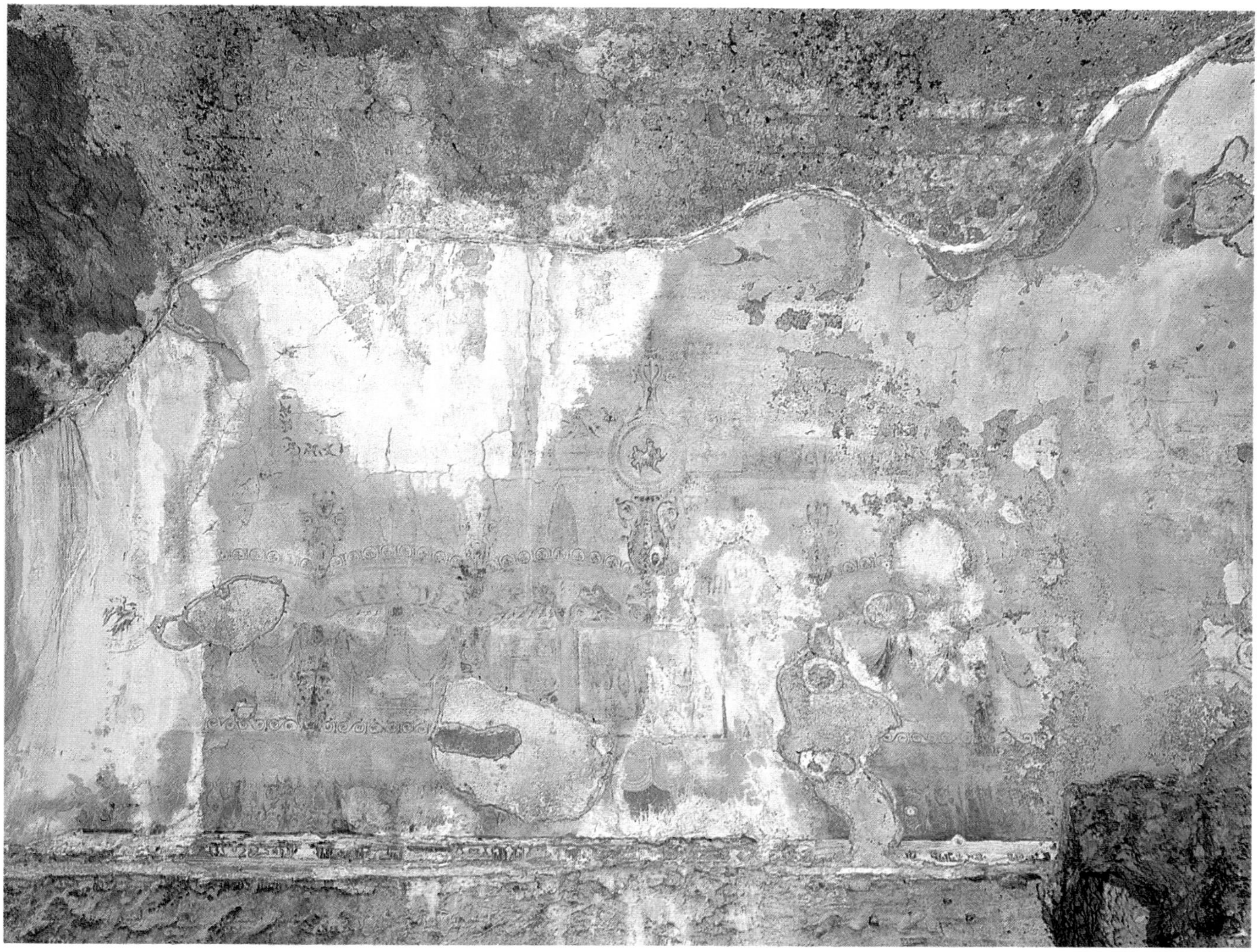

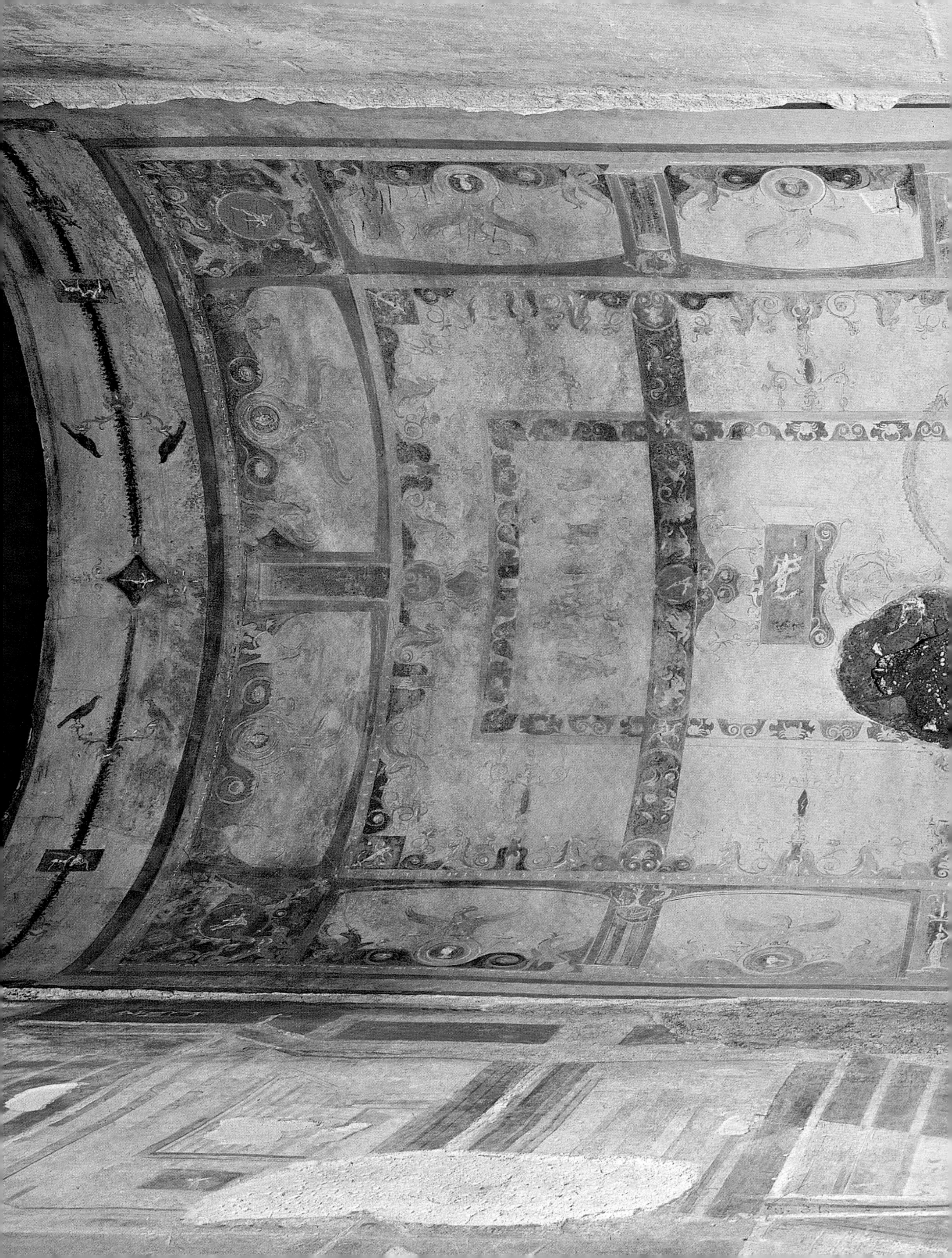

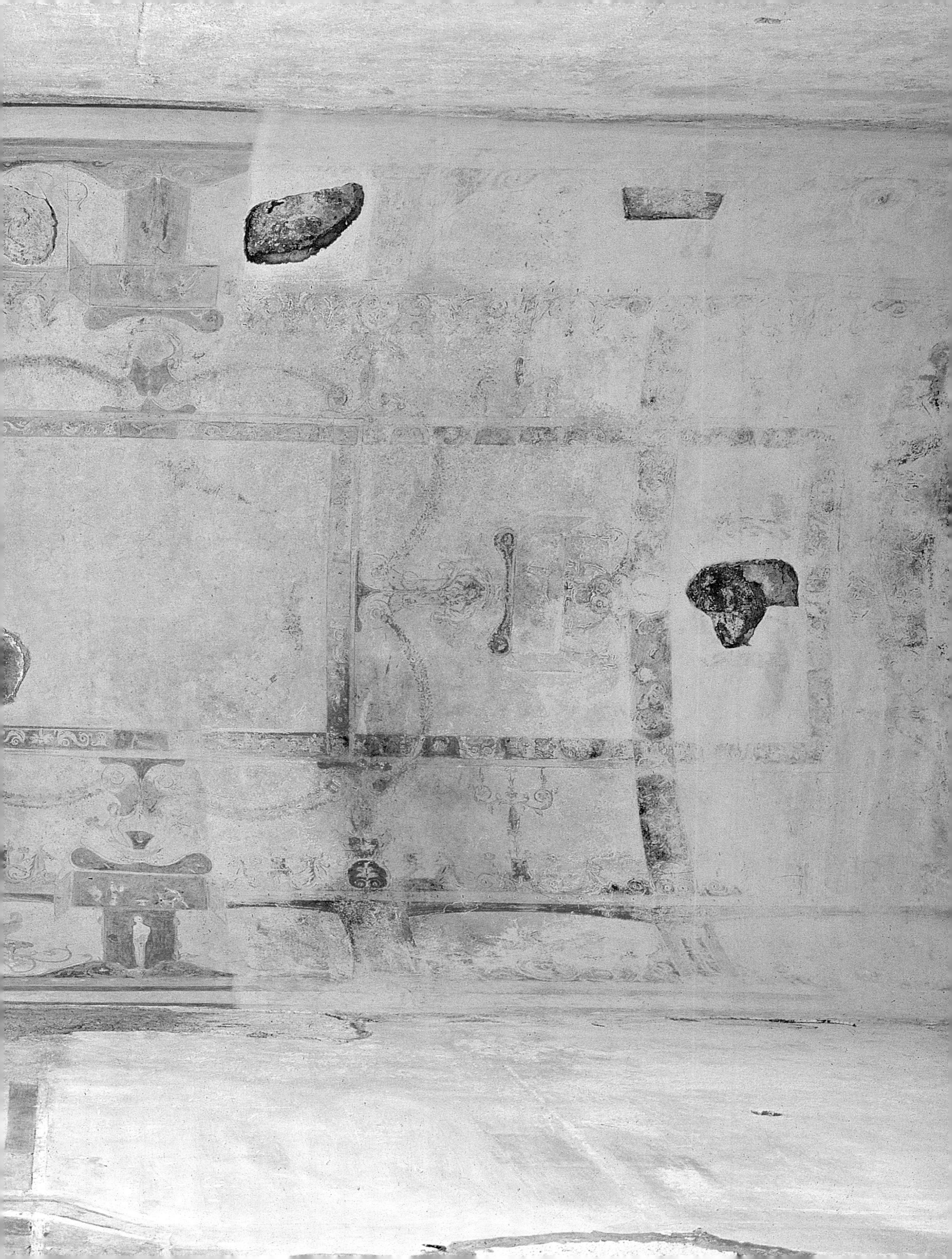

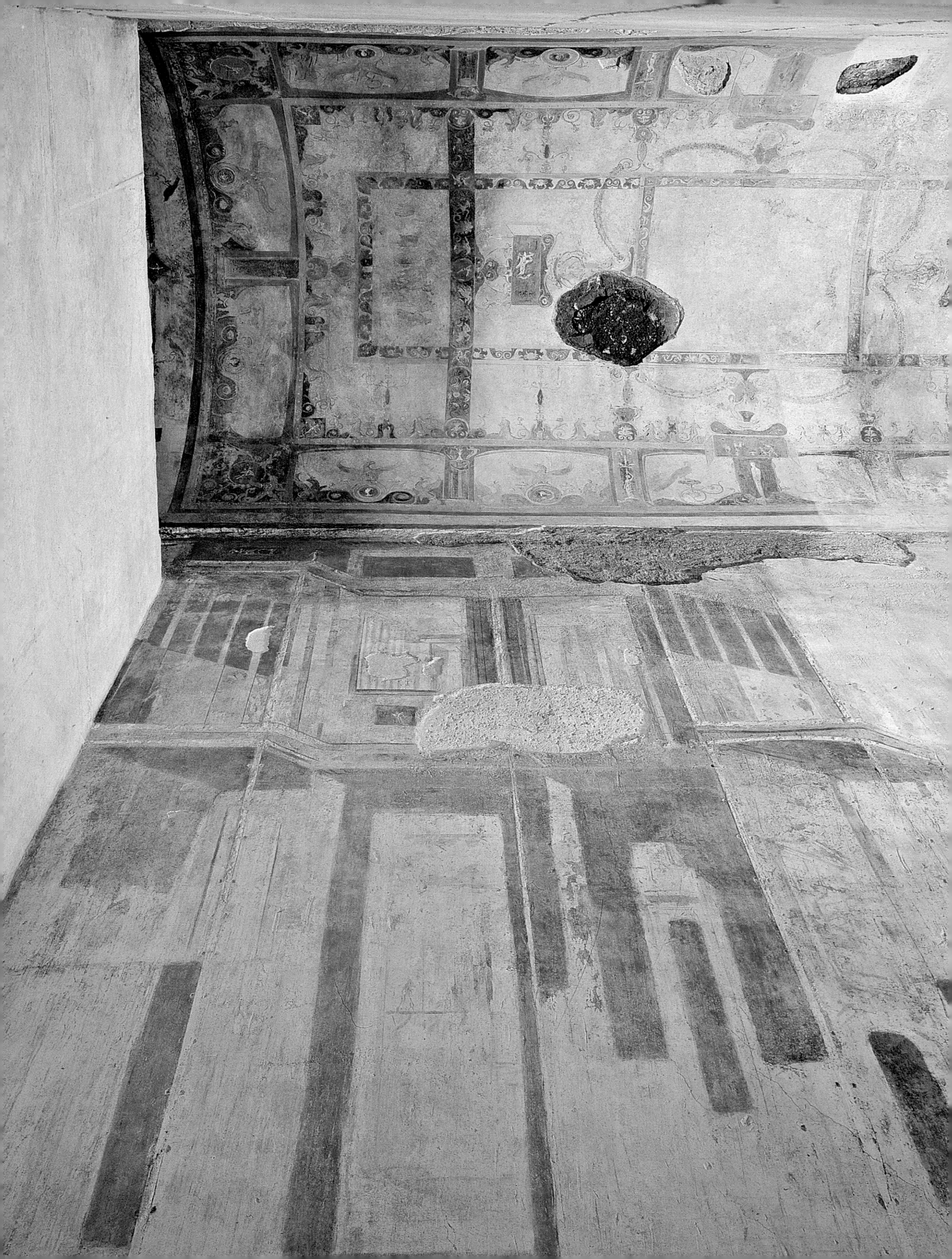

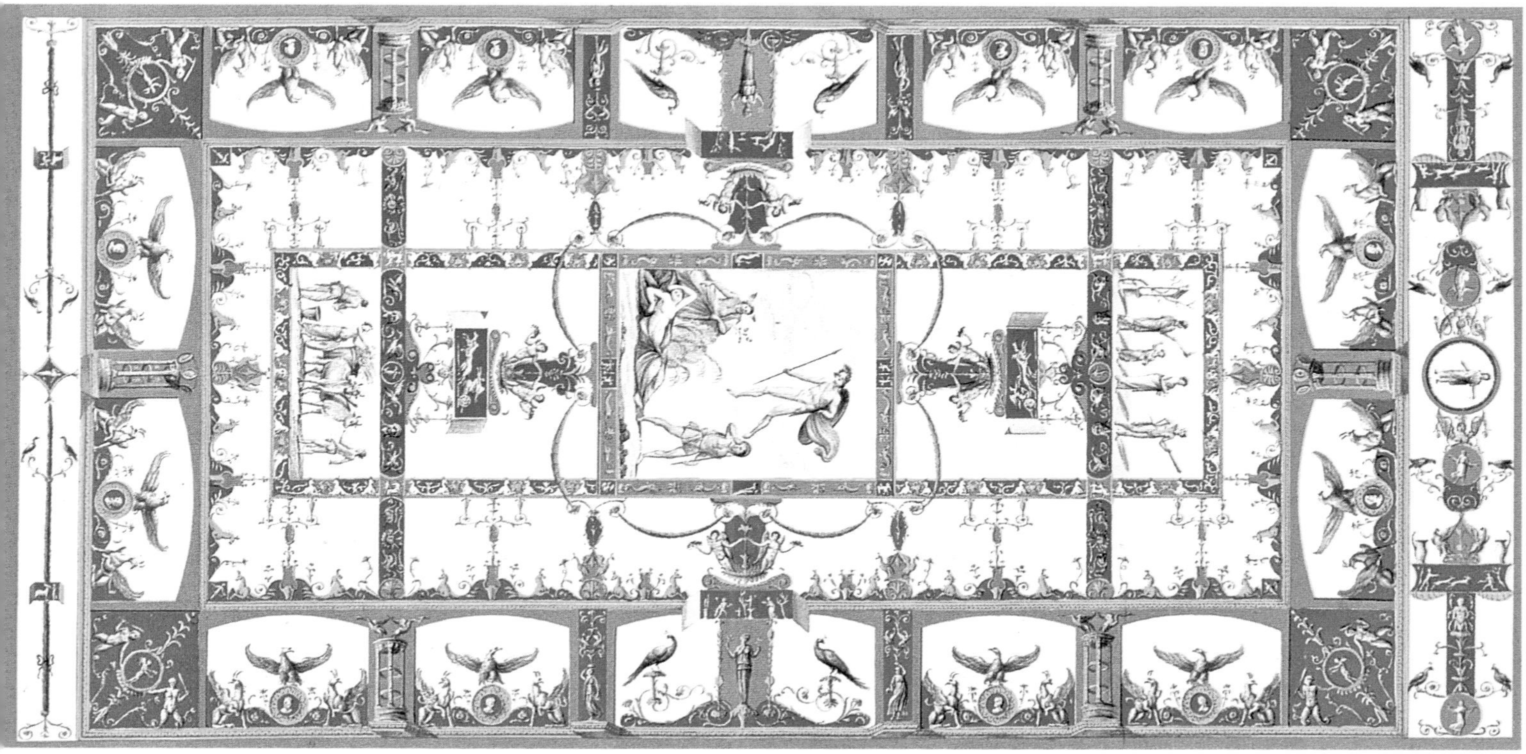

31. Corridor no.50 'of the eagles', wall and vault decoration

32. Corridor no.50 'of the eagles', decoration of the vault with the central scene (now lost) of the abandonment of Ariadne by Theseus on the island of Naxos (Mirri 1776)

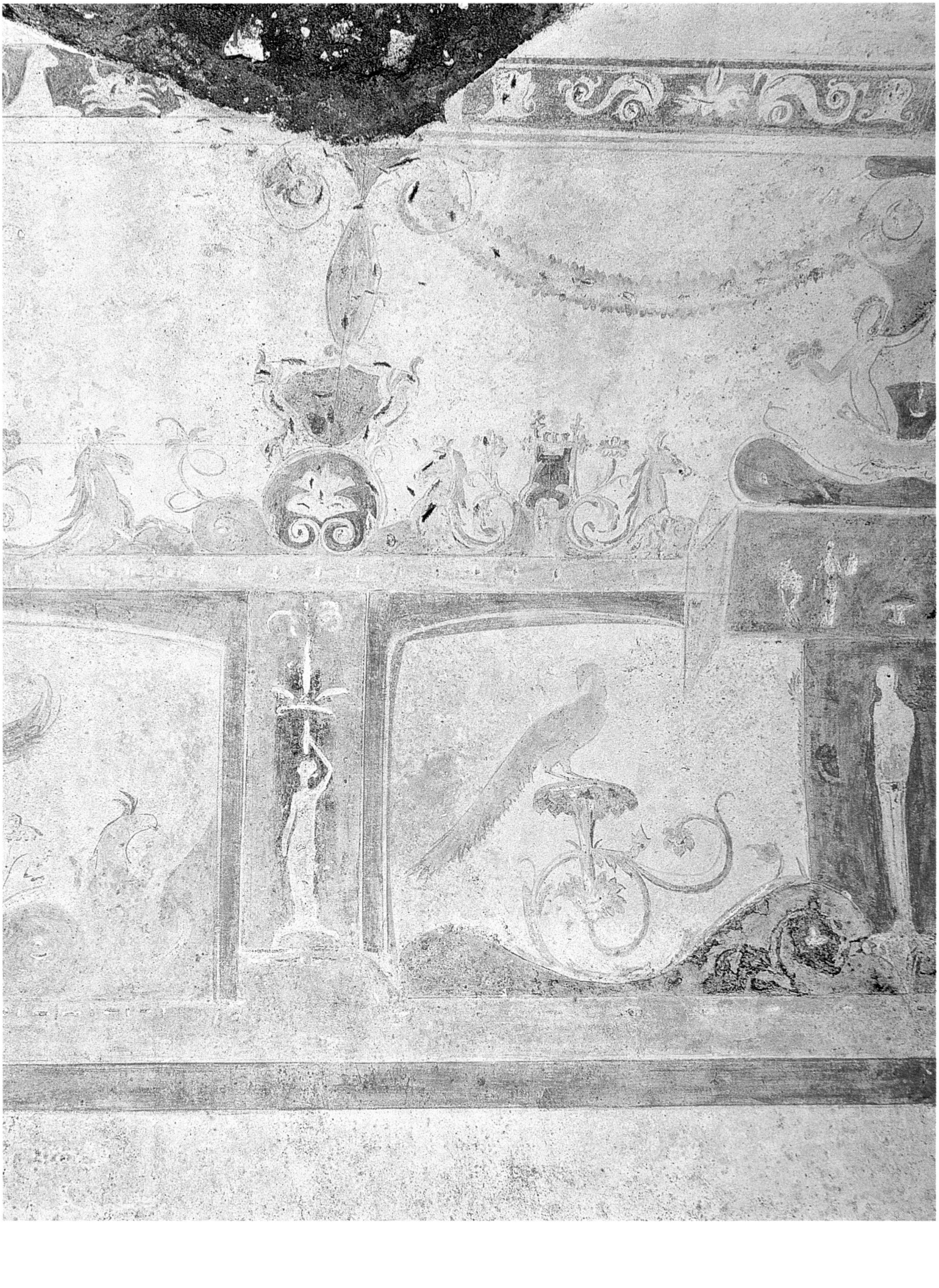

33. Corridor no.50 'of the eagles', detail showing a peacock, alternating with tripods and caryatids, in one of the panels which surround the vault

34. Corridor no.50 'of the eagles', vault, tritons with shouldered oars, placed at the corners of a series of panels containing the repeated motif of the imperial eagle on clipea, *with griffons to each side*

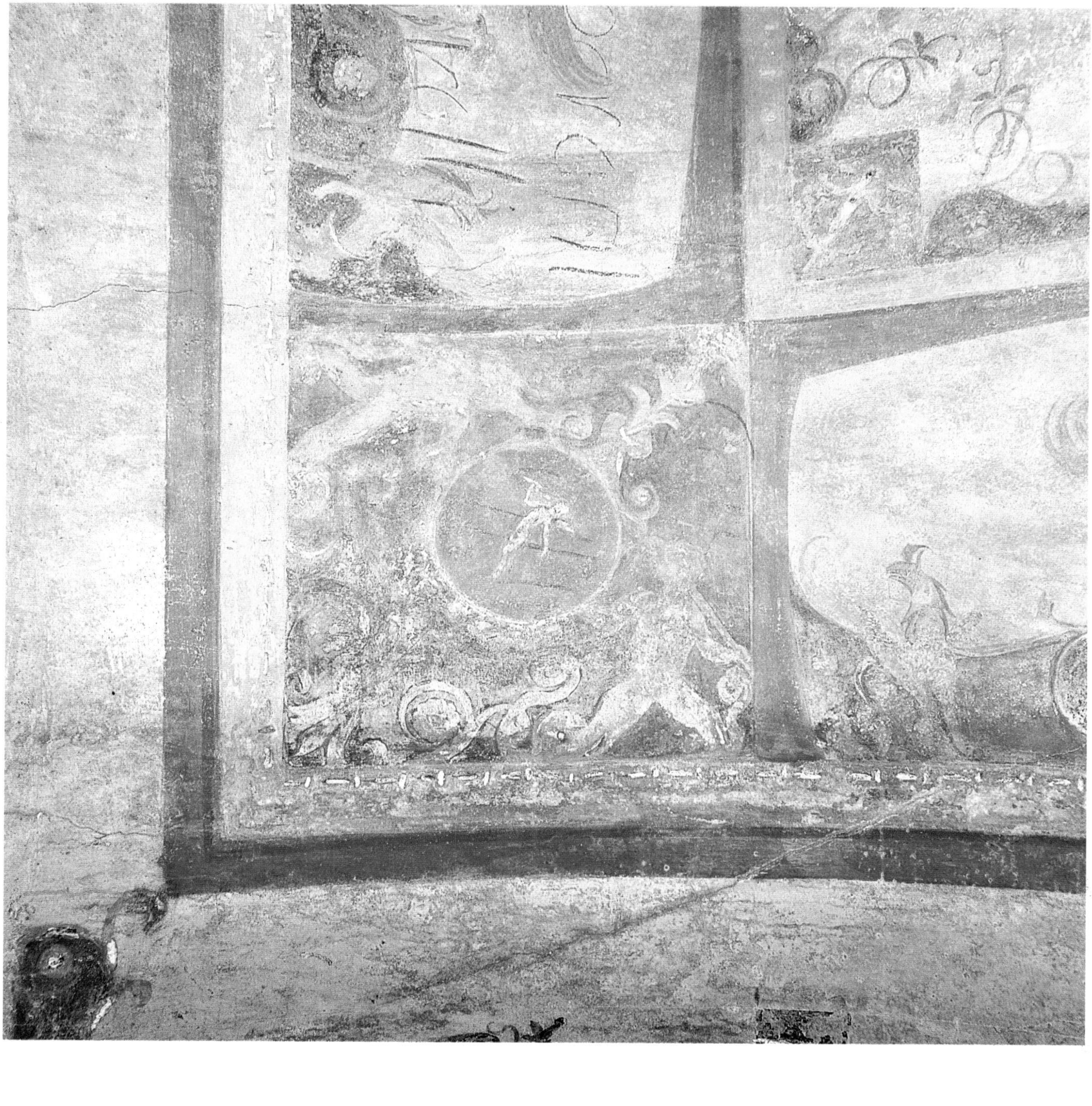

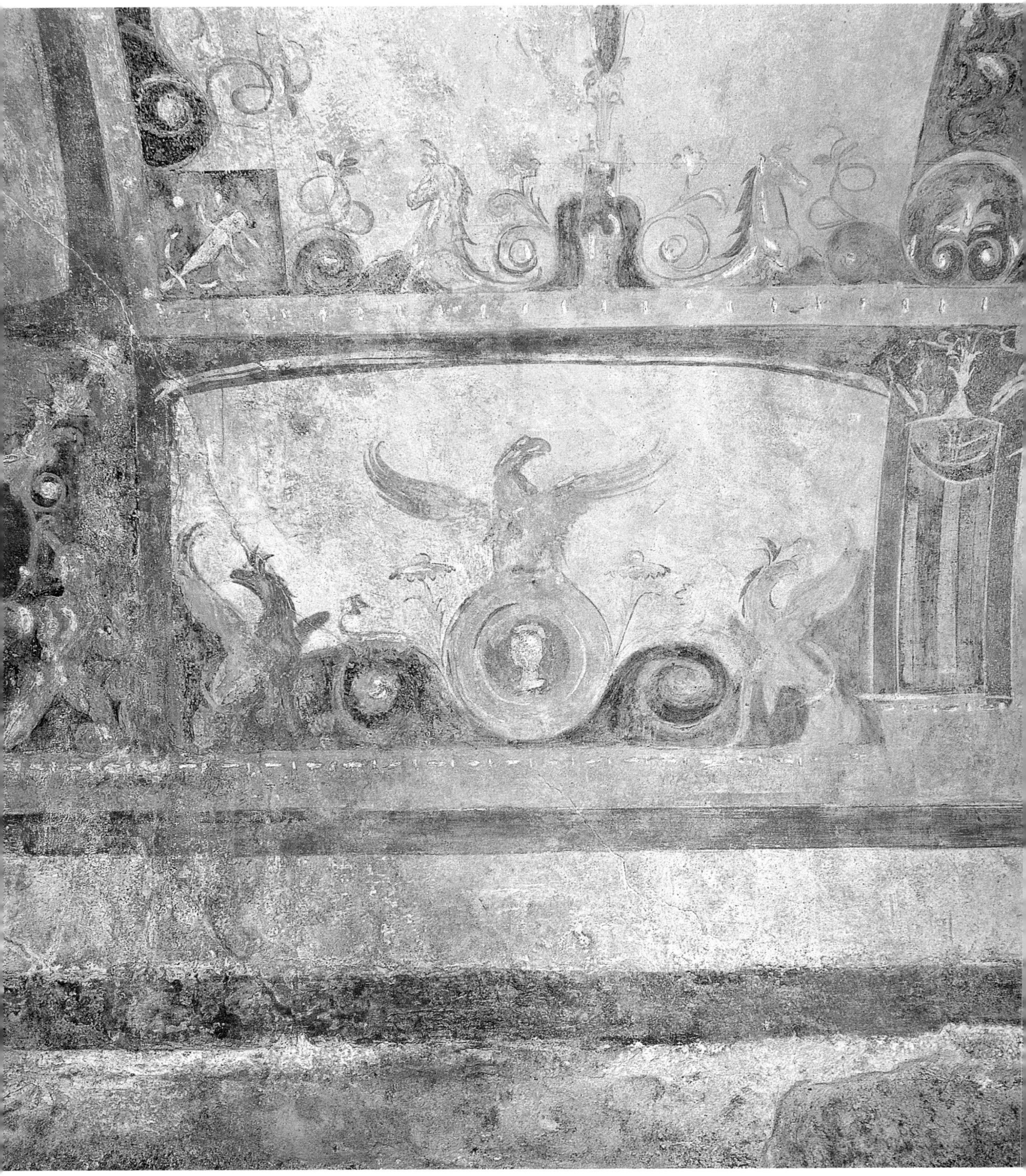

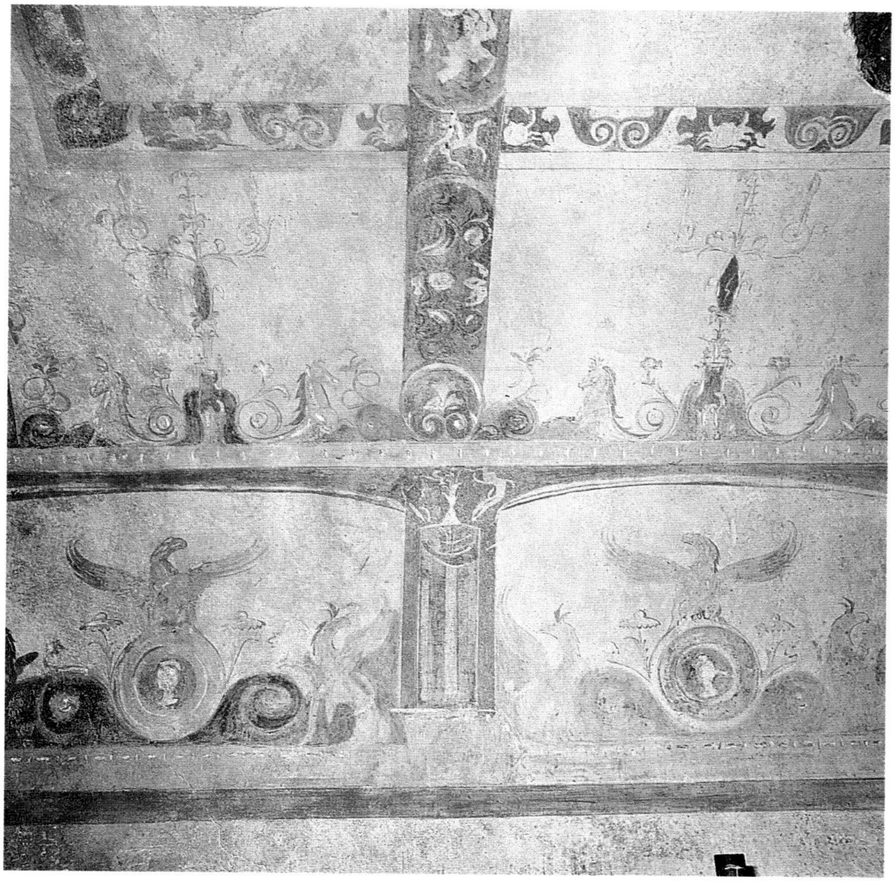

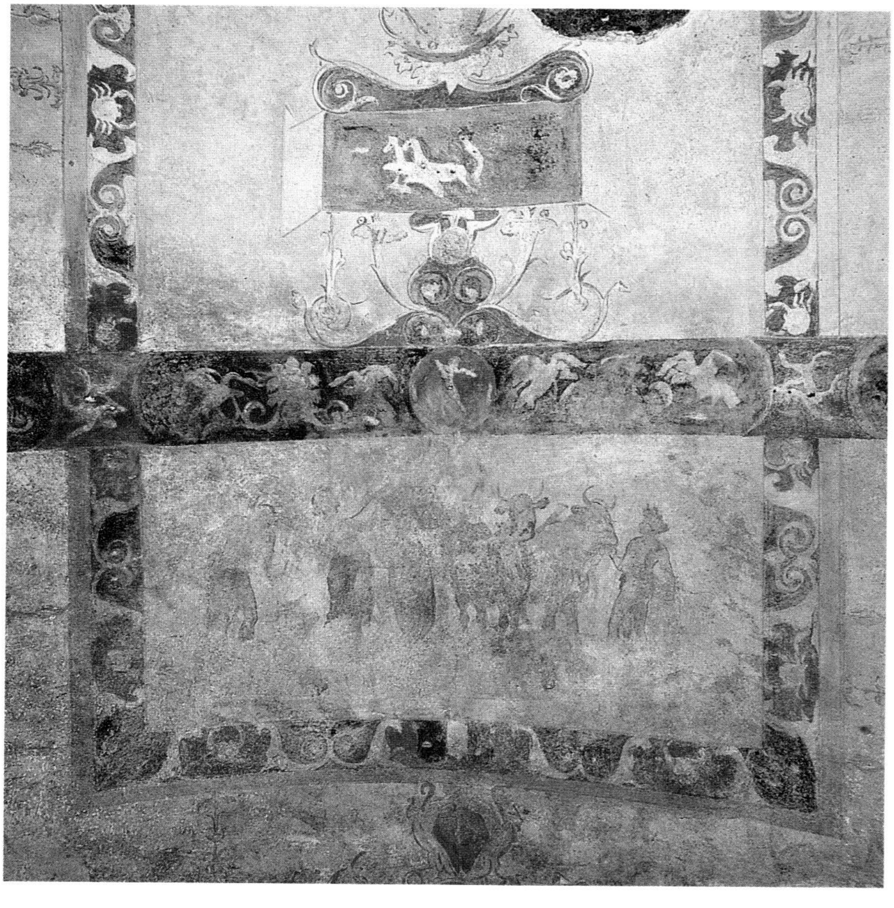

35-36. Corridor no.50 'of the eagles', vault, decorative details

37. Corridor no.50 'of the eagles', vault, rural scene

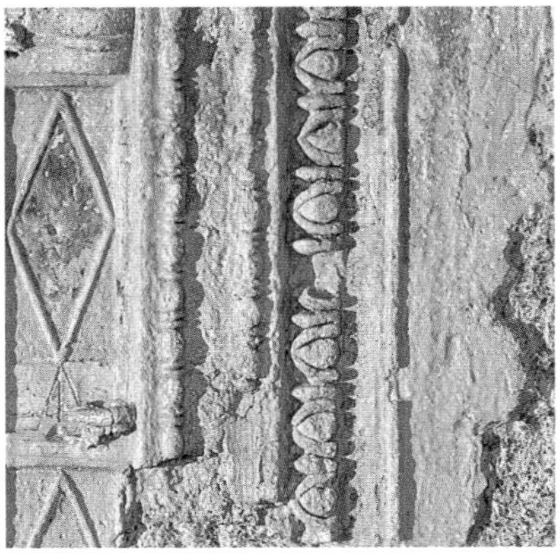

The Golden Vault (80)

In the 16th century the 'Golden Vault' still preserved the original complexity of its ornamental framework, fantastic character and brilliance of colour. These characteristics aroused great admiration from artists of the period, just as they had in the late 15th century. The artists were inspired by the exceptionally rich and varied composition and assimilated it completely, leading to adaptations of the ancient prototype that became, in effect, originals. This can be seen in the decorative schemes of Pinturicchio in the Palazzo Petrucci and in the Libreria Piccolomini of Siena cathedral, by Giovanni da Udine in the Stufetta Bibbiena in the Vatican, by Peruzzi in the Palazzo della Cancelleria, and by Raphael in the vaulted ceilings of the Vatican *Loggia*.

It is not surprising that, in his celebration of the 'Fasti' of the Farnese family, Taddeo Zuccari used the sumptuous decorative scheme of the most stunning, grandiose and ideologically significant room of Nero's palace as a model for the most public room of the Palazzo of Caprarola.

Its rich marble veneers, the sumptuous stuccowork and wall paintings, the magnitude and the axial position of the Golden Vault all manifest its importance in the palace. It is here, without doubt, that the most impressive celebration of Neronian ideology is found.

In addition to the interest of 16th century artists in elaborate reproductions of the refined ornamental grotesques on display in the buried ruins, figurative

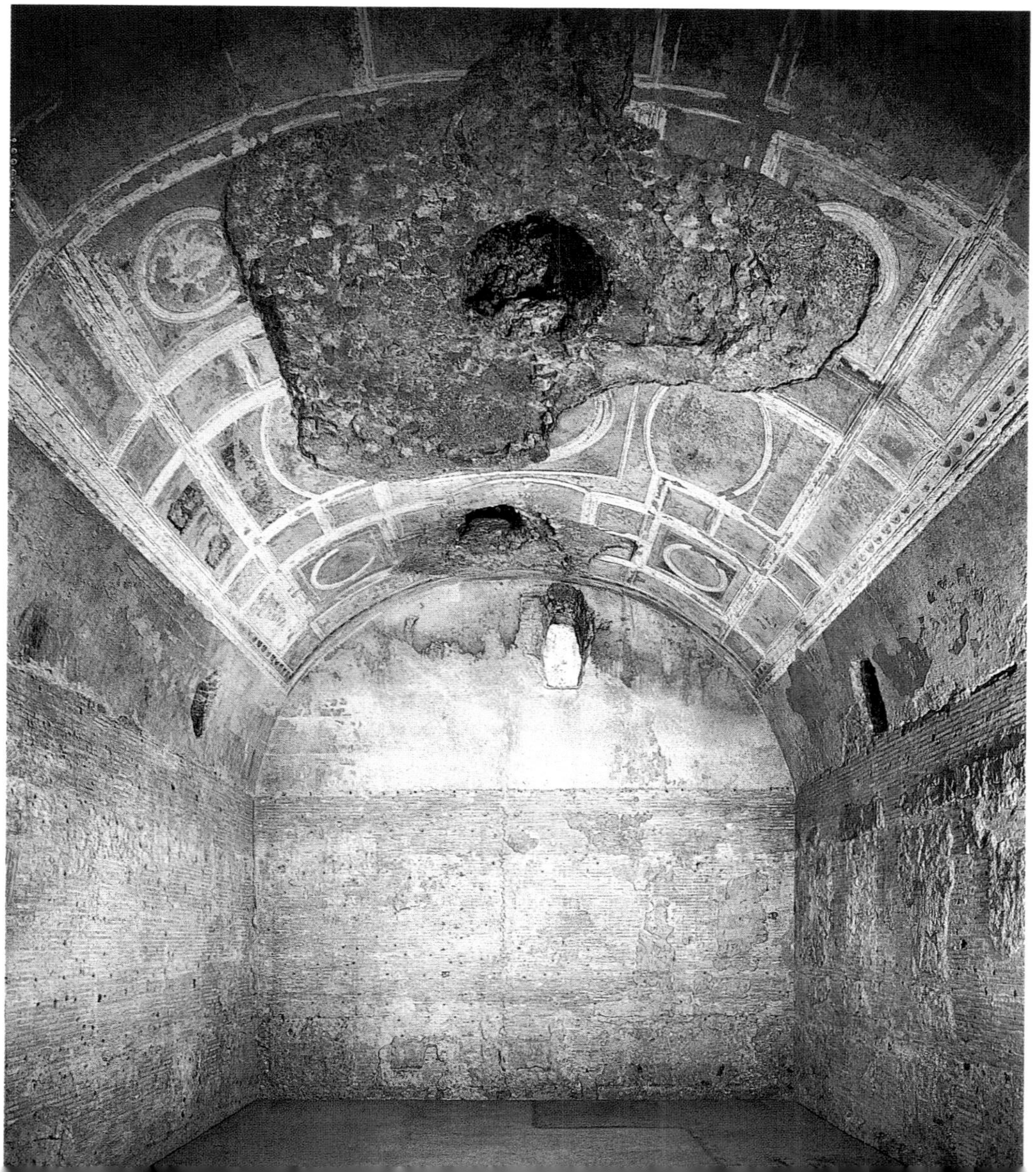

38. 'Golden vault', present condition of the decoration

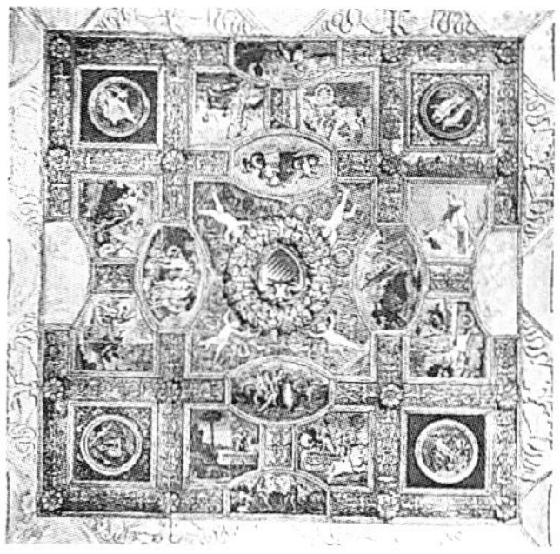

39. Pinturicchio, vault of the Palazzo Petrucci (New York, Metropolitan Museum)

40-41. 'Golden vault', detail showing the decoration divided into separate fields

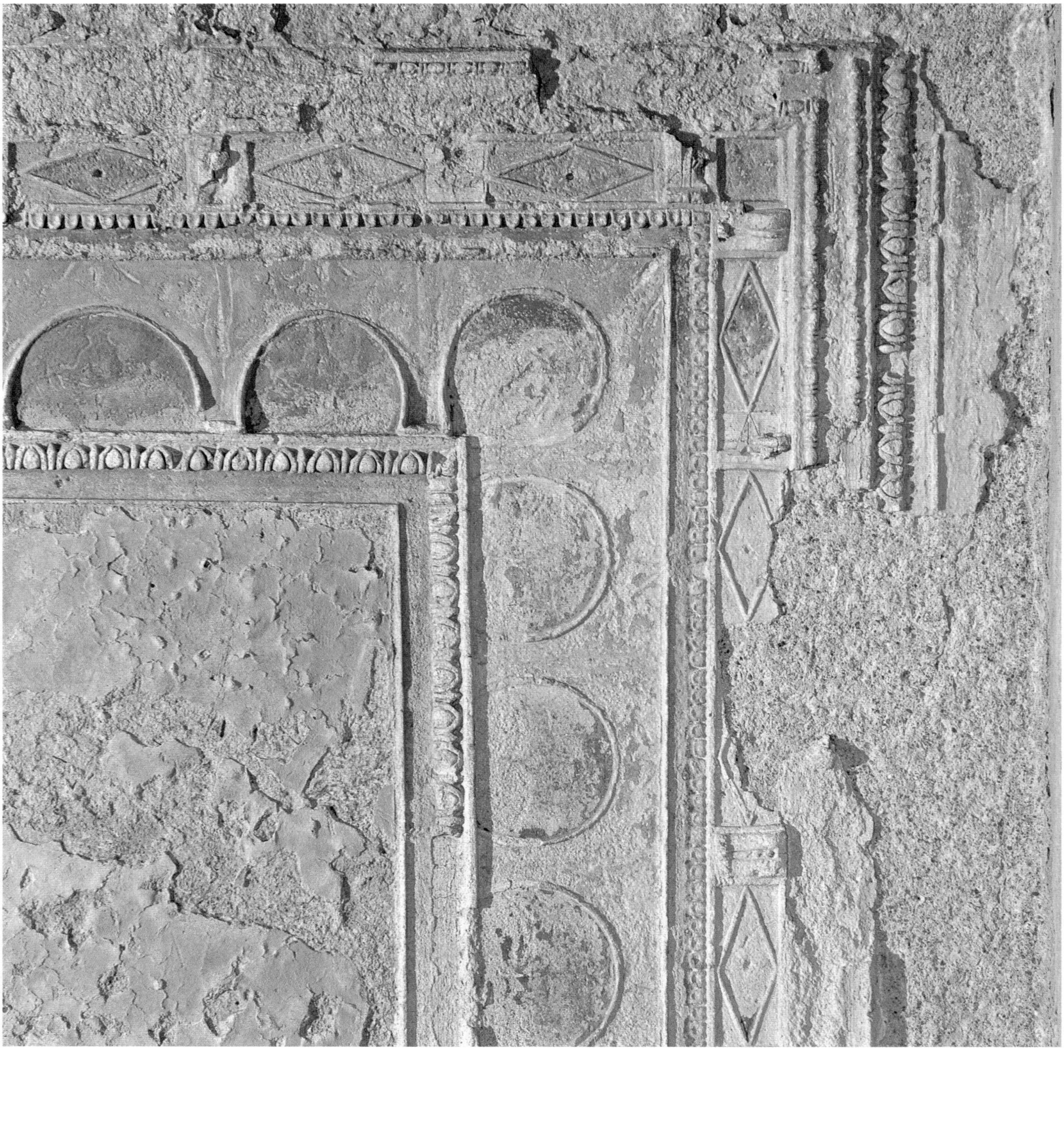

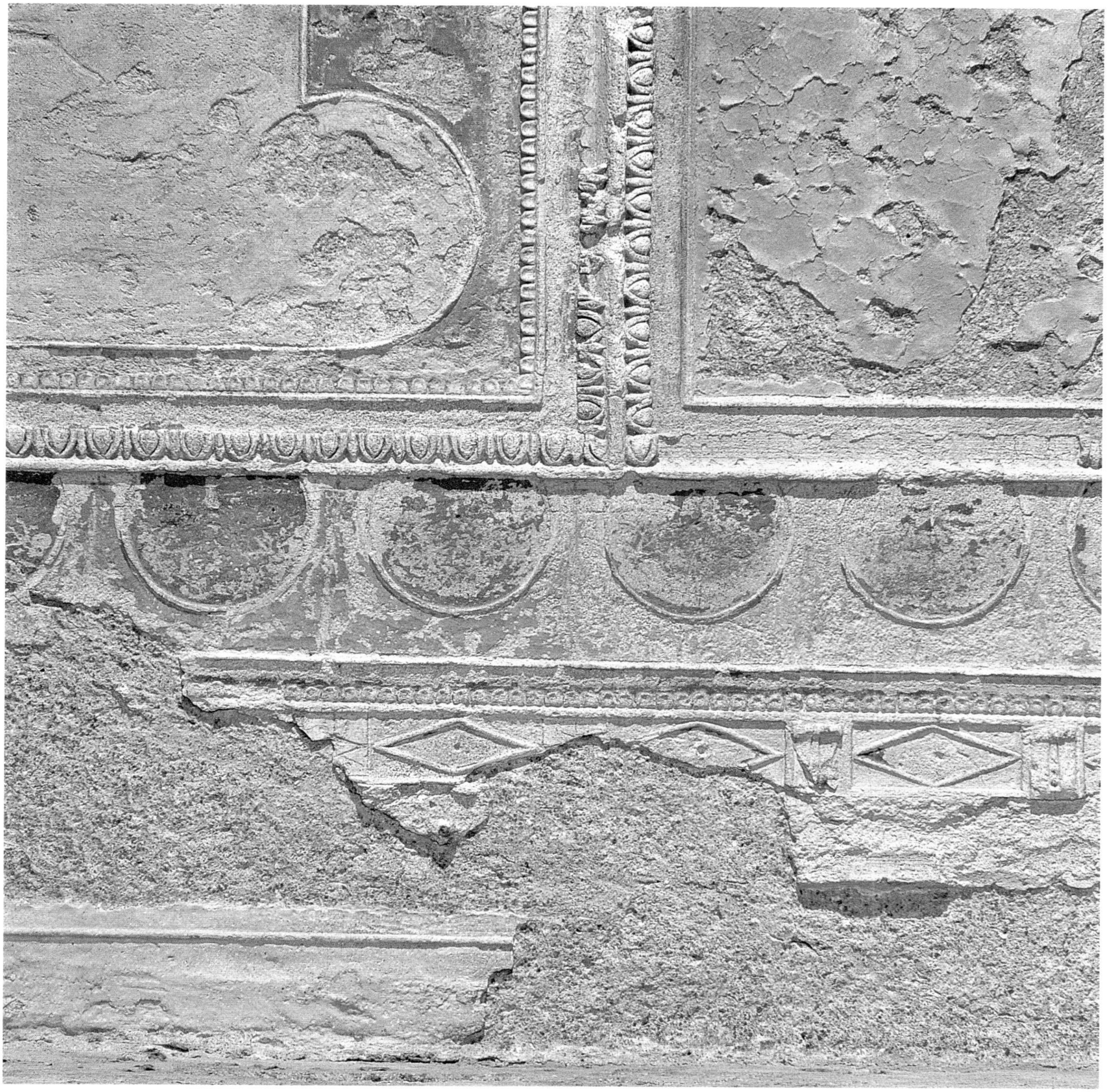

42. 'Golden vault', detail showing the decoration divided into separate fields

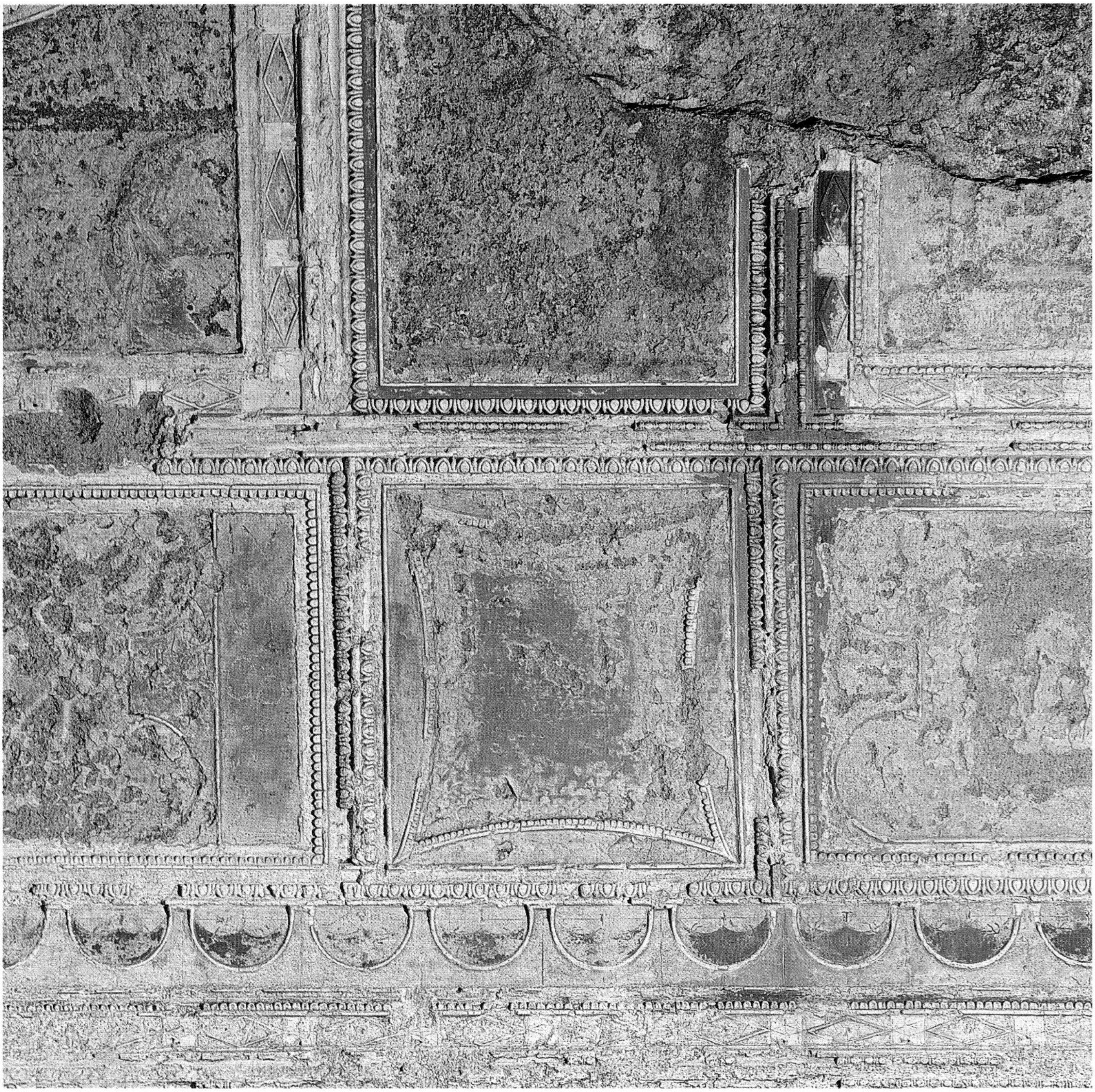

43. 'Golden vault', detail of the cornice relief moulded in gilded stucco

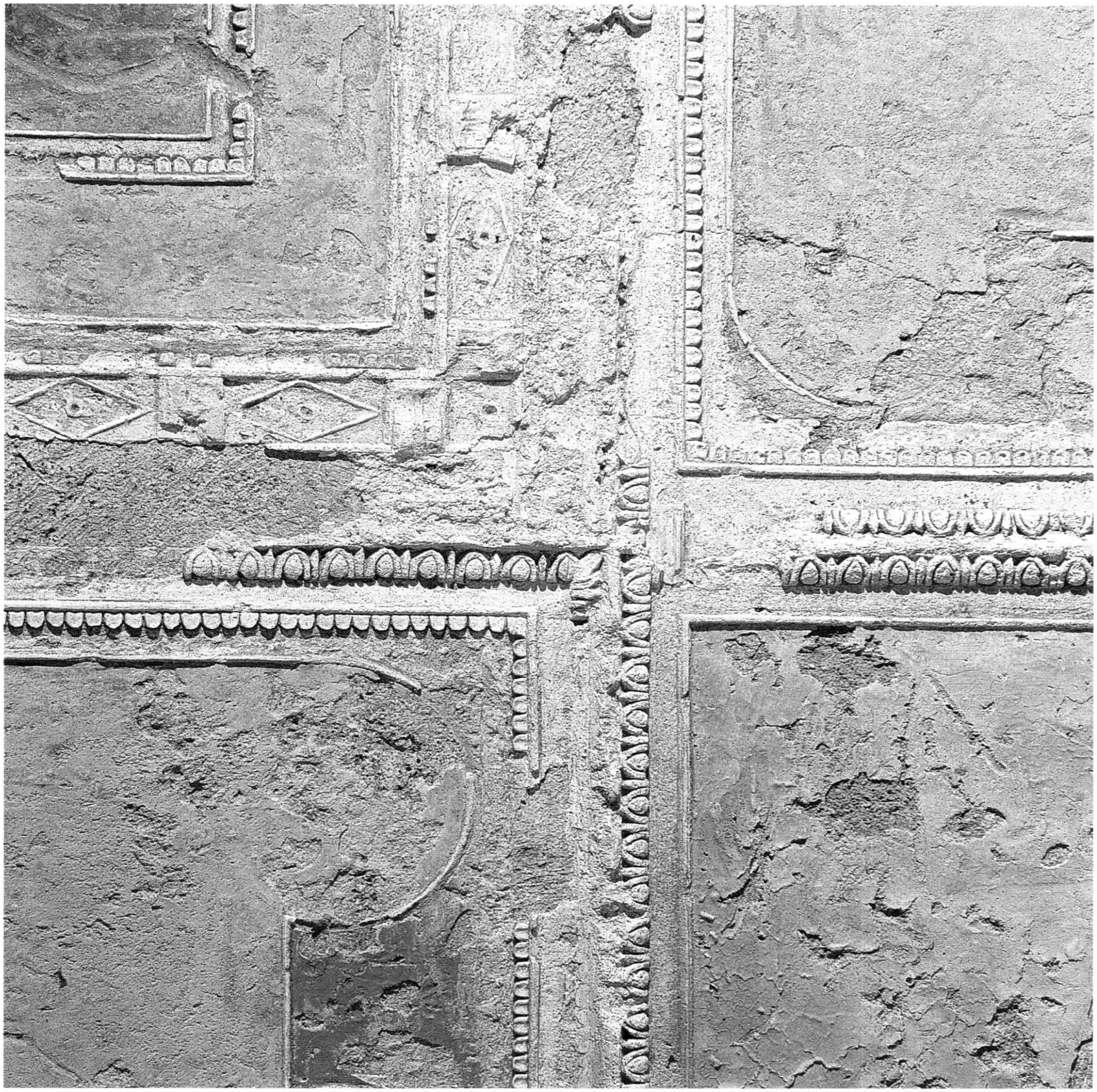

scenes (today almost completely lost) set within the multiple geometric fields dividing the ceiling of the vault were also reproduced and sketched in drawings. These drawings were not always faithful or trustworthy (relative to the original). Often they were anonymous, but some can be attributed to the hands or workshops of particular artists, such as Jacopo Sansovino (*Codice Fossombrone*) and Domenico Ghirlandaio (*Codex Escurialensis*).

A watercolour by Francesco de Hollanda (found in the *Codex Escurialensis* and from which derive loose copies, such as the prints of Cameron) illustrates to great effect the entire vault with its dazzling colours, and presupposes conditions of preservation no longer seen today. It enables us to appreciate more fully the original magnificence and complexity of the decorative scheme and the content of its figurative scenes than would be possible from just the remains that survive now.

The composition was of geometric form. Towards the walls, on the east and west sides, it was bordered by a band decorated by large figures. At its centre was a circle within a square that was set off by a stuccoed cornice. The circle contained a scene depicting the rape of Ganymede. This ornate version of the scene contrasts with the canonical version from the fourth century B.C. onwards which derived from the work of the Athenian artist Leochares, and which was perhaps inspired by a painted original. This must have been present in wall-paintings at Rome between the 3rd and 2nd centuries BC, as shown by some lines of verse by Plautus (*Menaechmi* V, 143).

In the Neronian depiction the handsome Trojan

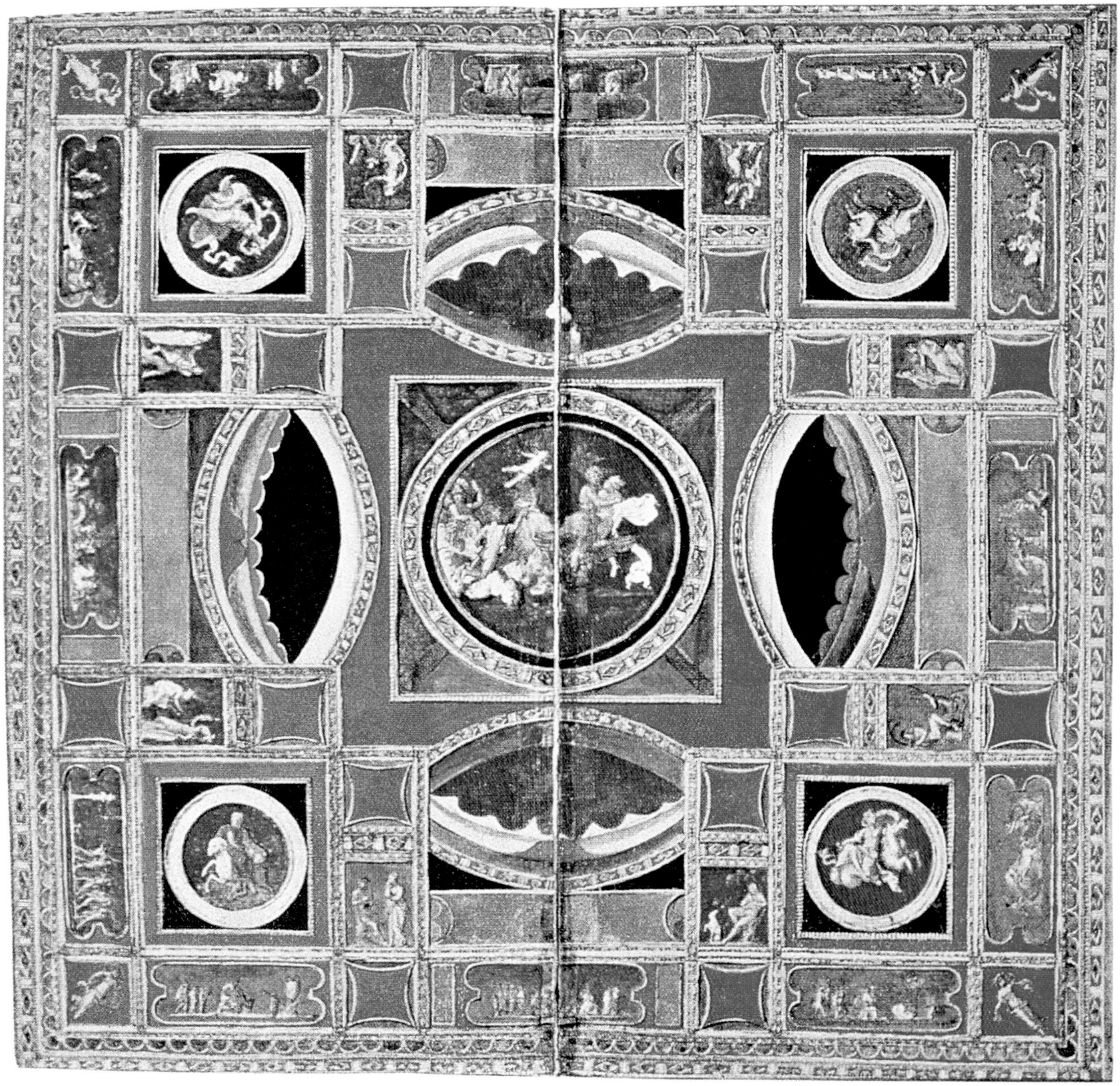

44. 'Golden vault', water-colour by Francisco De Hollanda (1538), El Escorial, Library

prince is seen together with Zeus carried through the air by an eagle, which is messenger and hypostasis in the depiction of the myth of Zeus in Classical art. The topic was created by Lesches of Lesbos, who belonged to a circle of poets who wrote about mythological cycles. Its symbolic significance concerns the afterlife; it relates to the ascension of the spirit to the sky, and its depiction was more often employed in a funerary context in Roman art.

Around the central composition a series of geometric motifs was developed, establishing a repeated image of a circle contained within a square. As well as dominating the centre of the composition, this motif was also repeated at the four corners and appears within a framework of rectangular and square panels which covers the entire surface of the vault.

Within these panels figurative scenes rendered in stucco or with simple strokes of colour are depicted in silhouette. These scenes are framed by elaborate cornices of gilded stucco, and are on neutral backgrounds with bright colours, although, in that *compendiaria* style which characterises the entire decoration of the palace, they lack any hint of spatial context. As can be seen in the 16th century drawings and etchings of Turnbull (based on the drawings of Pietro Sante Bartoli), Mirri and Ponce, which document the picture's gradual decay, the scenes deal with some of the most popular mythological subjects at Rome – such as the 'Departure of Hippolytus for the hunt'. These figurative scenes date back to a famous prototype which itself was inspired by the work of Euripides. They were common, not just in paintings (mostly Pompeian) but

45. 'Golden vault' (Mirri 1776). In the centre the scene of the abduction of Ganymede has been replaced with another depicting Demeter and the young Triptolemos, son of the king of Eleusius

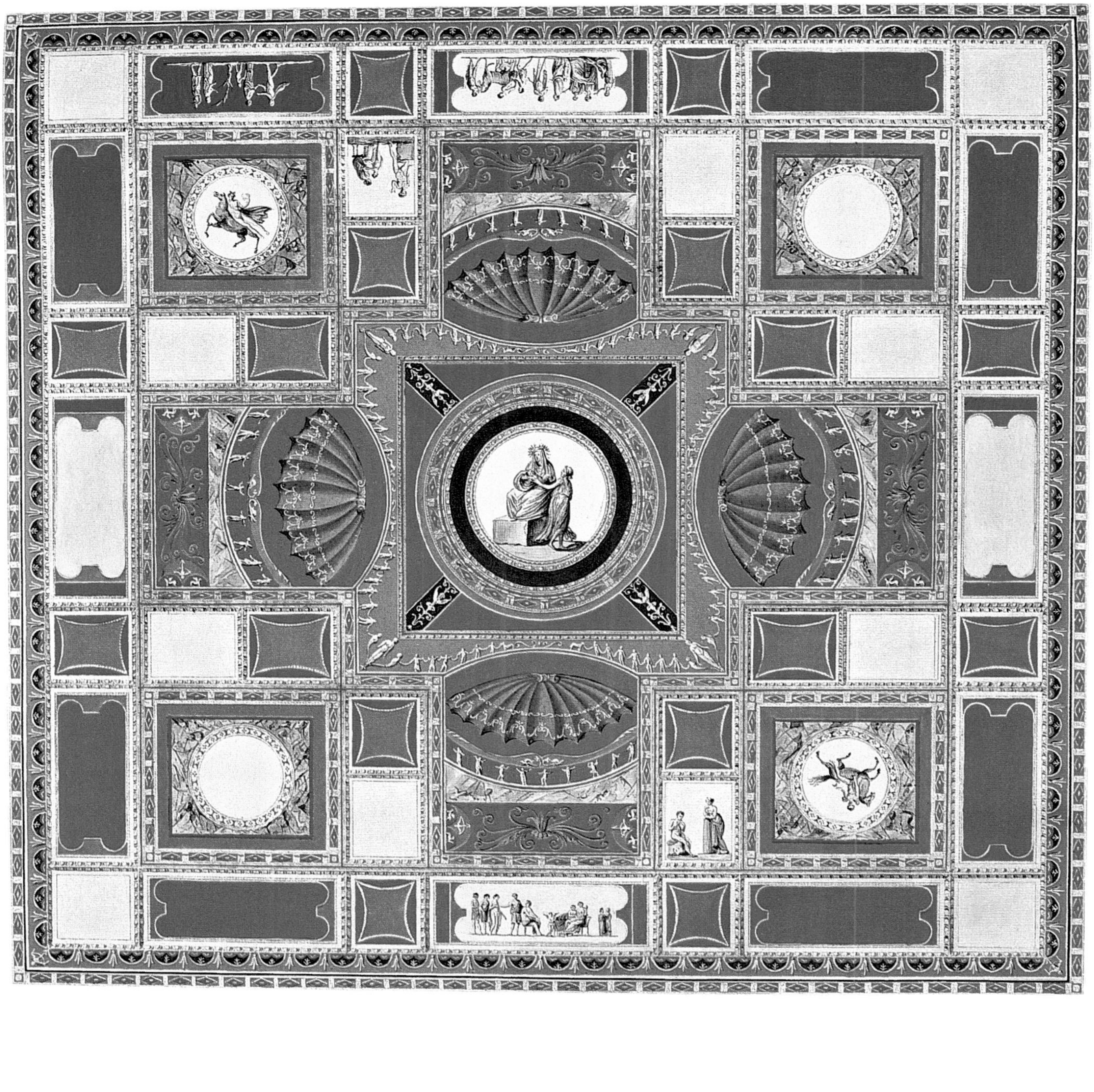

46. 'Golden vault', corner medallion, detail showing a youth on a horse (Mirri 1776)

also in funerary reliefs and particularly on sarcophagi, due to their inherent symbolism deriving from the destiny of the hero.

Recently it has been reasserted that Hippolytus and Phaedra are also the protagonists of the second mythological scene (the most accurate reproduction of which are the drawings of the Codice di Fossombrone), which was previously identified as the story of 'Ares and Aphrodite surprised by Hephaestos'. Comparable in its iconography to the so-called 'Nozze Aldobrandini' (Aldobrandini Wedding, a panel depicting preparations for a nuptial, or perhaps religious, ceremony, found in the neighbouring Gardens of Maecenas), the scene is repeated in Pompeian paintings and on sarcophagi.

In addition to the marine and Dionysiac processions found in the rectangles at the edges of the vault, the mythological scenes are most commonly integrated with depictions of one or two figures representing nymphs or ephebes on rams or horses, placed in the medallions in the four corners, and groups with Satyrs and Muses in the small frames closest to the large central panel. These, along with others of uncertain identification, are included among the drawings of the Codice di Fossombrone. These were copied directly from the original and reproduced by copyists of the 18th century, albeit with a certain license and in any case in neoclassical style.

The elaborate decoration of the hall has led to the identification of an artistic personality of great skill, a *maestro* corresponding to Pliny's description

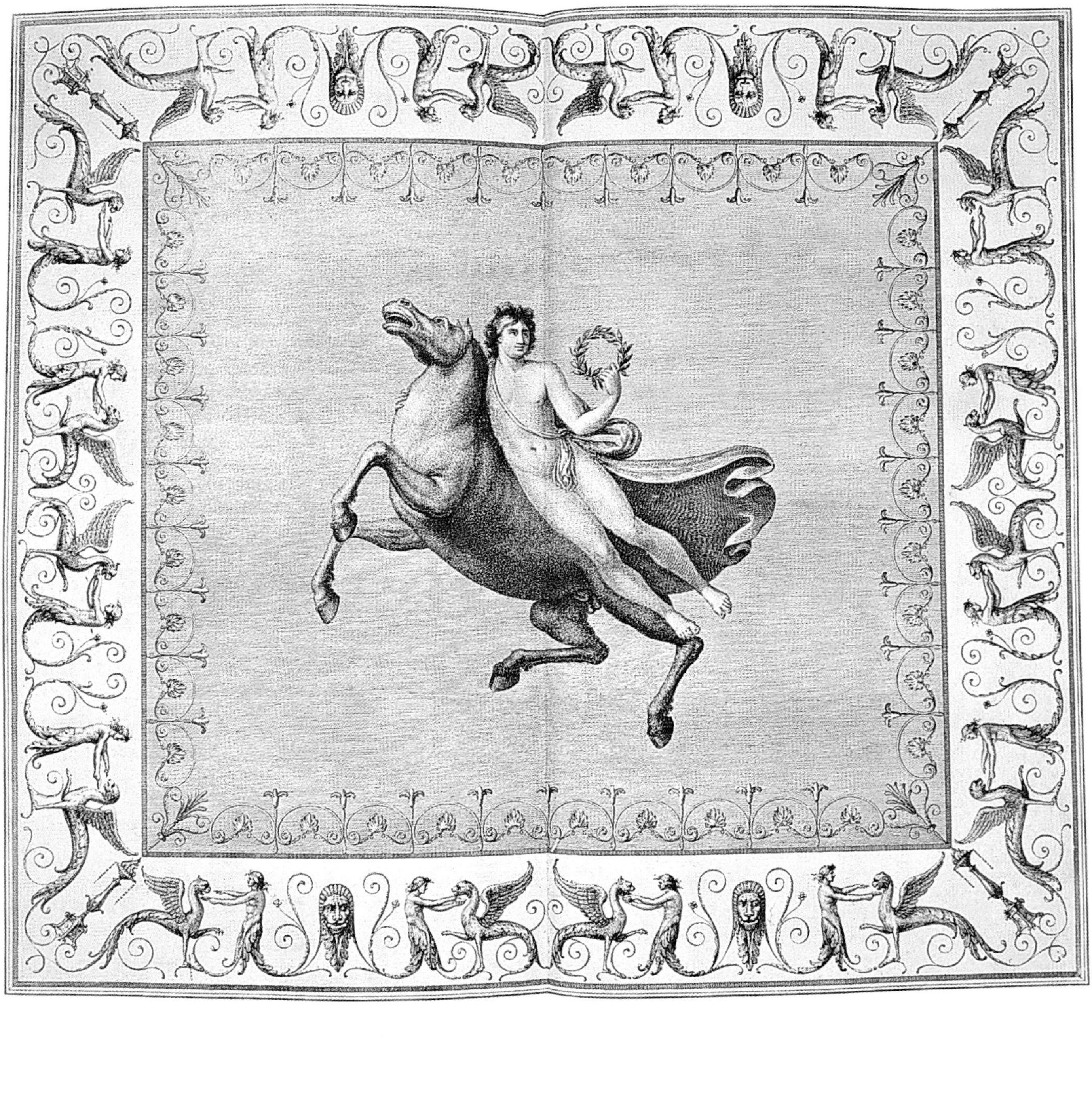

of the art and personality of Fabullus. Fabullus was Nero's reserved official painter, who, by his mastery of the use of colour, achieved contrasts between red and blue backgrounds, his best-known characteristic. With clever combinations of strongly tinted colours, he created decorative schemes which were novel and extremely magnificent, and interpreted well his imperial client's inclination towards the grandiose and fantastic. This was in perfect harmony with the extravagant taste of his time, the reflection of which can be seen equally in the literature of the period.

The *Maestro* who decorated the golden vault can be seen as the originator of a new artistic trend, in antithesis to the simplicity of Augustan artistic restraint. He knew how to impress a stamp of originality and grandeur not found in contemporary, painted, artistic expression in the Vesuvian cities. Despite this, studies (such as that of Ragghianti) ignore the artistic superiority of Rome and its simple imitation by local workers in their attempt to identify individual Campanian artists. Instead they identify (particularly in the cycle of Pompeian paintings in the House of Loreius Tiburtinus depicting the story of Laomedon) the style of an artist, the 'Neronian' or 'Palatine' *maestro*, not only similar to the *Maestro* of the Domus Aurea, but even more incisive and original than him.

47. 'Golden vault', detail showing a satyr and muse (Mirri 1776)

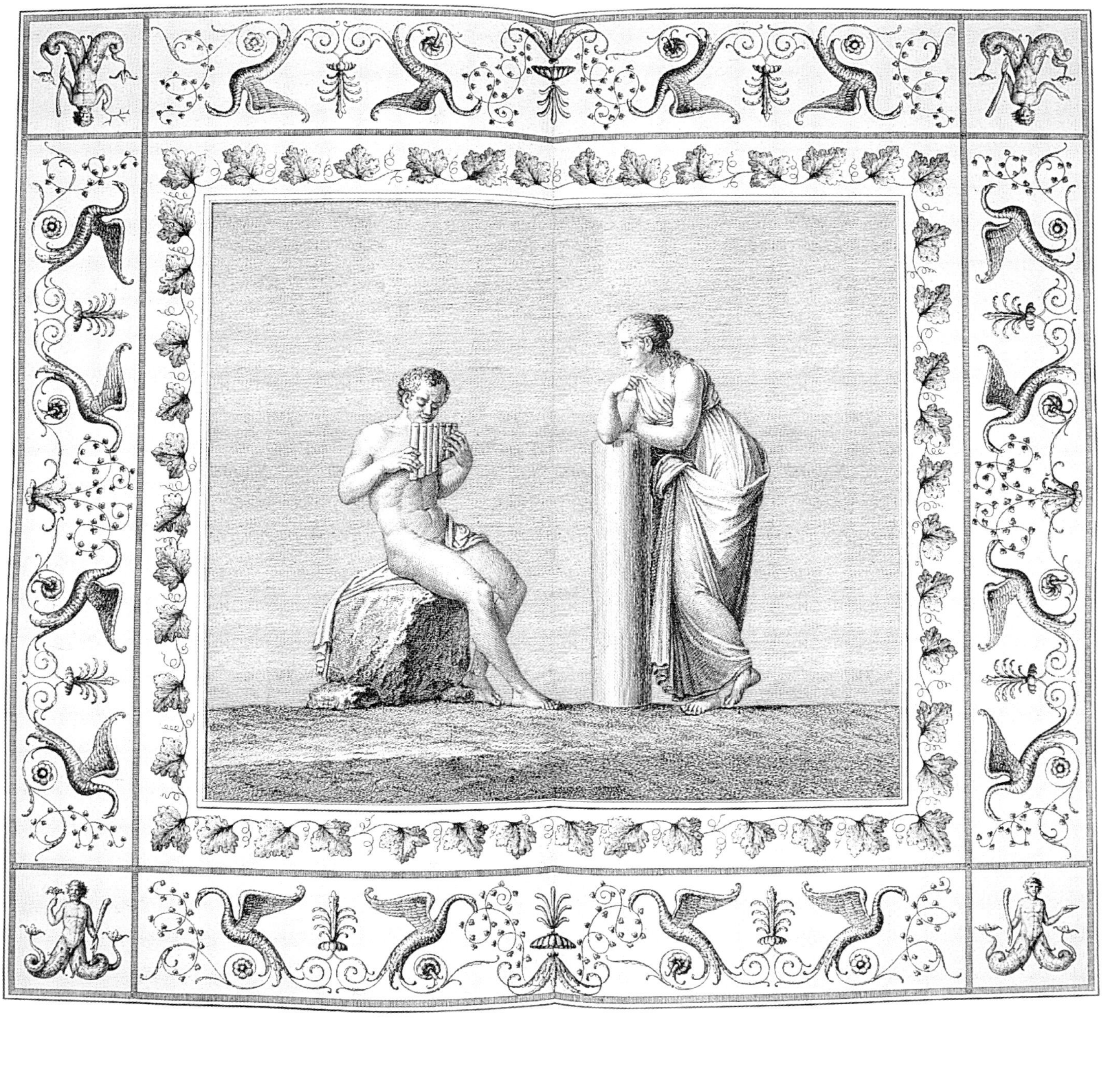

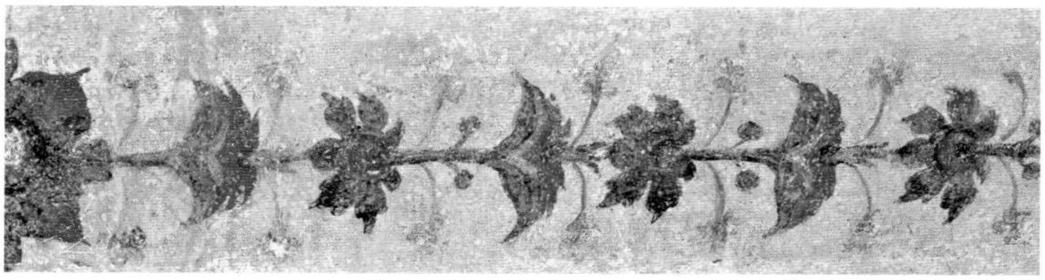

The Hall of Achilles at Skyros (119)

The lavish ornamentations of the ceilings of the Neronian palace is particularly interesting for the study of a complete decorative scheme. Few examples of such a thing are handed down to us from the Roman world and such evidence is rare even in Pompei. Of particular relevance are the decorative schemes of the public halls of the *Domus*, executed in mixed techniques using paint and stucco. In the hall of Achilles at Skyros (so named from the depiction, at the centre of the vault, of Achilles among the daughters of king Lycomedes of the Dolopes at the island of Skyros, where he had been hidden by his mother Thetis to prevent him participating in the Trojan war) the stucco embellishes the elaborate paintings, and emphasises the public function of the room. Stucco in the form of moulded cornices sets off the geometric composition of the decoration of the vault, it is used to produce small moulded figures and adds depth to columns and capitals. In addition, it outlines the architecture which divides the upper parts of the walls (the remnants of which are covered with exquisite marble veneers).

Partitions framed by painted bands and by moulded stucco cornices contain Bacchic figures standing and holding *kantharoi* (scenes of generic subjects or of purely decorative interest). Along with Dionysiac *thiasoi*, these symbolise the golden age. These partitions articulate the vault as a fake coffered ceiling. Bands with figured panels (these scenes are now almost completely lost) close the composition on the long sides performing the usual function of rendering square the decorated space.

The imagination of the artist is freely expressed in the profusion of friezes and ornamental elements, such as floral candelabra set with harpies and winged sphinxes, gilded *kymatia*, and various filling motifs. He first defined the spaces, then framed the panels and figurative scenes, and with a sense of *horror vacui*, did not even spare the surfaces of the architectural elements.

From this derives a decorative style of notable magnificence, which reflects the quality of *luxuria* aspired to by the *princeps* in his constant emulation of oriental dynasties, the basis of the luxuriant new Golden Age, of the *felix saeculum* which the court panegyrists and Seneca himself anticipated.

The decorative arrangement of the walls (in identical form on opposite walls) allows us to see how a new, growing feel for spatial illusion developed in contrast with the layout of previous styles. It offers an example of the specific characteristics of fourth style, illusionistic opening up of the walls onto architectural backgrounds with broad vistas. The stage-like composition is enlivened by emblems at the apexes of different levels and by the insertion of single, emphasised 'living' figures, standing or seated, of philosophers, poets and worshippers. These are positioned behind the architecture or visible through open panels in glimpsed views that break up the upper part of the wall and repeat themselves in sequence the entire length of the wall.

In the foreground, slender stucco and painted pilasters are illusionistically differentiated from their background. They are depicted as if they had a structural function and as if they support, by means of an architrave, the entire vault.

While the emphasis on depicting an illusionary spatial environment is new, the illustration of the Homeric story placed at the centre of the arrangement is completely original. This bears testimony to the independence of the artist from Greek prototypes which Pliny (*Natural History*, 35.134) attributed to the painter Athenion of Maronea, known to us from numerous Pompeian versions such as that in the House of the Dioscuri.

Such individuality leads one to attribute the lavish decorative programme of the hall to an artist of distinction, who left the mainly ornamental parts to the simplest *parietarii* and undertook himself the execution of the figured scenes, impressing on them a personal and vigorous style based on impressionistic technique. His originality can be seen also in the setting together of contrasting, bright colours such as red, blue and gold, the distinctive trademark of the *pictor imaginarius Fabullus,* the famous painter of Nero's reign (Pliny, *Natural History*, 35. 120).

The rendering of drapery and the bare flesh of the figures who populate the mythological scene lacks contrasts but is cleverly shaded. This scene culminates in the dynamic rendering of the central group, consisting of Deidamia seated with her torso slightly twisted and Achilles leaning at a sharp angle and grasping the spear and shield hidden among the women's gifts by the cunning Ulysses. (In the Pompeian version, Deidamia is depicted afraid and retreating behind Achilles who, along with Ulysses

48. Hall of Achilles at Skyros, vault, detail with a Bacchic figure

49. Hall of Achilles at Skyros, vault, detail with a generic scene

and Diomedes, occupies the centre of the scene.) The composition adheres to the formal classical tradition in which symmetrically grouped figures are placed on a neutral background without scenic elements. It is characterised by an outline style, the figures depicted by quick, dabbed strokes of the brush and beautifully set off by painted highlights.
The content and the aesthetic impact of the depiction of this particular myth, makes it clear that it has programmatic significance. This depiction of the least significant and least heroic episode of the hero's life celebrates, according to some, the most essential aspects of Nero's new values, and according to others, the simple imitation of Achilles that was a theme of Neronian propaganda.
Despite this, the episode, already dealt with in the Greek painting by Polygnotos in the 5th century (Pausanias, I. 22. 5), came to be used frequently by Roman decorators as the decorative subject of sarcophagi and mosaics.

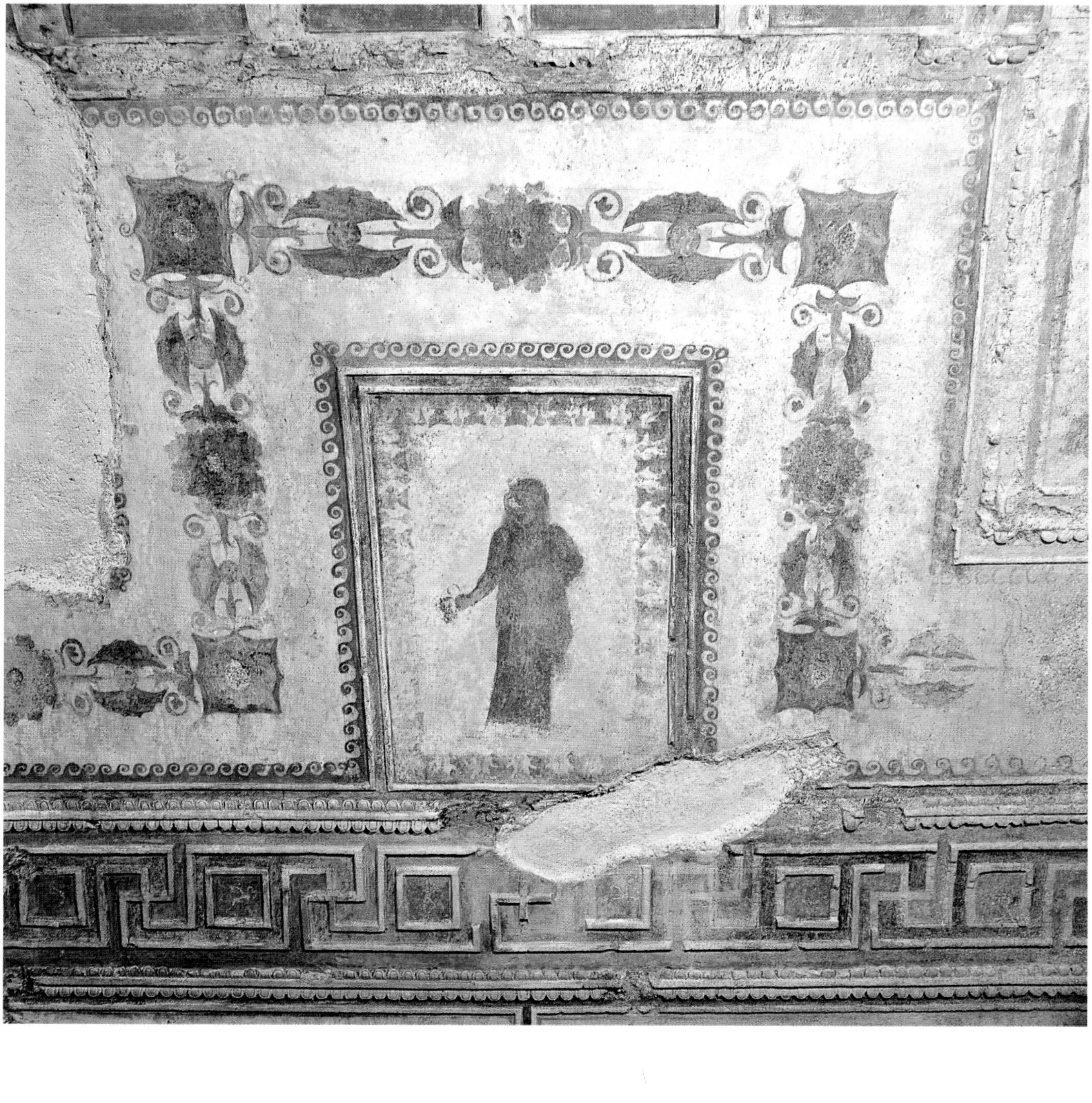

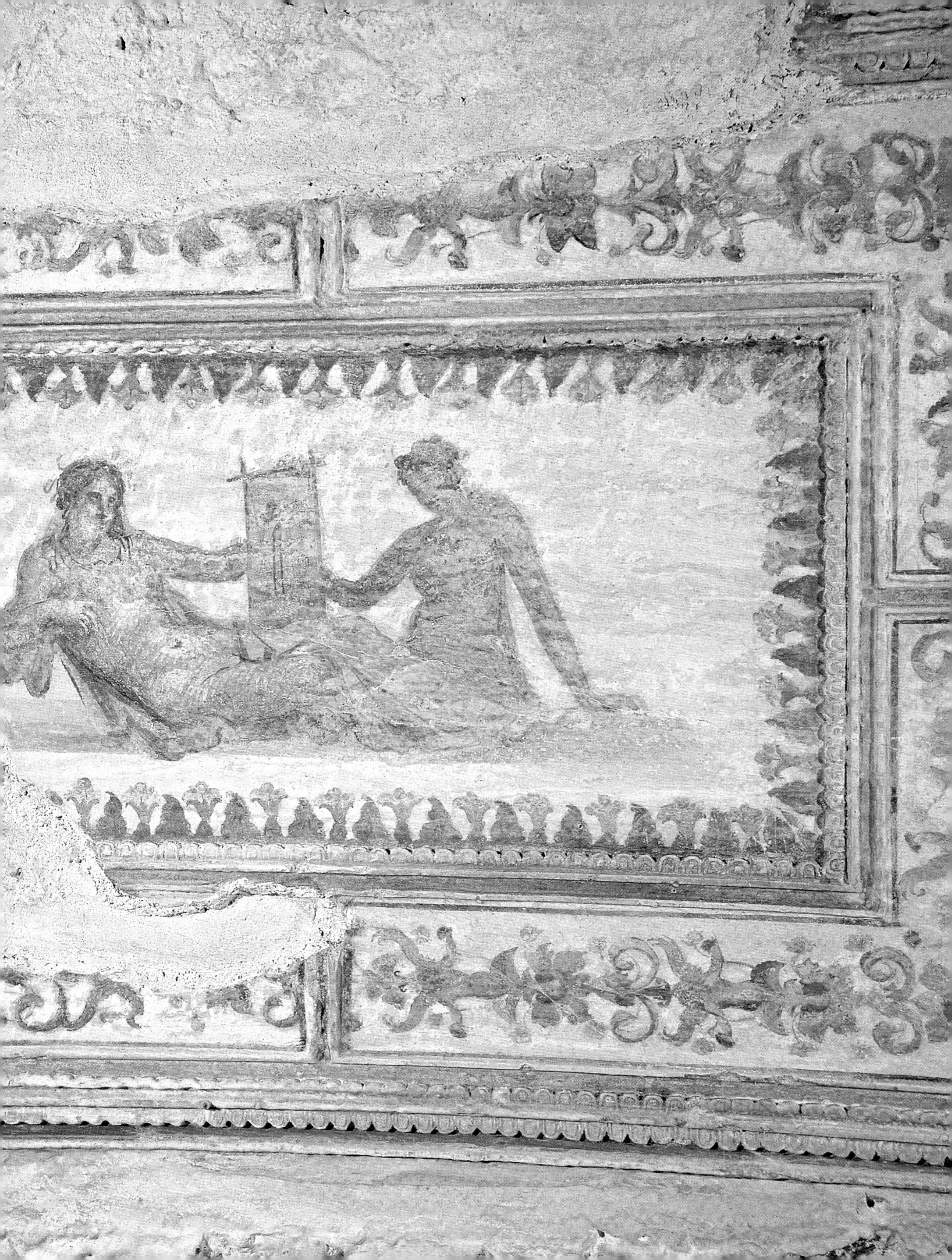

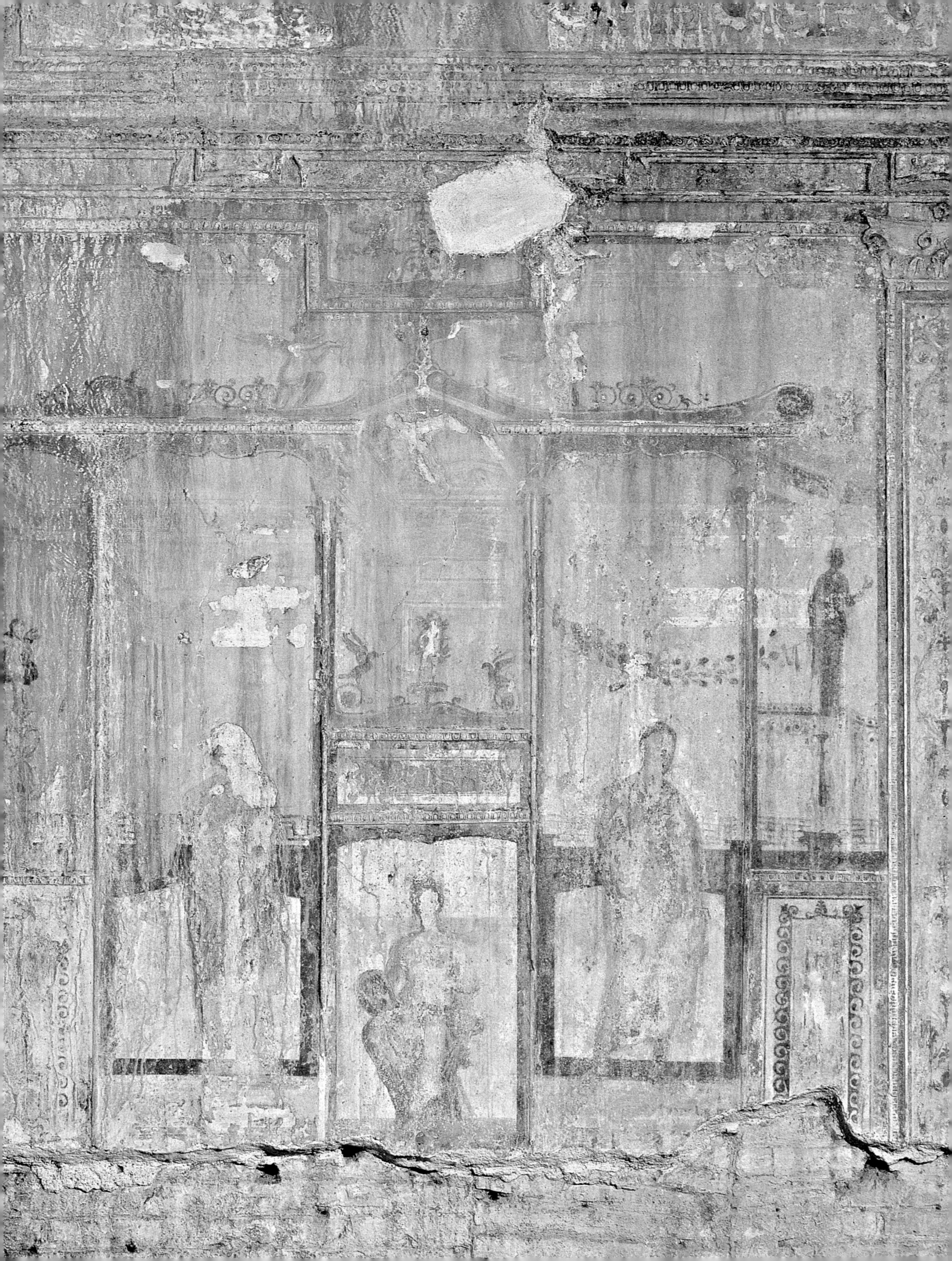

50. Hall of Achilles at Skyros, wall decoration with fantasy architecture inhabited by figures

51. Hall of Achilles at Skyros, fourth style architectural wall decoration, detail

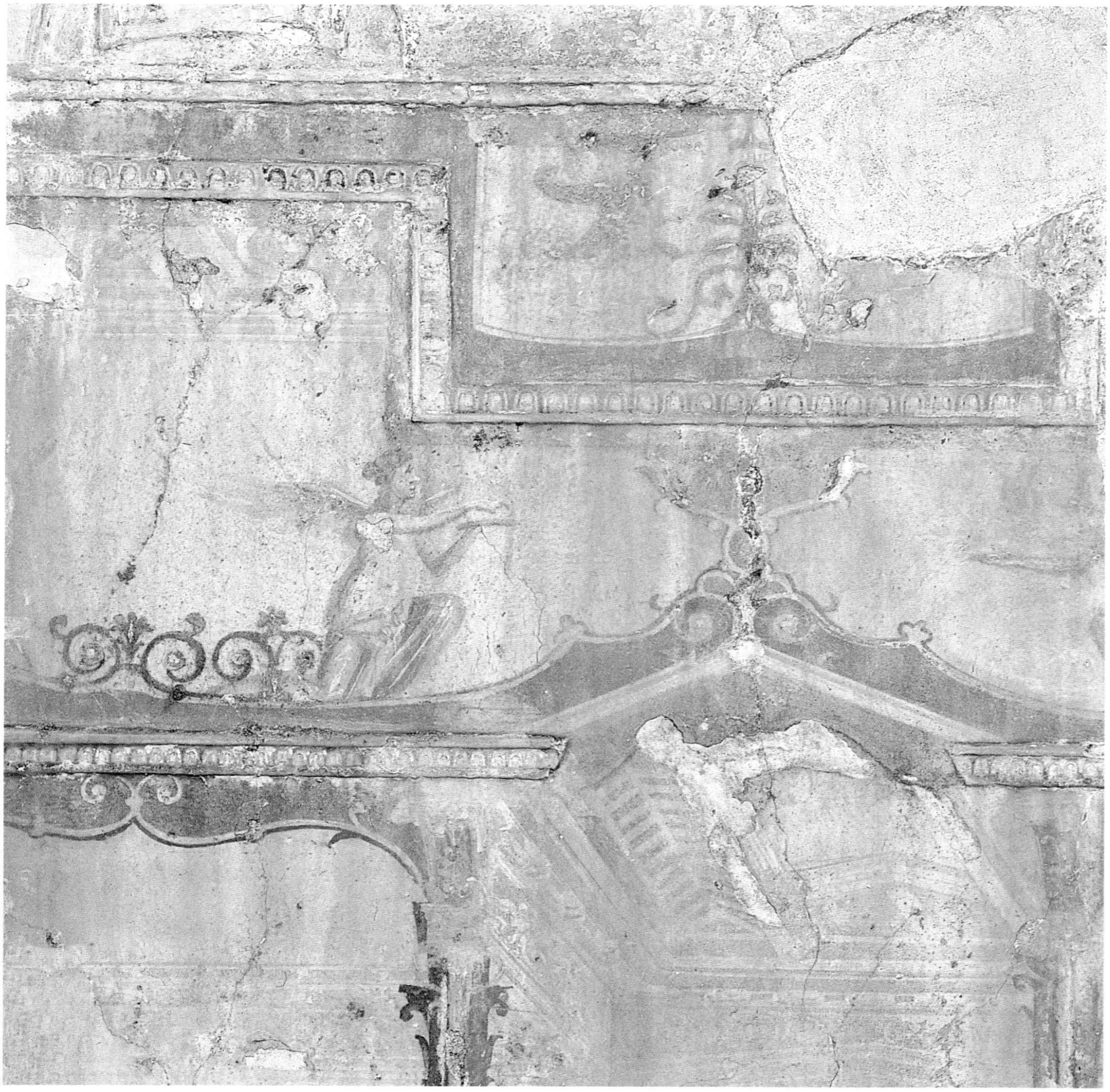

52. Hall of Achilles at Skyros,
detail of pilaster in painted stucco

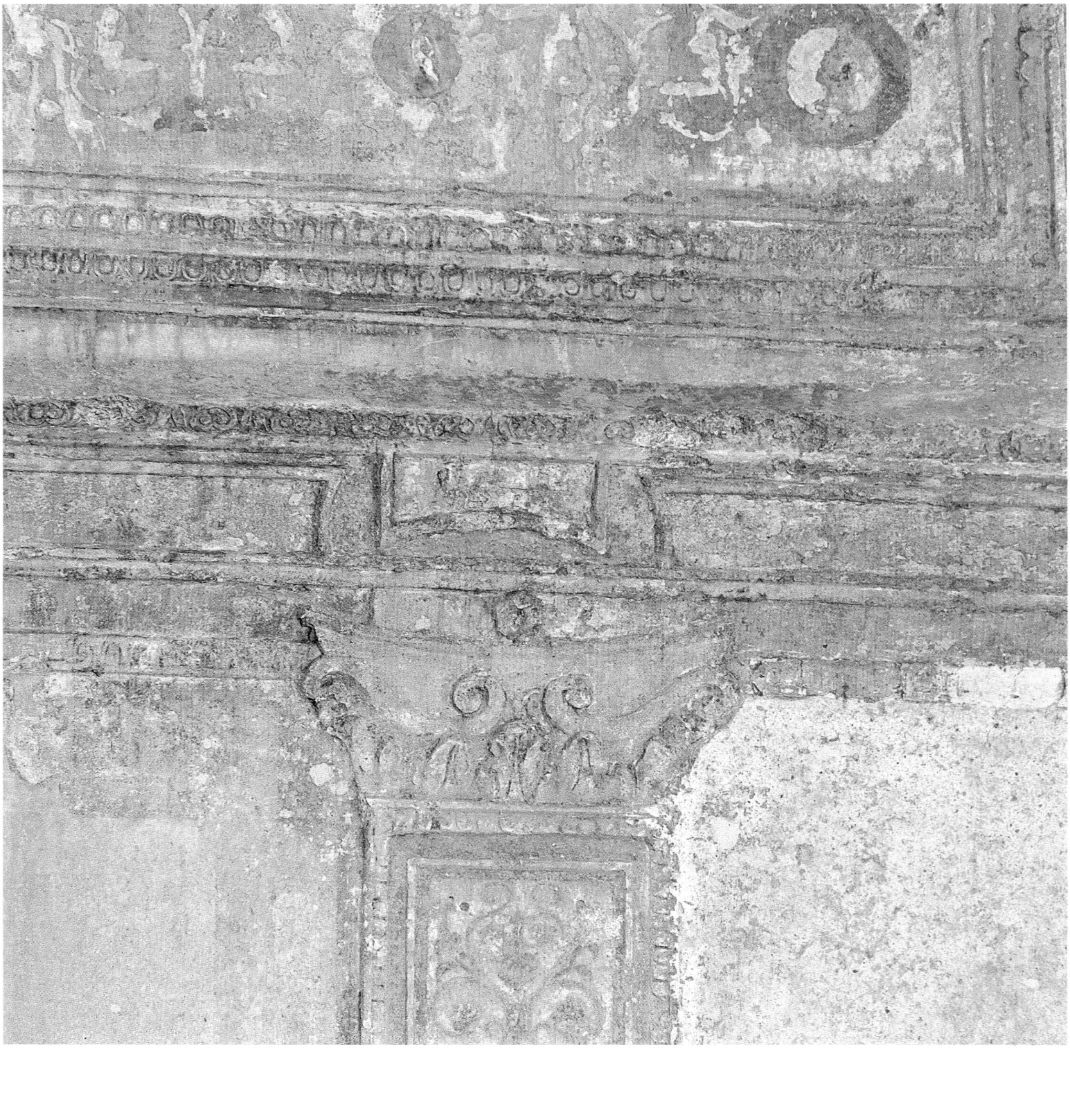

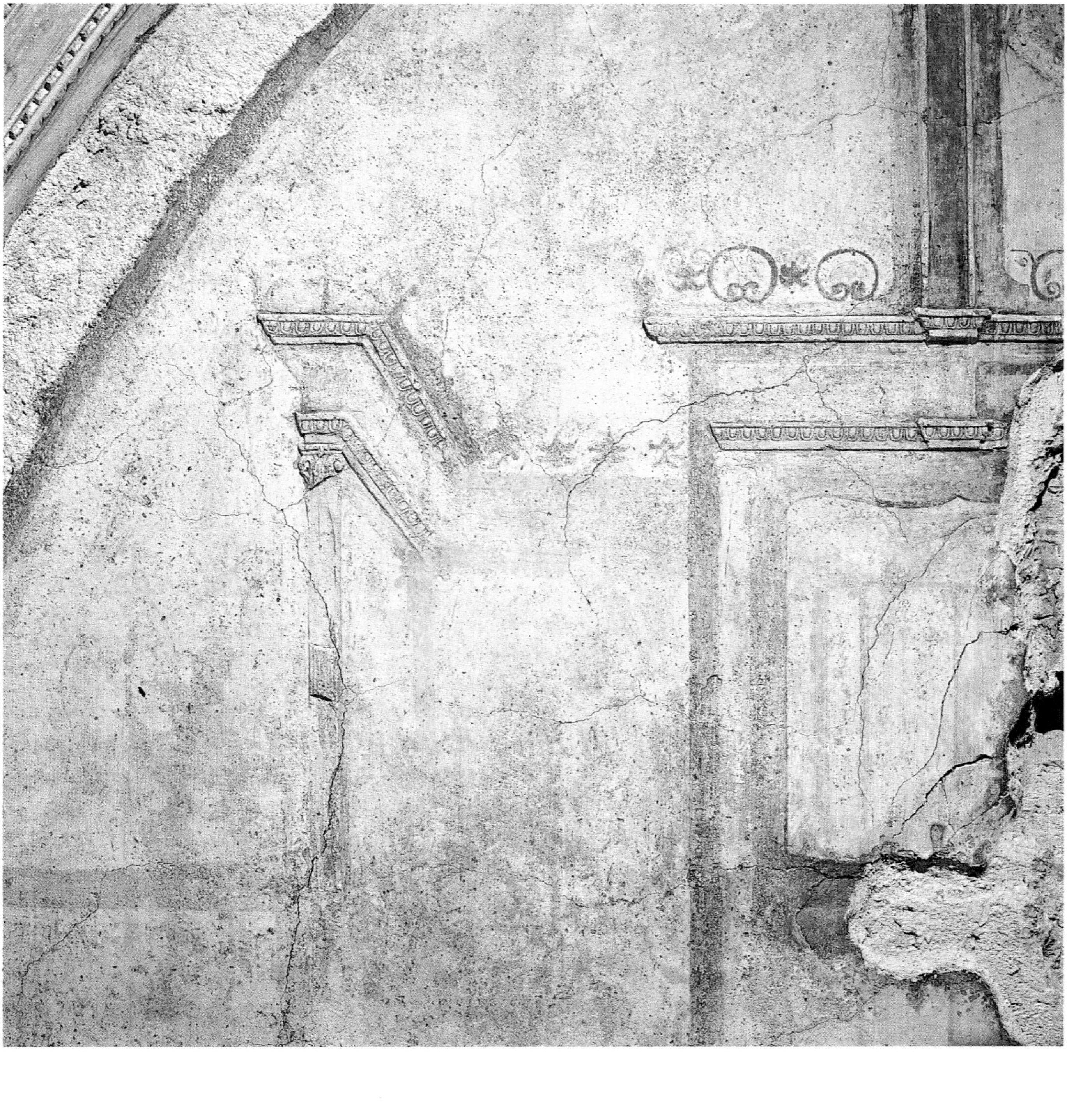

53. Hall of Achilles at Skyros, lunette, fourth style architectural decoration

54. Hall of Achilles at Skyros, detail of fourth style wall decoration

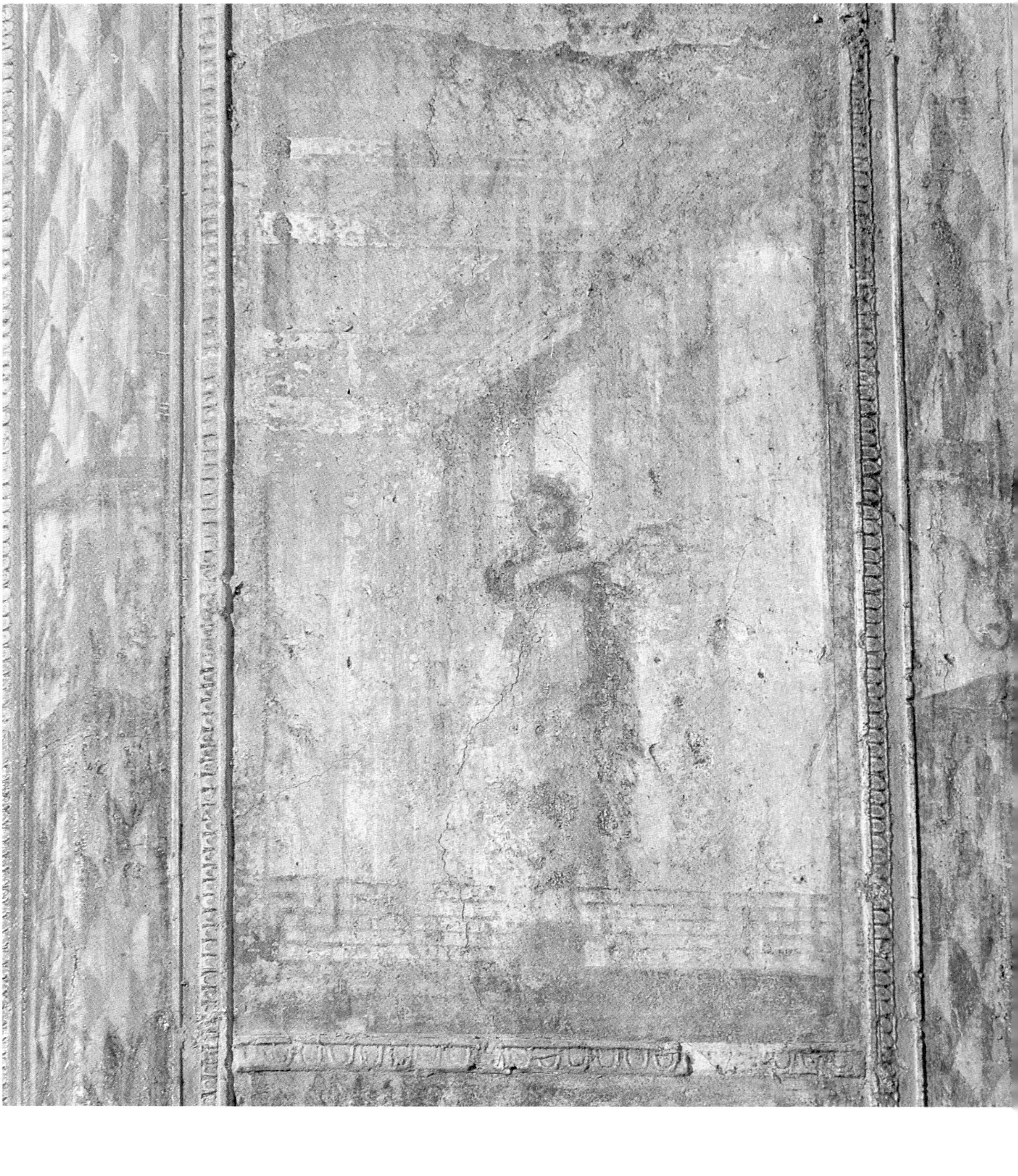

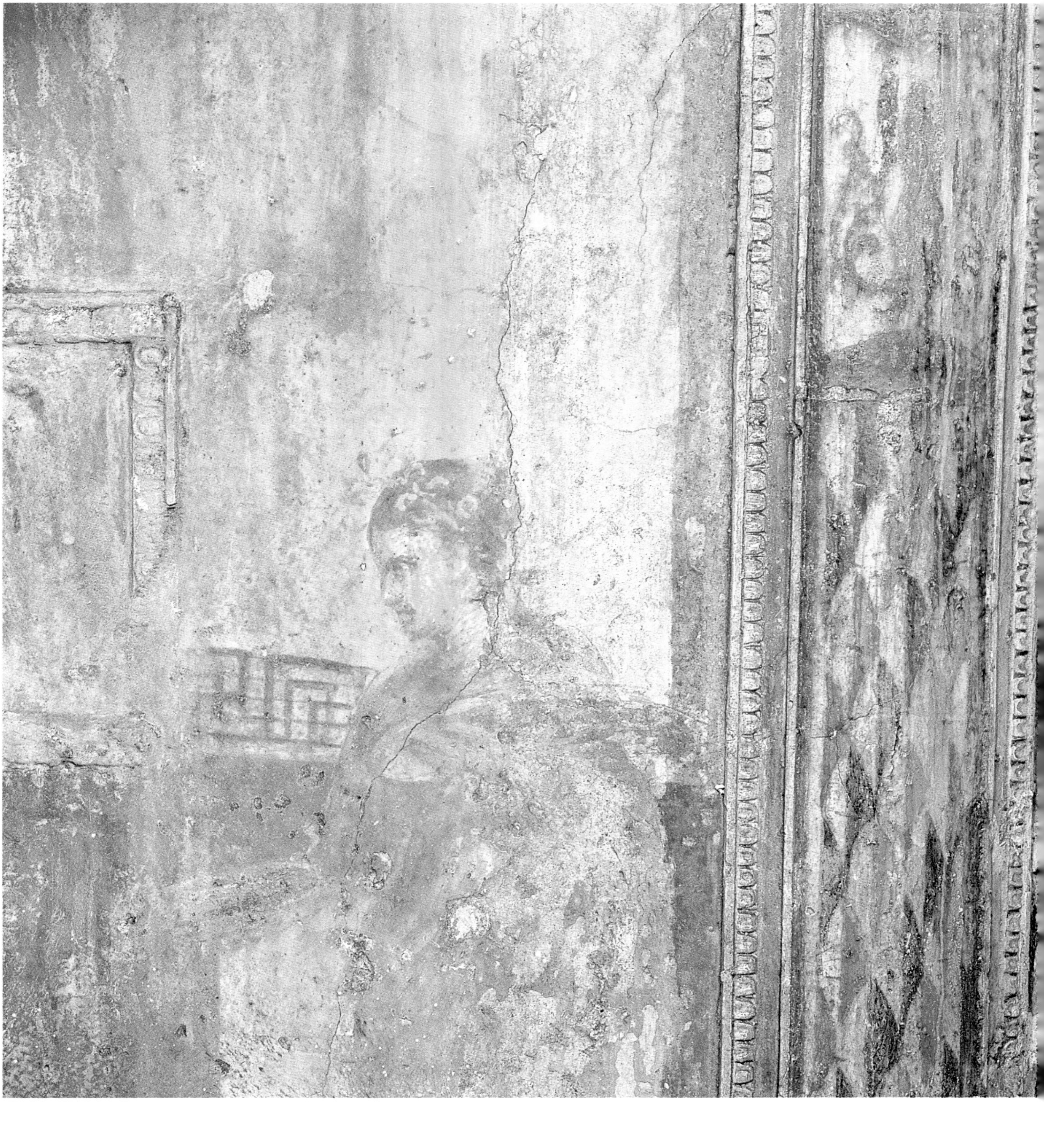

55. Hall of Achilles at Skyros, figure making an offering, from the wall decoration

56. Hall of Achilles at Skyros, central scene with Achilles between the daughters of King Lykomedes

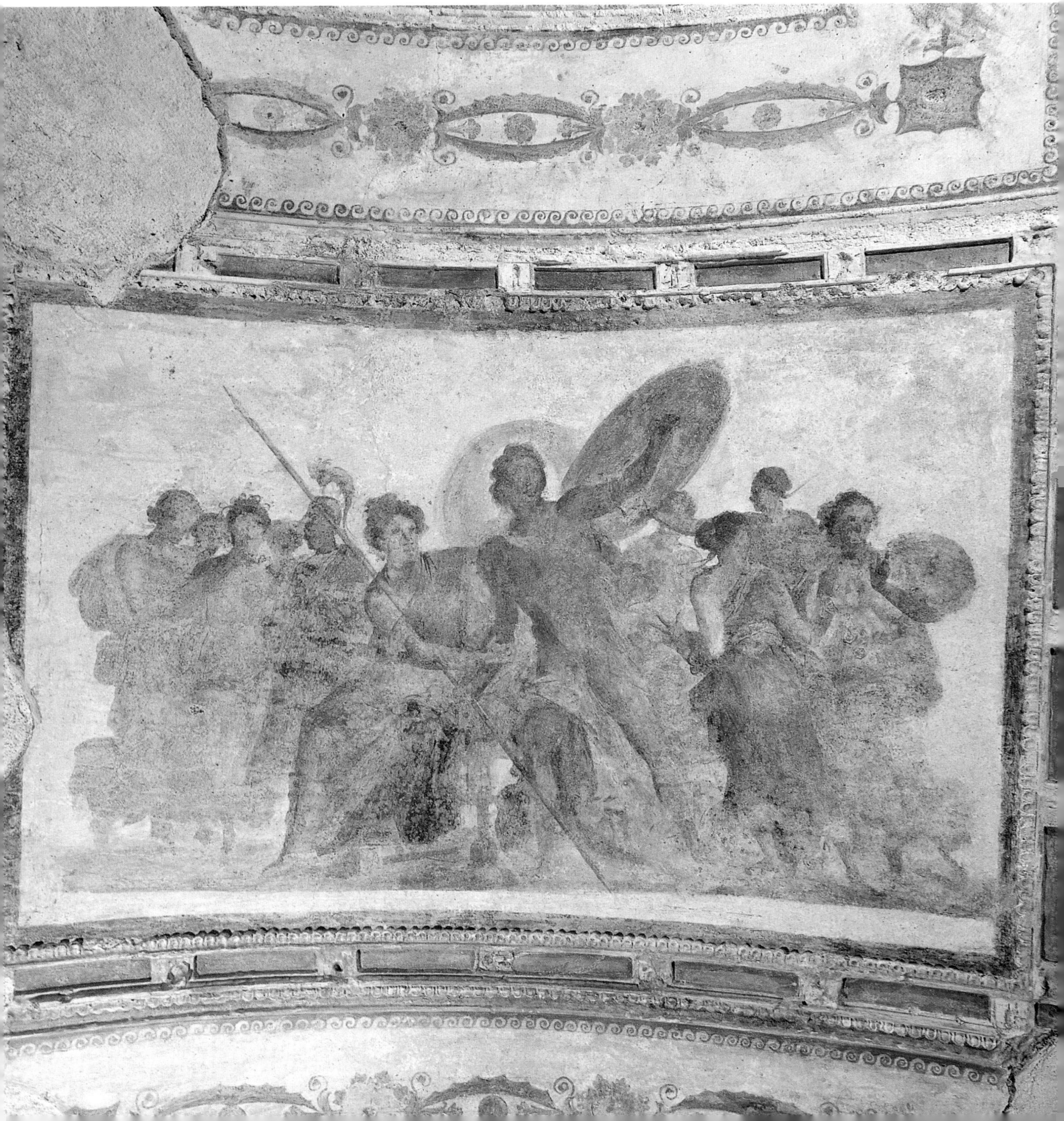

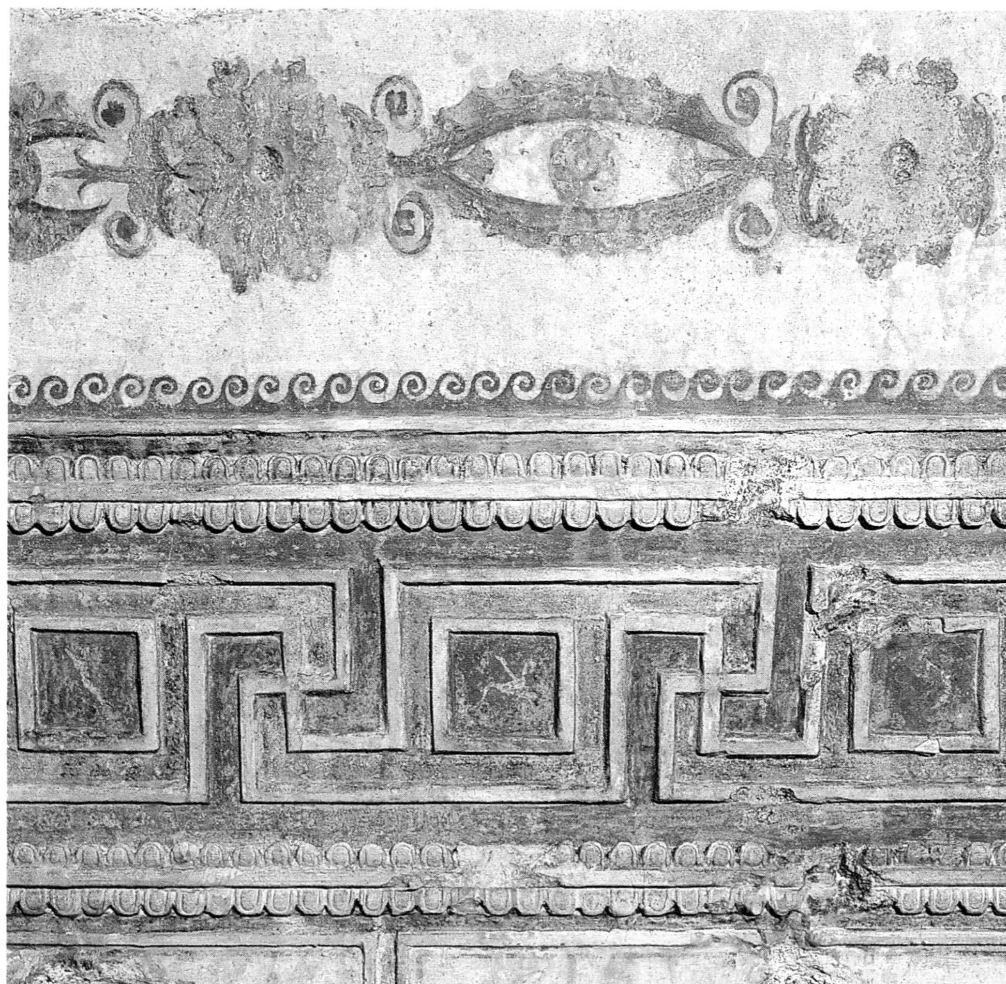

57. Hall of Achilles at Skyros, vault, detail of decorative friezes

58-59. Hall of Achilles at Skyros, vault, detail of scene with Achilles between the daughters of King Lykomedes

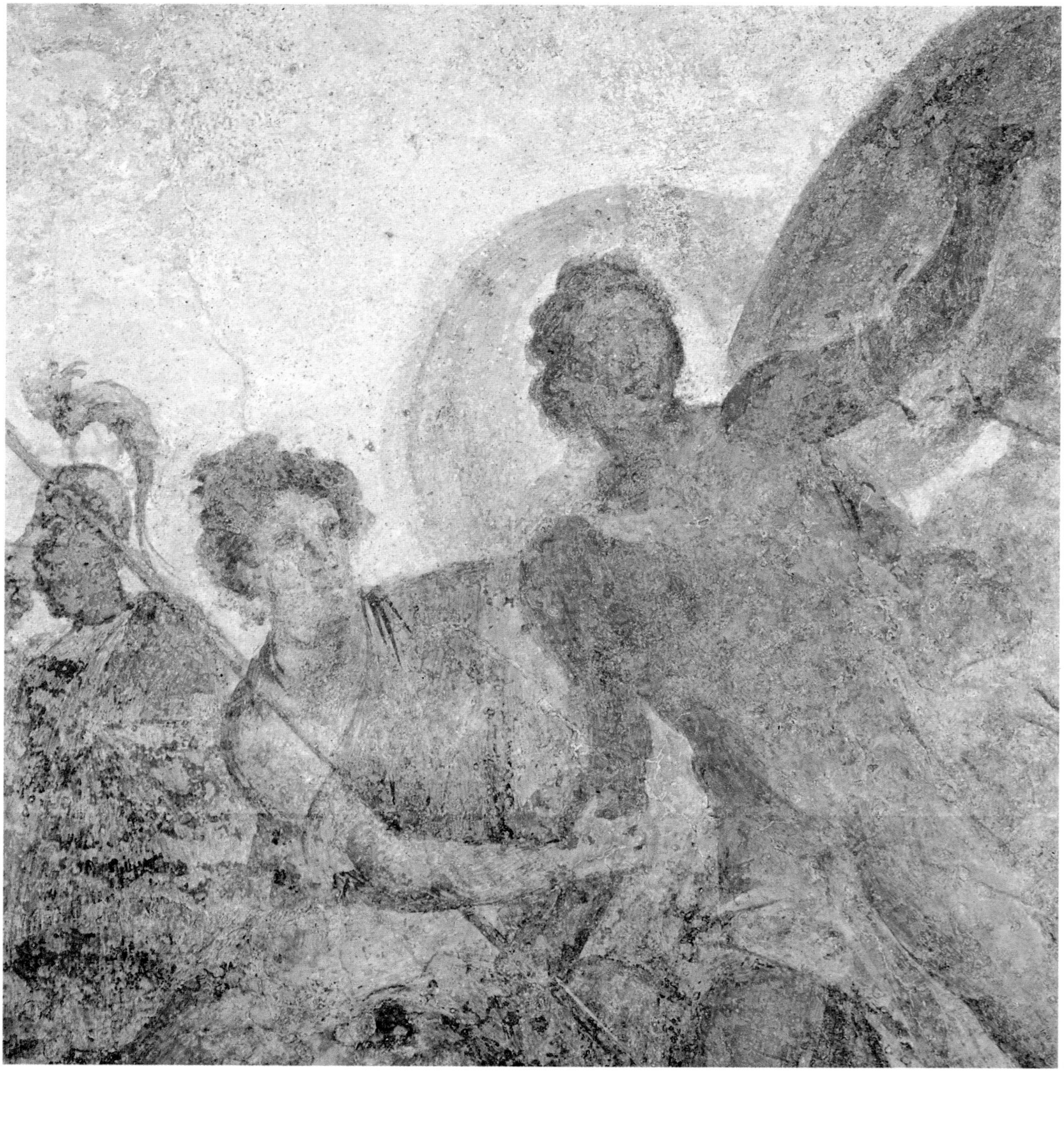

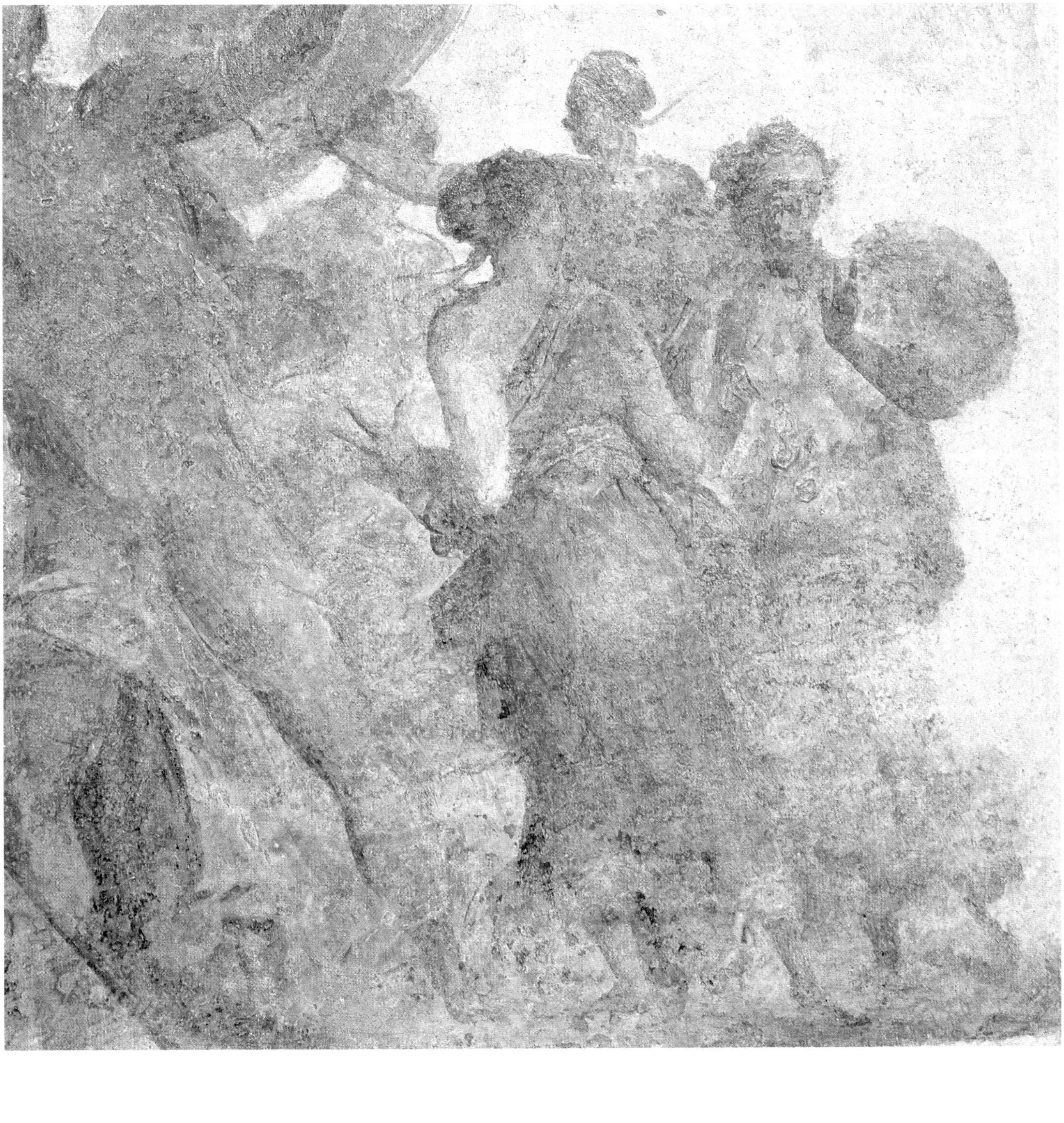

60. Hall of Achilles at Skyros, vault, detail with Dionysiac thiasos

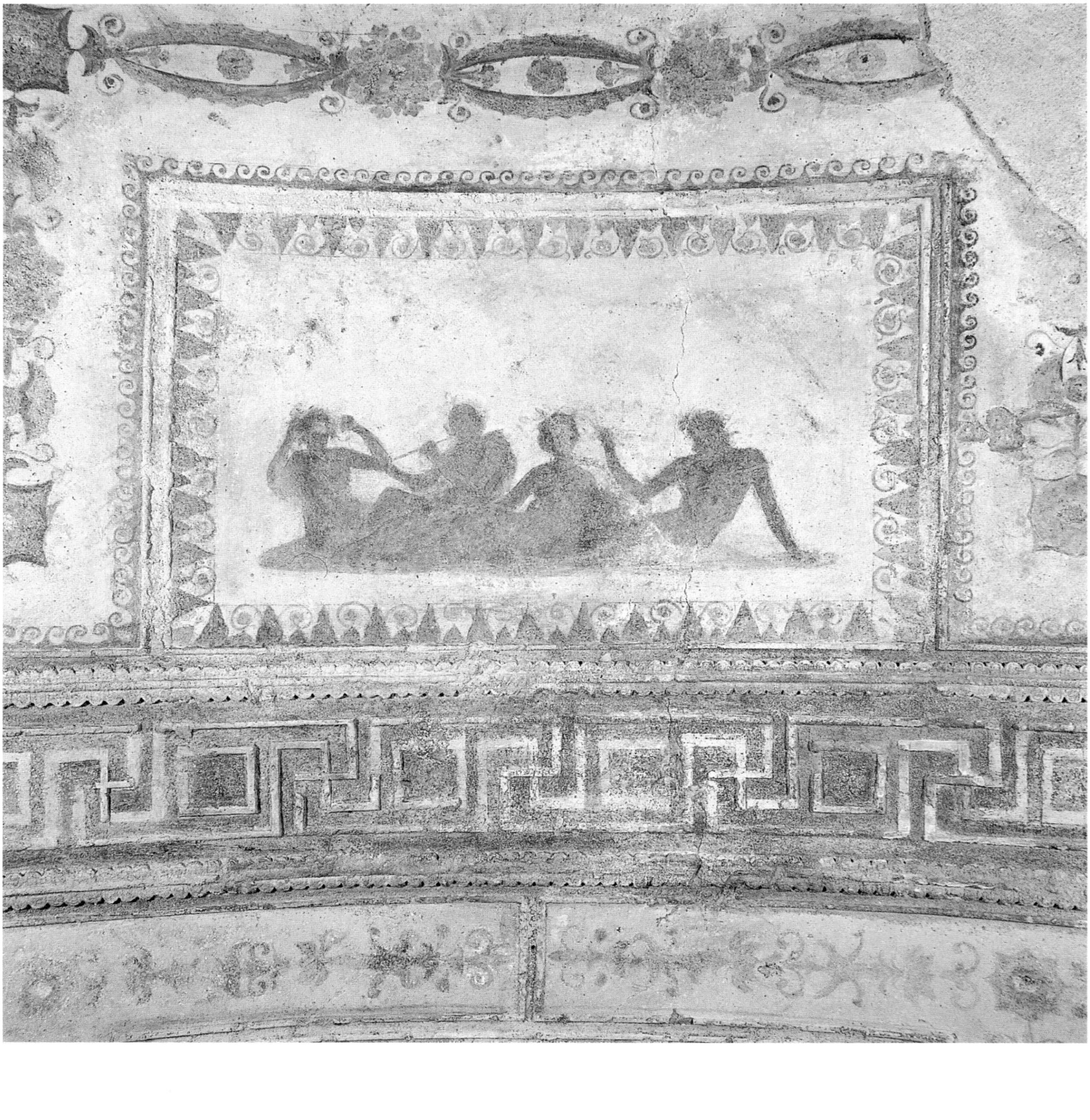

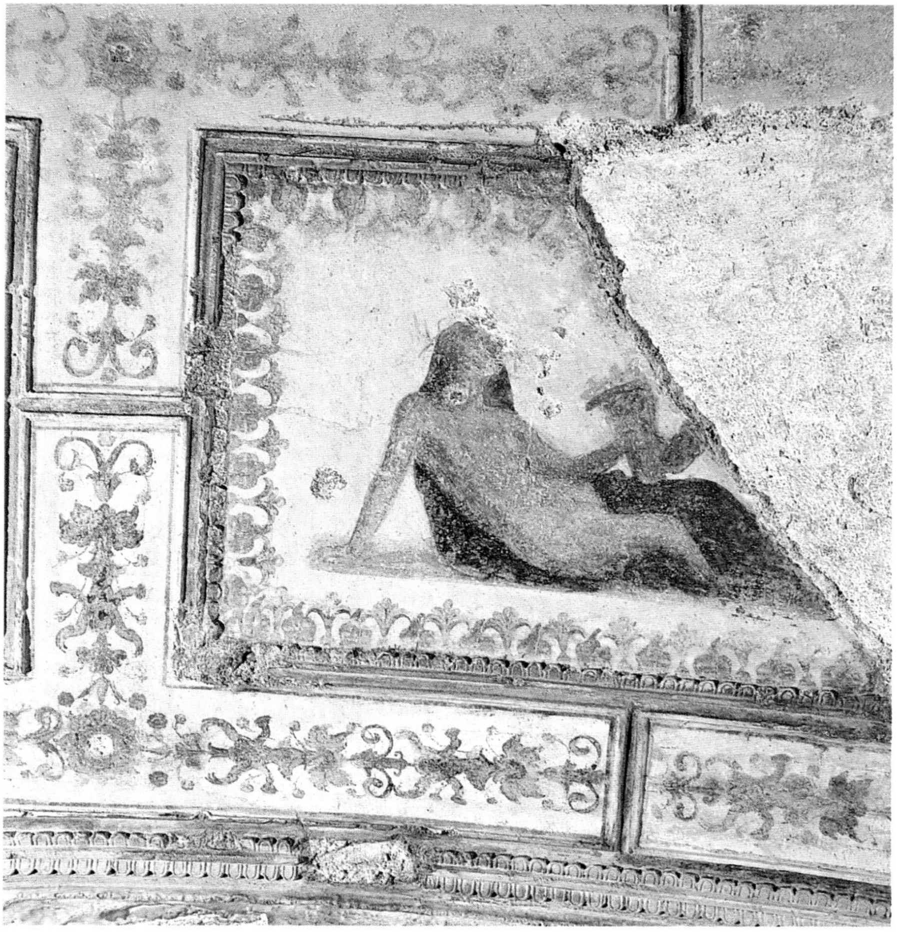

61. Hall of Achilles at Skyros, vault, detail, Dionysiac scene

62. Hall of Achilles at Skyros, vault, detail, Dionysiac scene

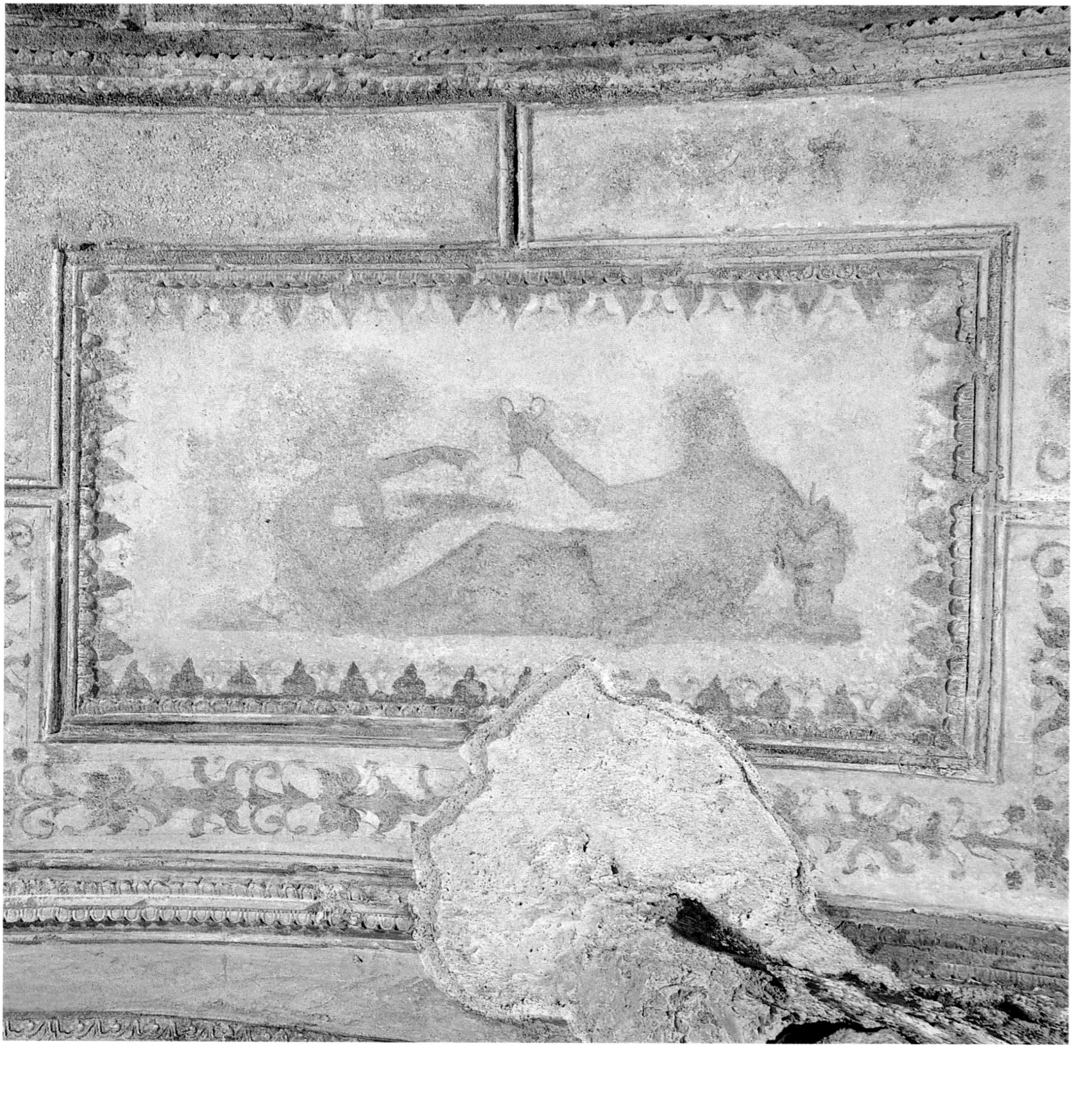

63. Hall of Achilles at Skyros, detail of the decoration of the shell in the apse of the room

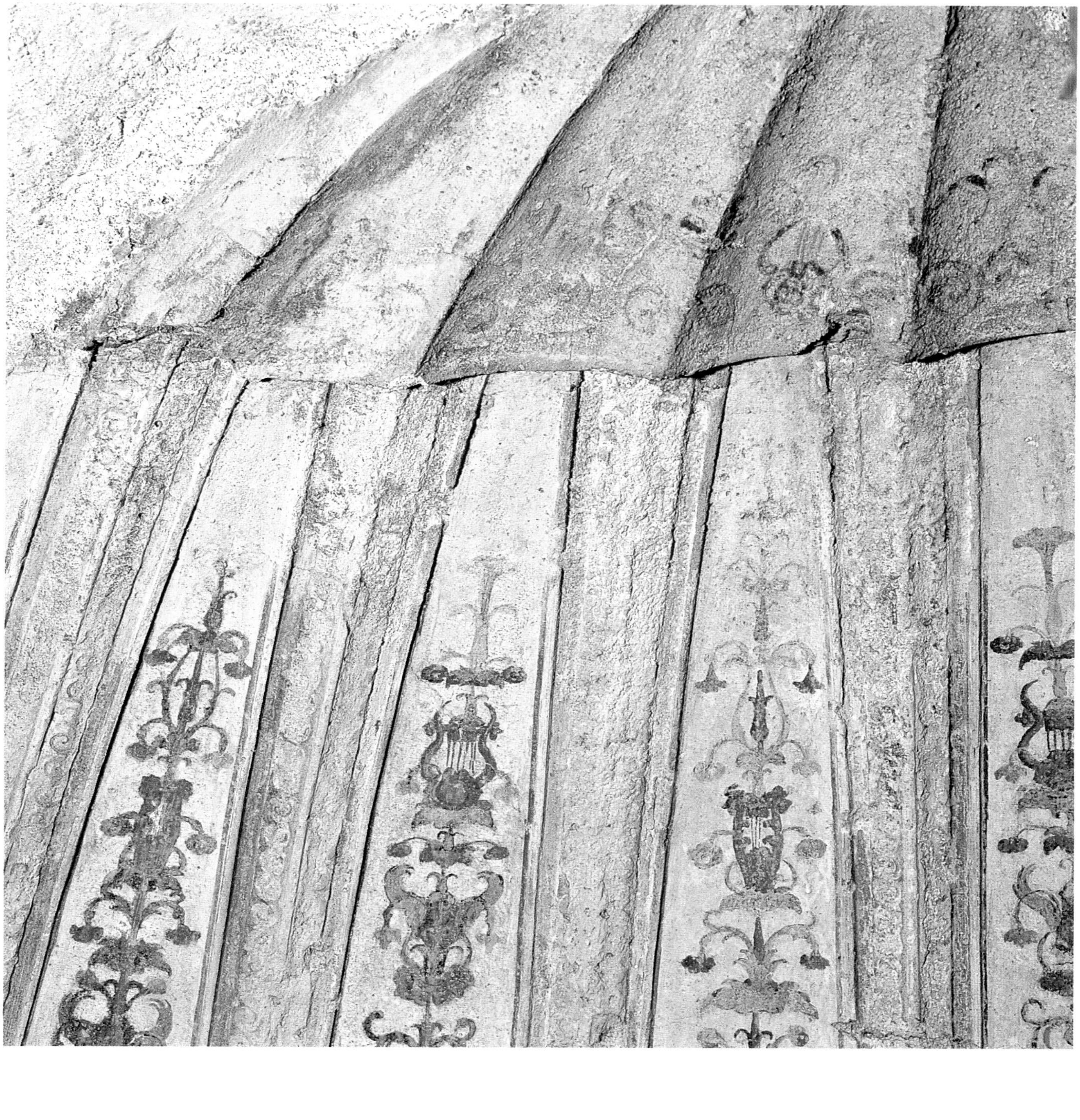

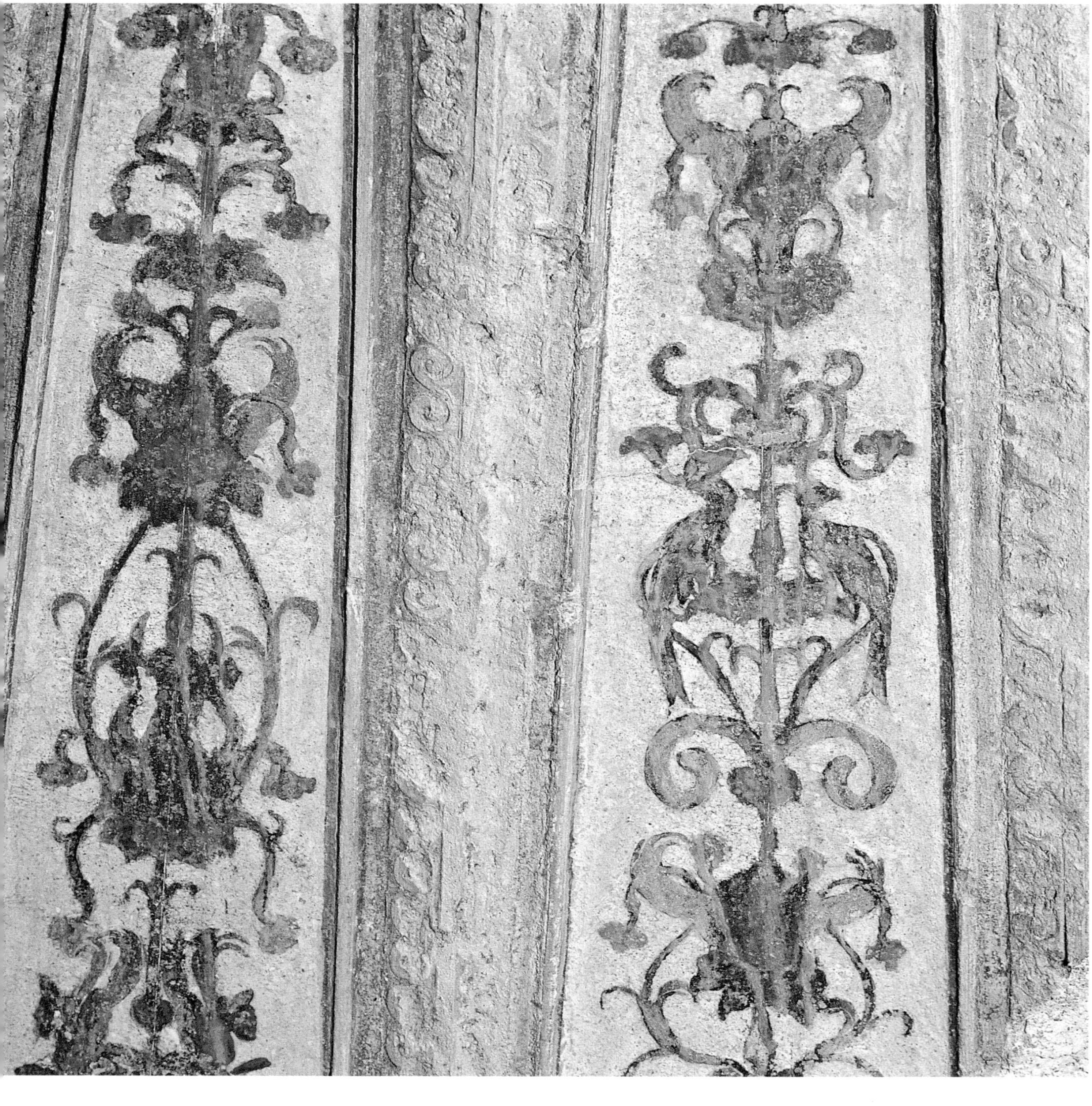

64. Hall of Achilles at Skyros, detail of the decoration of the shell in the apse, with harpies and animal motifs

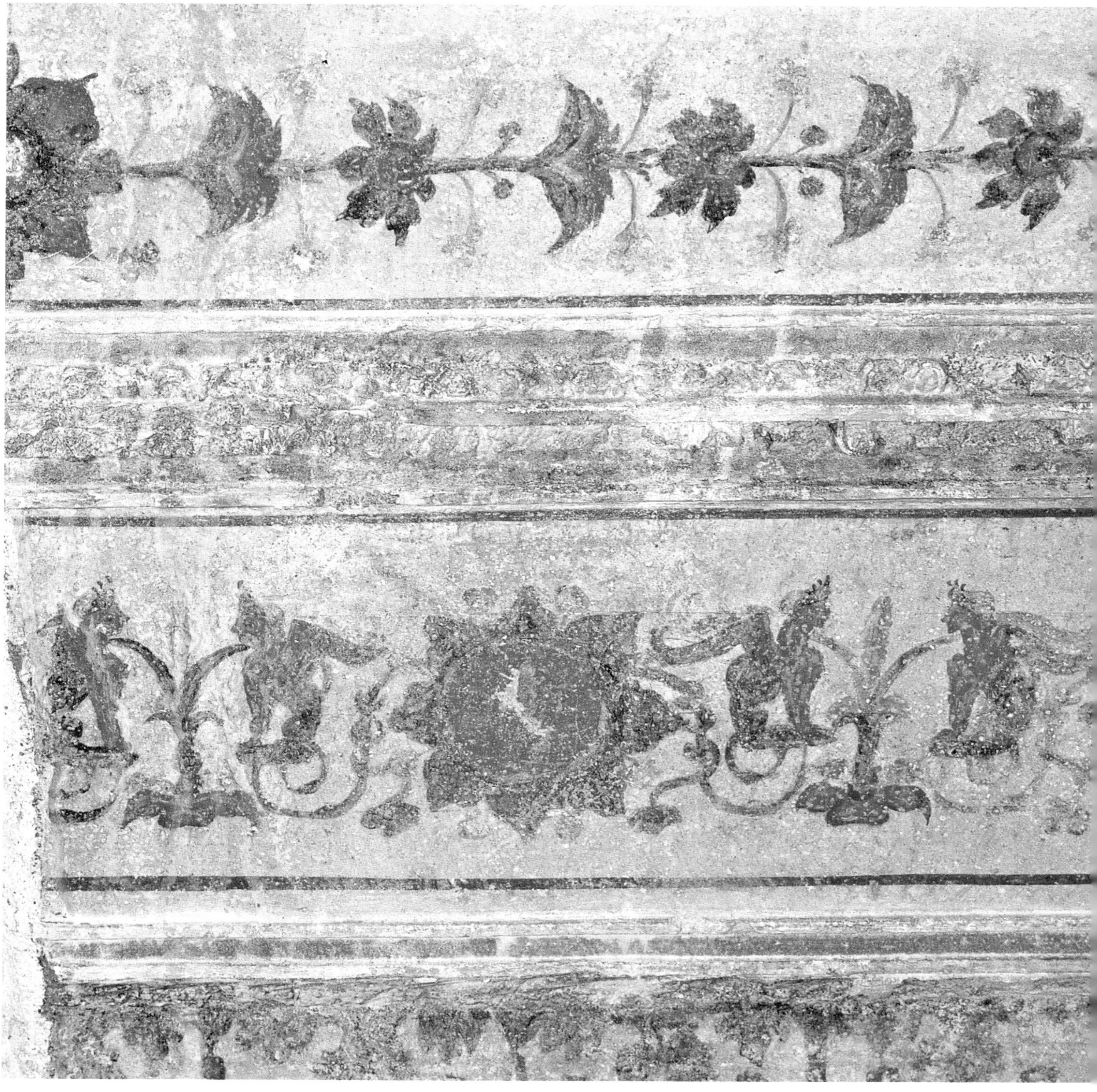

65. Hall of Achilles at Skyros, detail of the decorative and 'grotesque' friezes

66–67. Hall of Achilles at Skyros, vault, detail of the decorative friezes

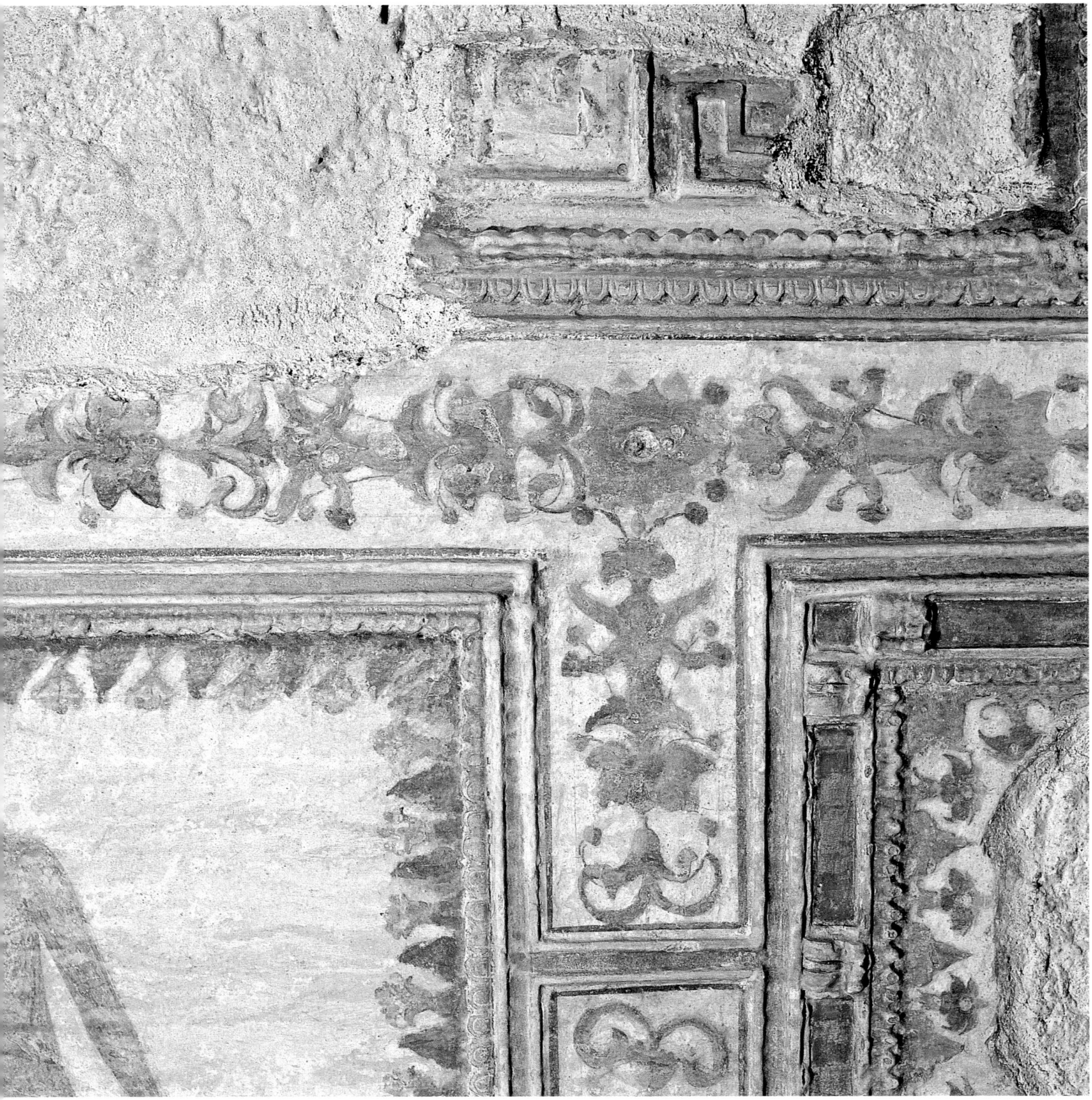

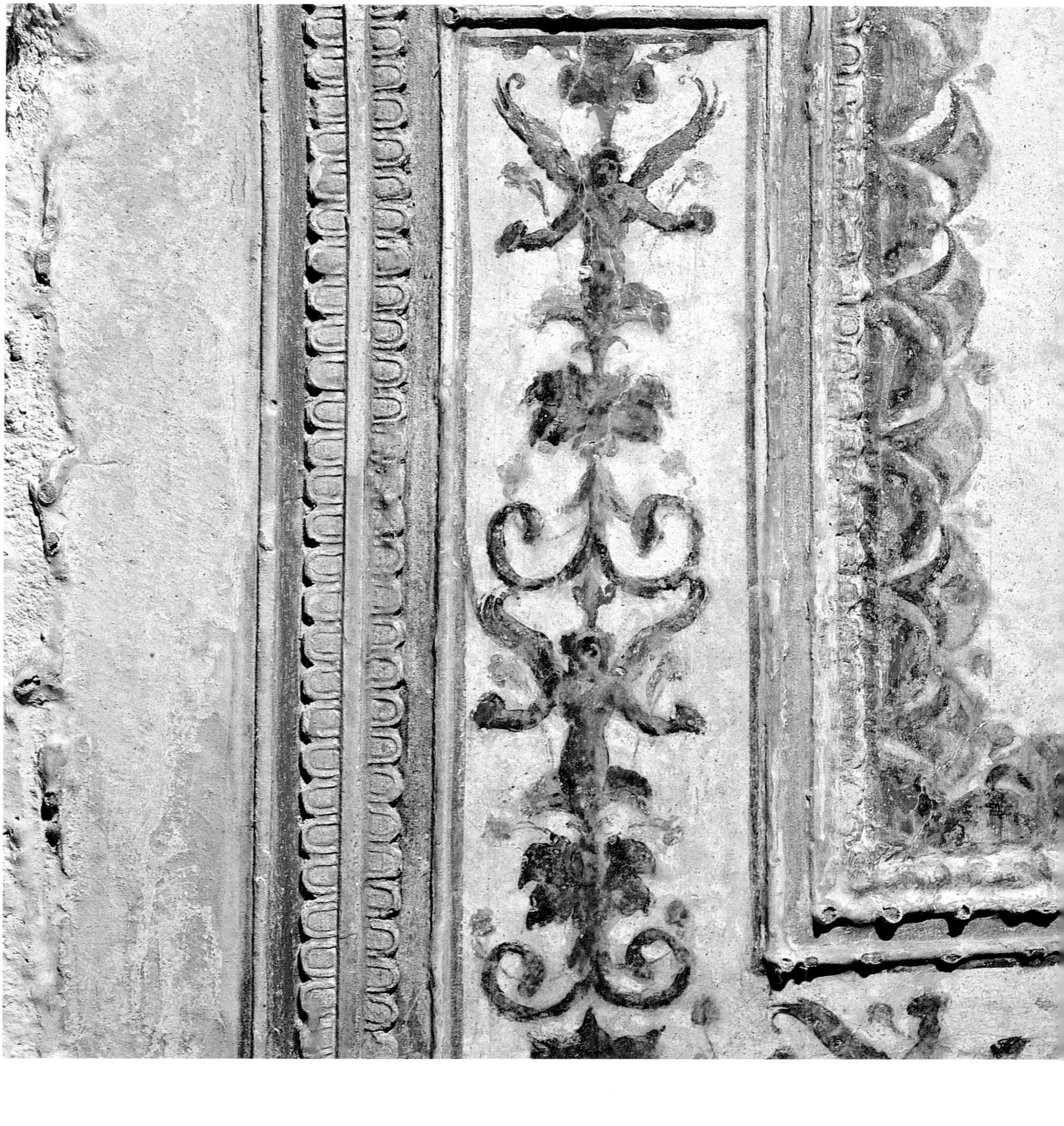

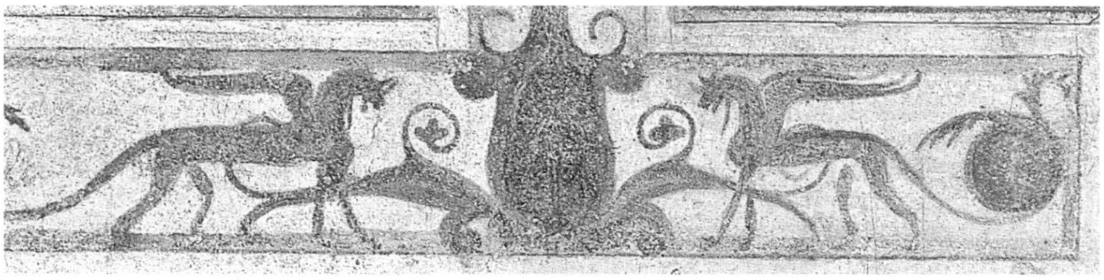

The Hall of Stuccoes, or the Hall of Hector and Andromache (129)

This room is iconographically and decoratively similar to room 119, the 'Hall of Achilles at Skyros'. The elegance of its workmanship is based on the extensive use of stucco (both in the small figured friezes and depictions of architecture on the walls, and for the cornices framing the divided panels of the ceiling) and on a luxurious series of colours such as bright red and the less intense blue and gold. The tone of the decoration relates to the official function of the room and emphasises its importance in the most architecturally advanced part of the *Domus*, which centres on the octagonal room.

The similarity of the decorative composition of the two rooms can be seen in the geometric style of the vault and in the architectural arrangement of the wall-painting with its fourth style vistas. These have similar formal and stylistic characteristics to those of the 'Golden Vault'.

The great decorative ability of the artist can be seen in the fine and varied friezes that frame panels as well as the composition of the whole vault which comprises groups of panthers, Erotes (?) and flying *Psychai* flanking an incense-burner or candelabra within a floral frame. They are separated by a type of *pinax* and by pairs of winged griffons (of probable Dionysiac symbolism), elegantly styled and heraldically set on the sides of a floral motif. In the vertical spaces between the panels (whose contents, decorated in stucco and gold leaf, were probably partially stripped away in the 16th century), harpies rise above amphoras decorated with plant-like volutes. *Kymatia*, cornices in a meandering pattern, with repeating

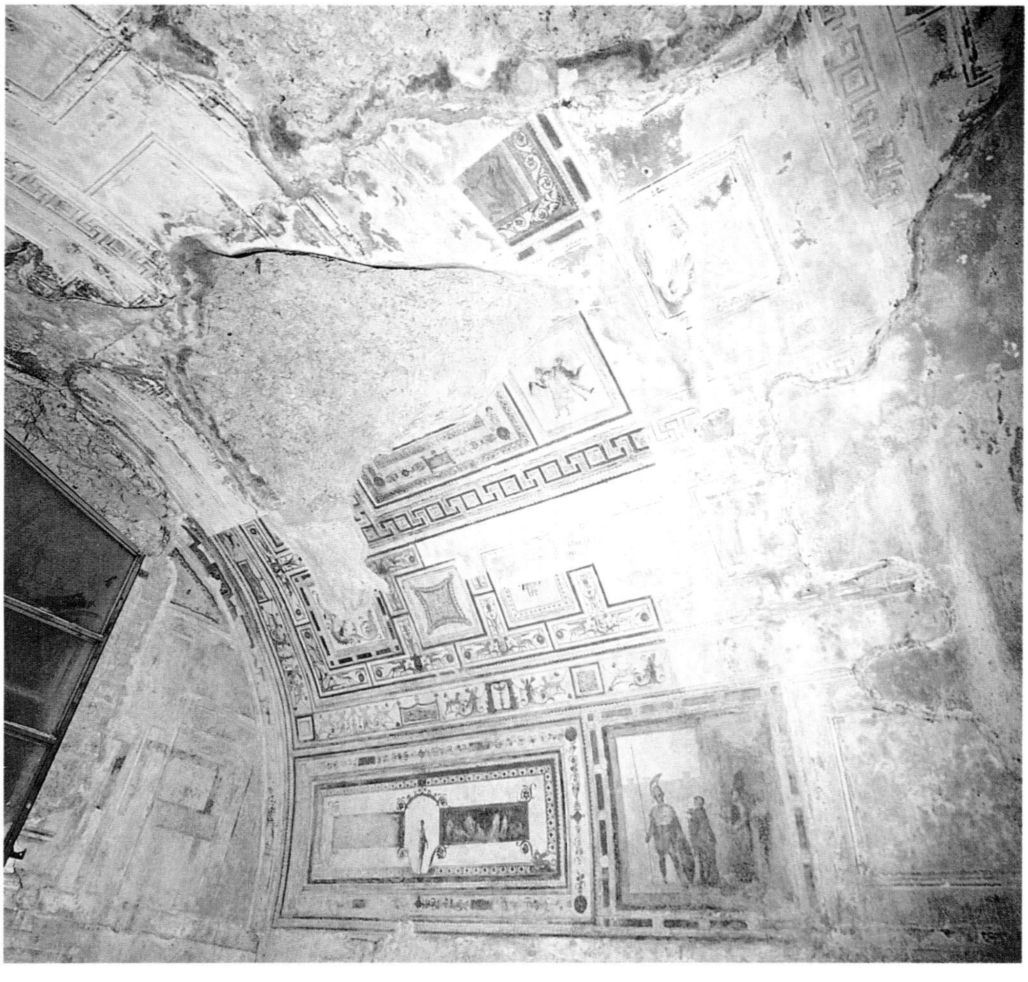

68. Hall of Hector and Andromache, geometric design of the decoration of the vault

69. Hall of Hector and Andromache, wall decoration with architectural prospect outlined in stucco

waves, plant-like spirals and floral calices, moulded in stucco or painted, help to emphasise the redundant baroque character of the decorative scheme.

This accounts for the fine ornate appearance of the surface of the splendid seashell of ribbed stucco which adorns the apse of the room (which is the mirror image of that in the Hall of Achilles at Skyros, located symmetrically opposite). Depictions of plaits are painted on it and interwoven with plant-like motifs and animal devices, including peacocks, sphinxes and swans. The shell is a repeated element in the architecture of the *domus*, as well as being connected to the goddess Aphrodite, who was born from a shell, it is a common Dionysiac motif found throughout the decoration of the palace. The stuccoes (which in the 16th century gave the room its name), together with the shell motif particularly drew the attention of artists. Until the end of the 15th century, they studied accurately the various versions of the decoration and produced their own versions, such as in the paintings of the chapel of Santa Maria del Popolo by Pinturicchio and those of the Vatican Loggia by Giovanni da Udine.

The clever rendering of the figured scenes, by means of an effective illustionistic impressionism, balances the formal elegance of the ornamental parts. This pre-

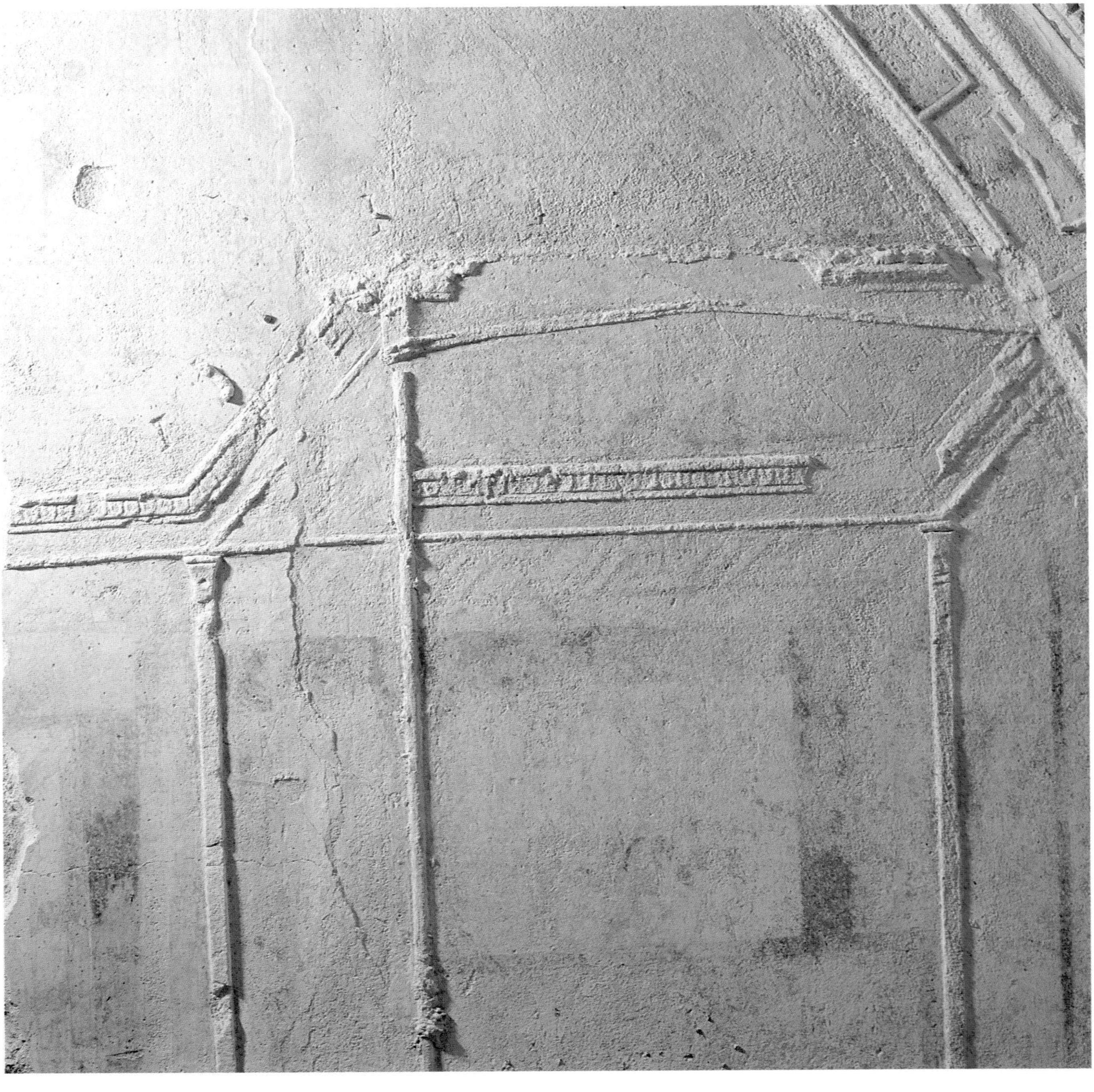

vents any imbalance between the ornamental parts and those with figures.

In his treatment of the marine topic that occupies the central panel of the vault, the artist succeeds in highlighting the moulded bodies of the figures which, by means of a masterful use strong shading, seem almost to break away from their background.

The figured scenes, classically conceived from Athenian (4th century BC) and Hellenistic prototypes, relate to the mythological sphere and to the epic of the Trojan world. These attracted the interest of copiers of the 17th and 18th centuries who reproduced them, in some cases in poorly interpreted form, despite the fact that they were already in a poor state of preservation.

The iconography of the central scene (reproduced in the 18th century by Francesco Bartoli, Windsor, 175, fol. 20 v, n. 9582; Eton Bn 5, fol. 25), relates to that of marine processions deriving from prototypes of the 2nd century BC. Two female figures can be recognised. The first is on a shell (no longer visible today), flanked by tritons in the presence of a cupid hovering in the air holding a small box. The second is riding a dolphin over the surface of the sea, and is identifiable as the sea goddess Amphitrite, rather than as Thetis (who would be carrying Achilles' weapons).

70. Hall of Hector and Andromache, vault, detail of friezes with griffons and harpies

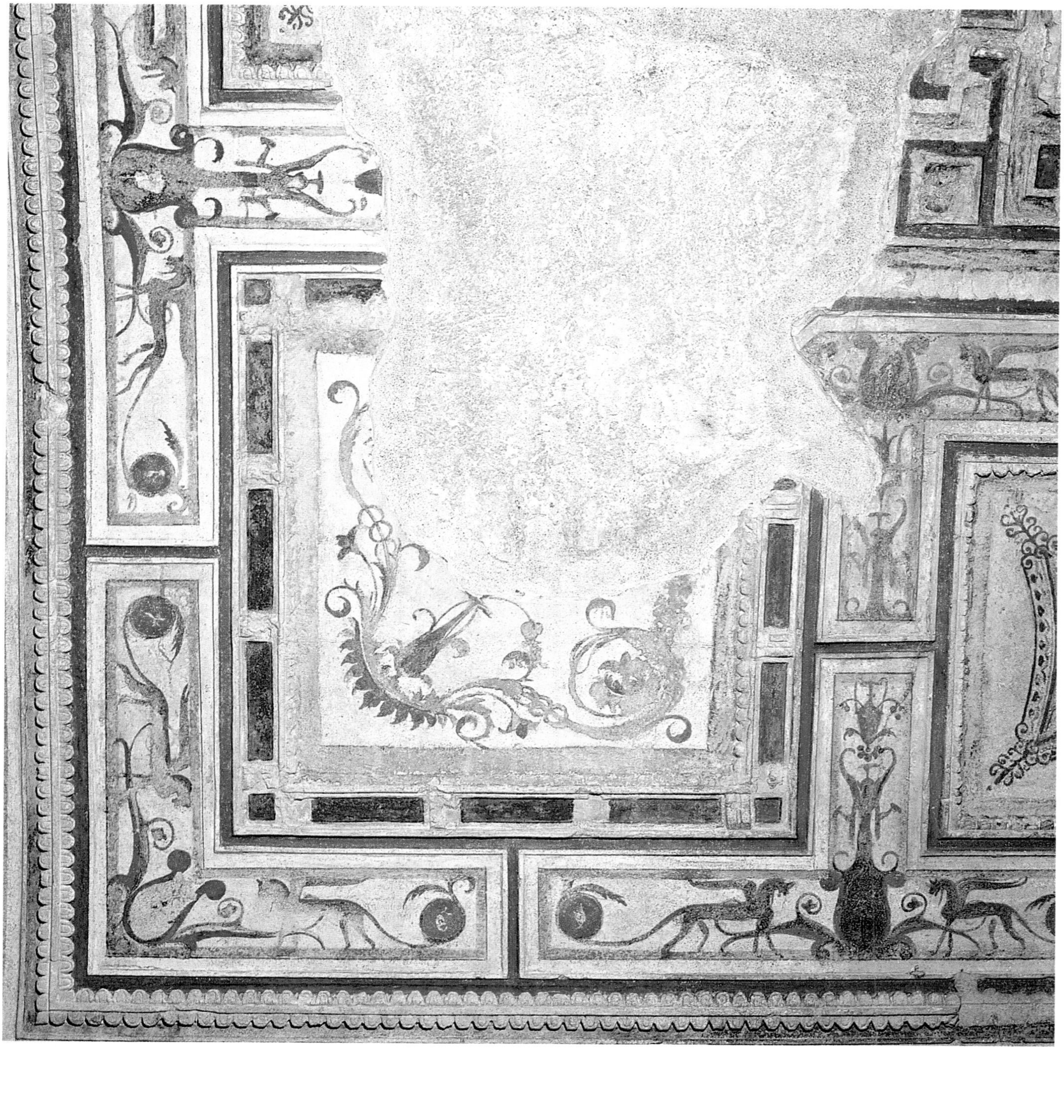

71. Hall of Hector and Andromache, friezes with griffons and harpies which frame the panels in sequence in the central band of the vault; in the panel can be seen the traces of where the gilded stucco was removed

72. Hall of Hector and Andromache, vault, sequence of decorative sections

The depiction of the farewell of Hector to Andromache, in contrast to the description in the poem, portrays the small Astyanax extending his arms to the hero 'of the waving helmet-crest', instead of turning away in fear 'from the horse-tail crest…and turning his head towards the breast of his wet-nurse'. Due to an erroneous interpretation in the 17th century restoration by Annibale Carracci (and also reproduced in the 18th century by other engravers) which omitted the figure of the young Astyanax, this scene was interpreted as the meeting of Coriolanus (the Roman conquerer who, subsequently banished, halted an attempt to conquer Rome after an encounter with his wife and his mother) and his wife Volumnia. Located in symmetry, on the opposite side, there is a scene of uncertain identity. This is set within the central panel of the three comprising the large lateral band surrounding the wall. At the beginning of the 20th century, Weege (who believed that the Laocoon group was discovered in this room in 1506) identified it as the depiction of the meeting of Paris with Helen, who is recognisable from the small cupid (who grasps her by her clothes), in the presence of Aphrodite, the protecting goddess of the Trojan prince.

This interpretation is supported by comparison with several depictions on vase-paintings (Chalcidian vases

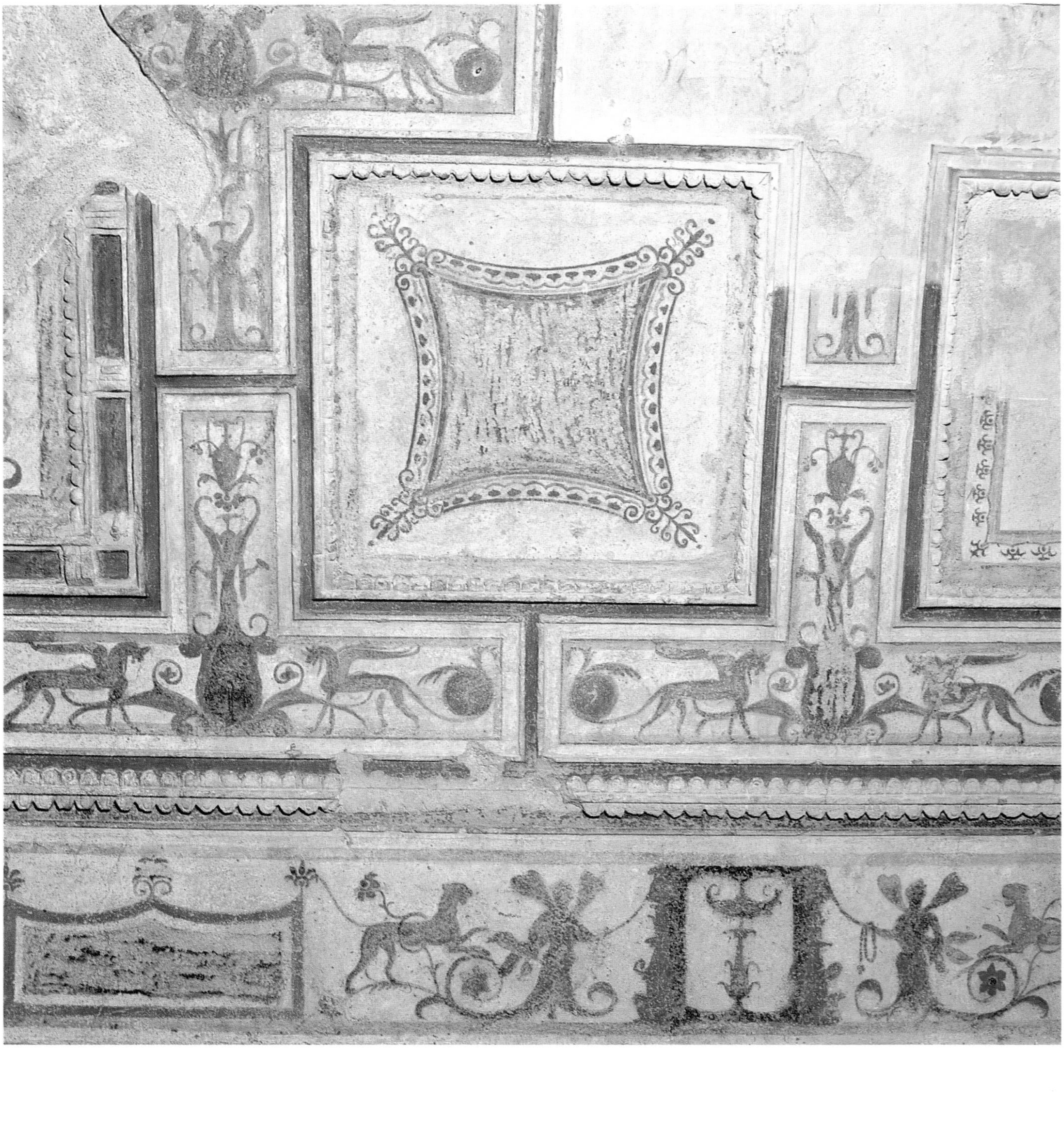

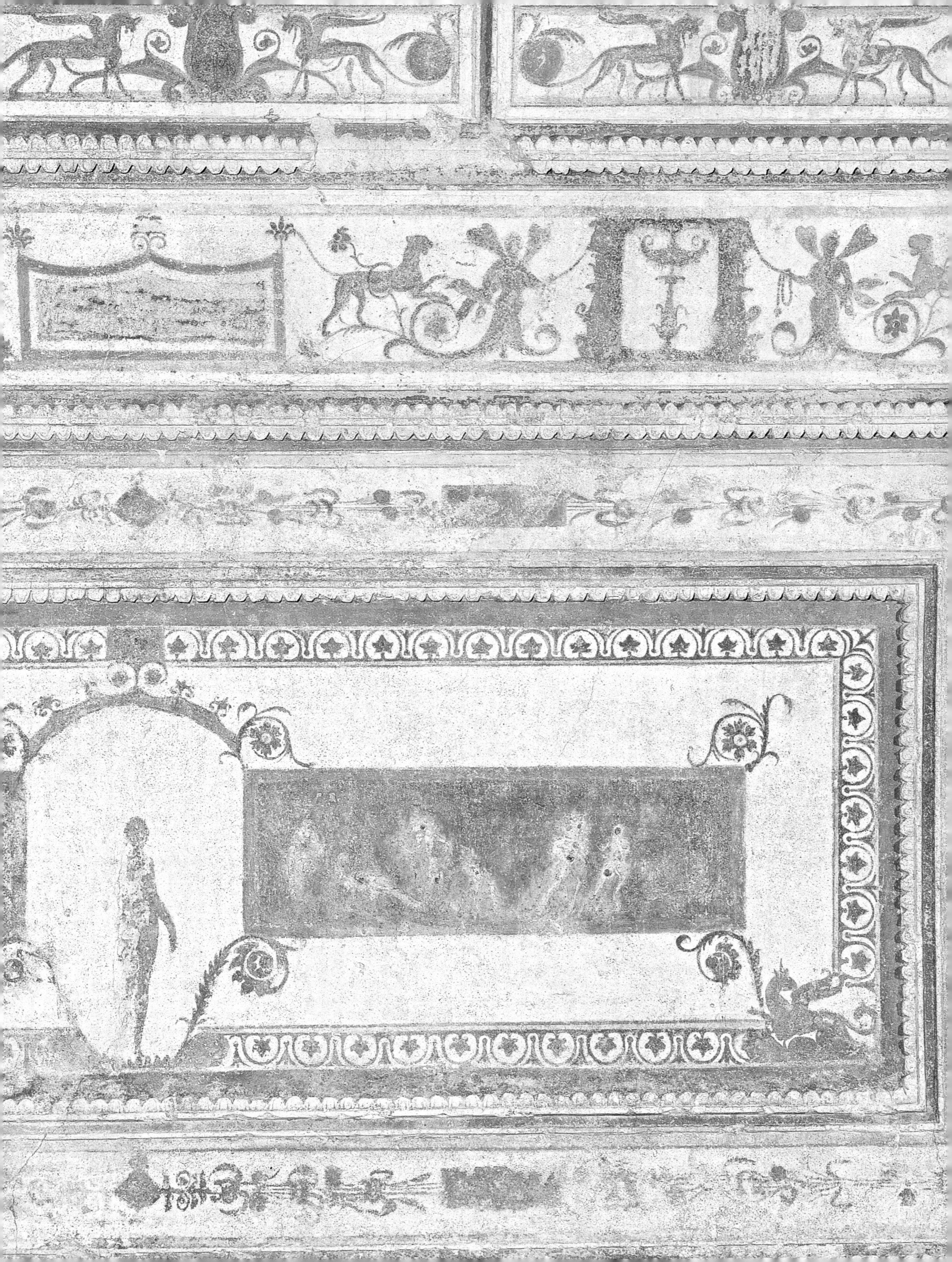

73. Hall of Hector and Andromache, vault, detail of sequence of decorative sections

74. Hall of Hector and Andromache, vault, detail of central panel with a triton and cupids

in Würzburg) in which the episode of Hector and Andromache is associated in particular with the figures of the two fatal lovers.

The remaining panels are framed by a series of painted and stucco cornices. They contain two small rectangular panels with a blue background, on which small stucco figures are silhouetted in different poses. These panels are connected from above by an elegant floral motif forming an arch, within which stands a female figure, also in stucco, and standing on a cluster of vines. Among the figured panels surrounding the central scene there are depictions of a satyr with maenad and a veiled female figure (possibly Europa) on the back of a bull.

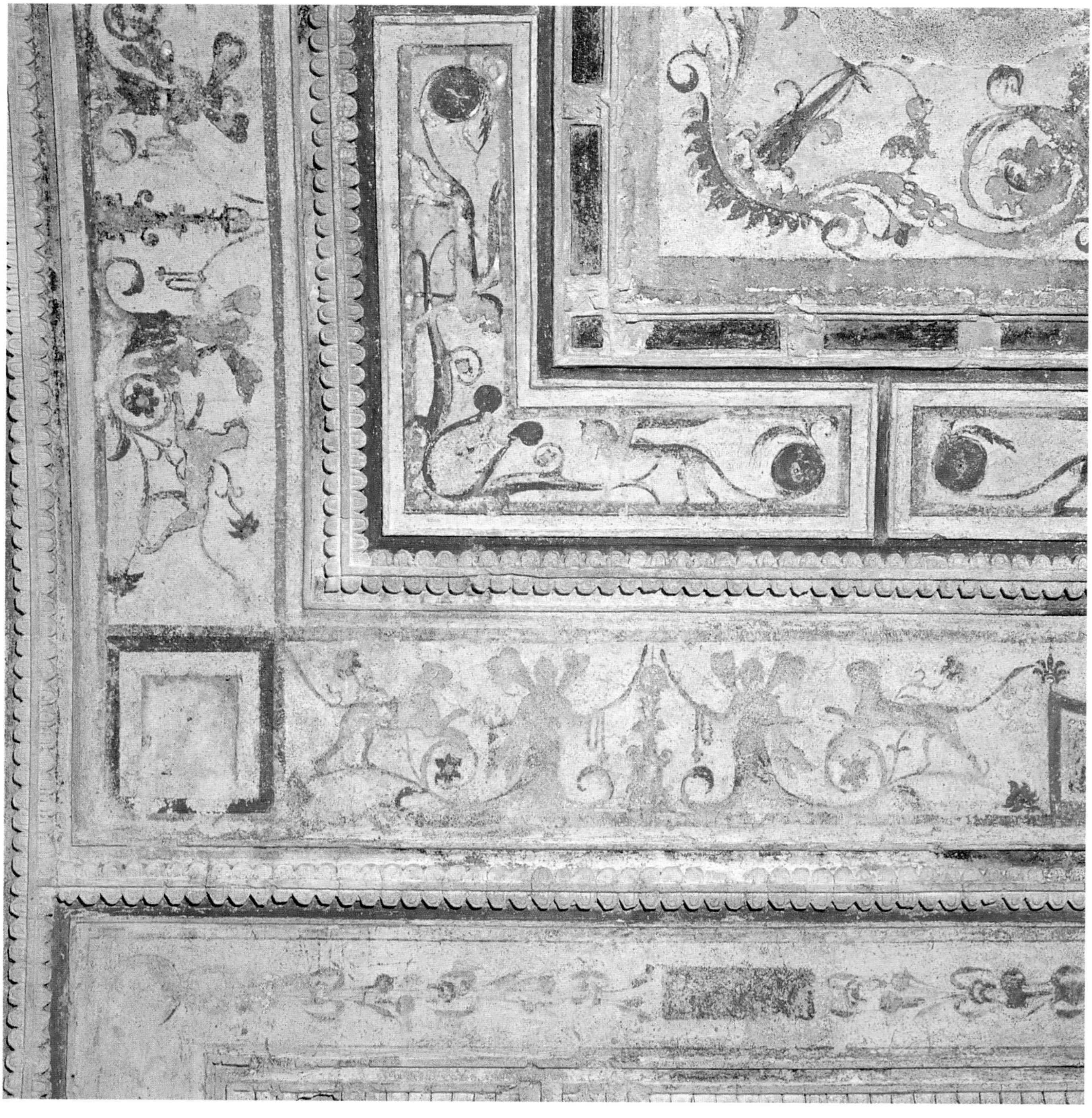

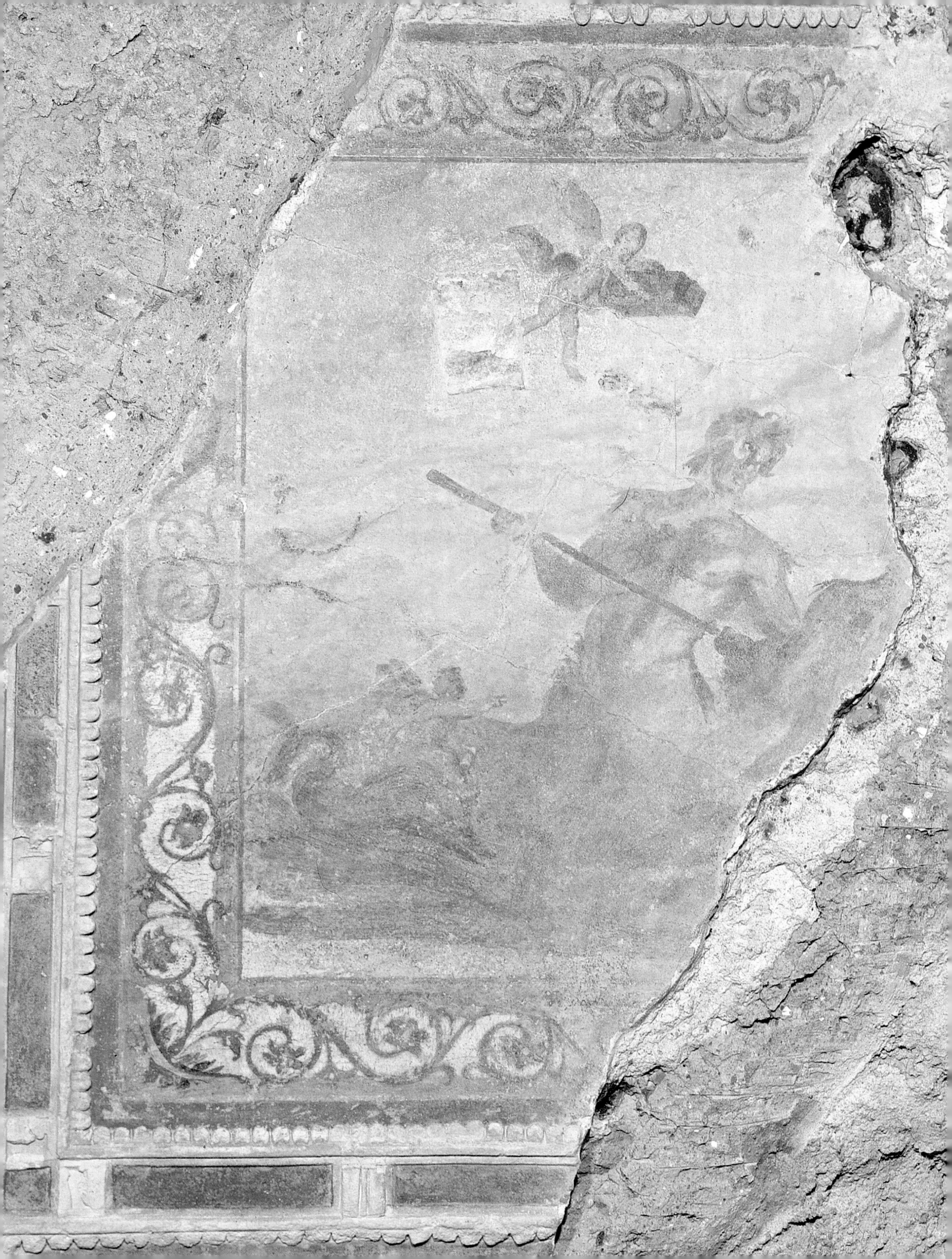

75. Hall of Hector and Andromache, side panel of the vault with scene of the farewell of Hector to Andromache

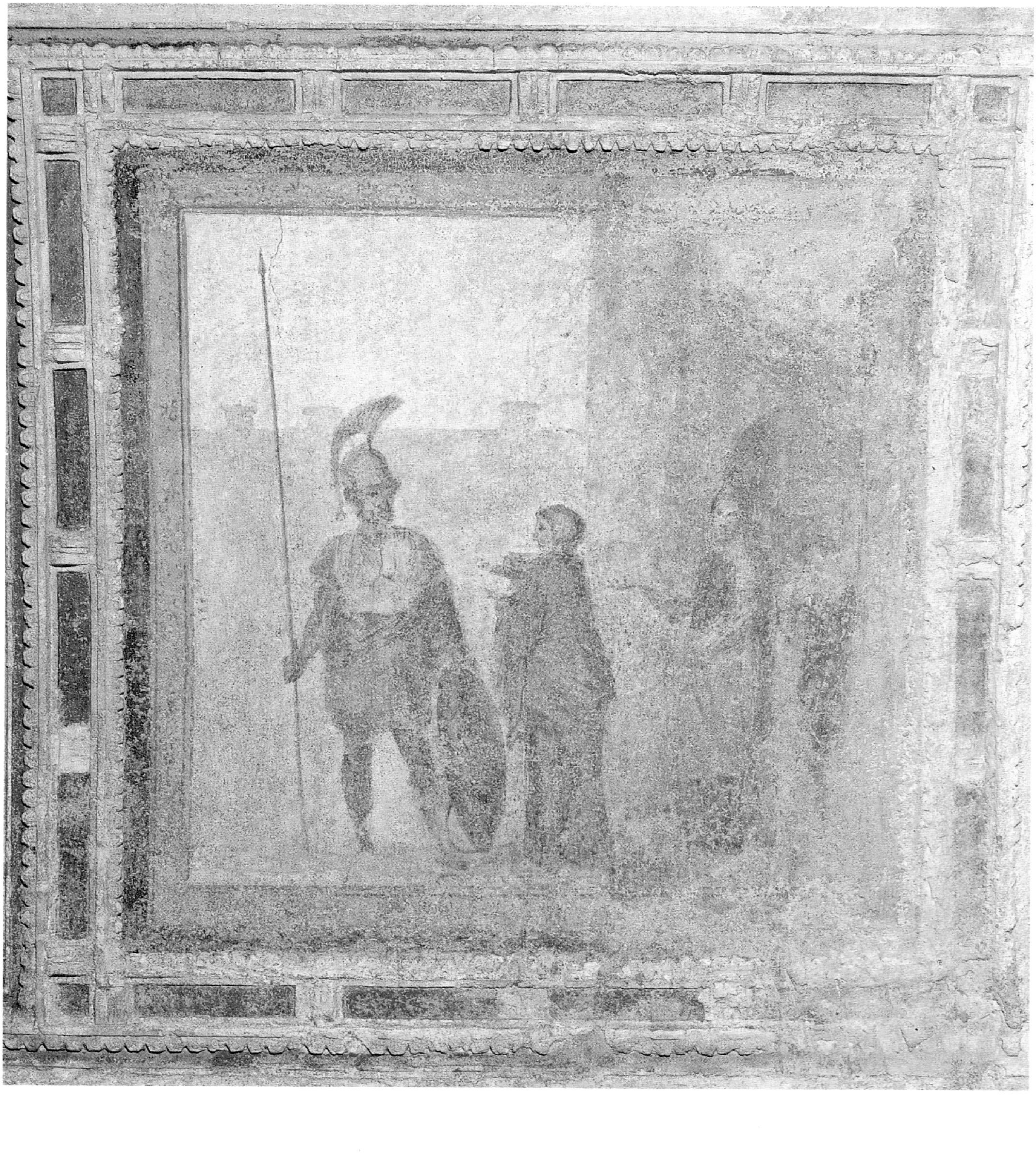

76. Hall of Hector and Andromache, side panel of the vault with scene of the meeting of Paris and Helen

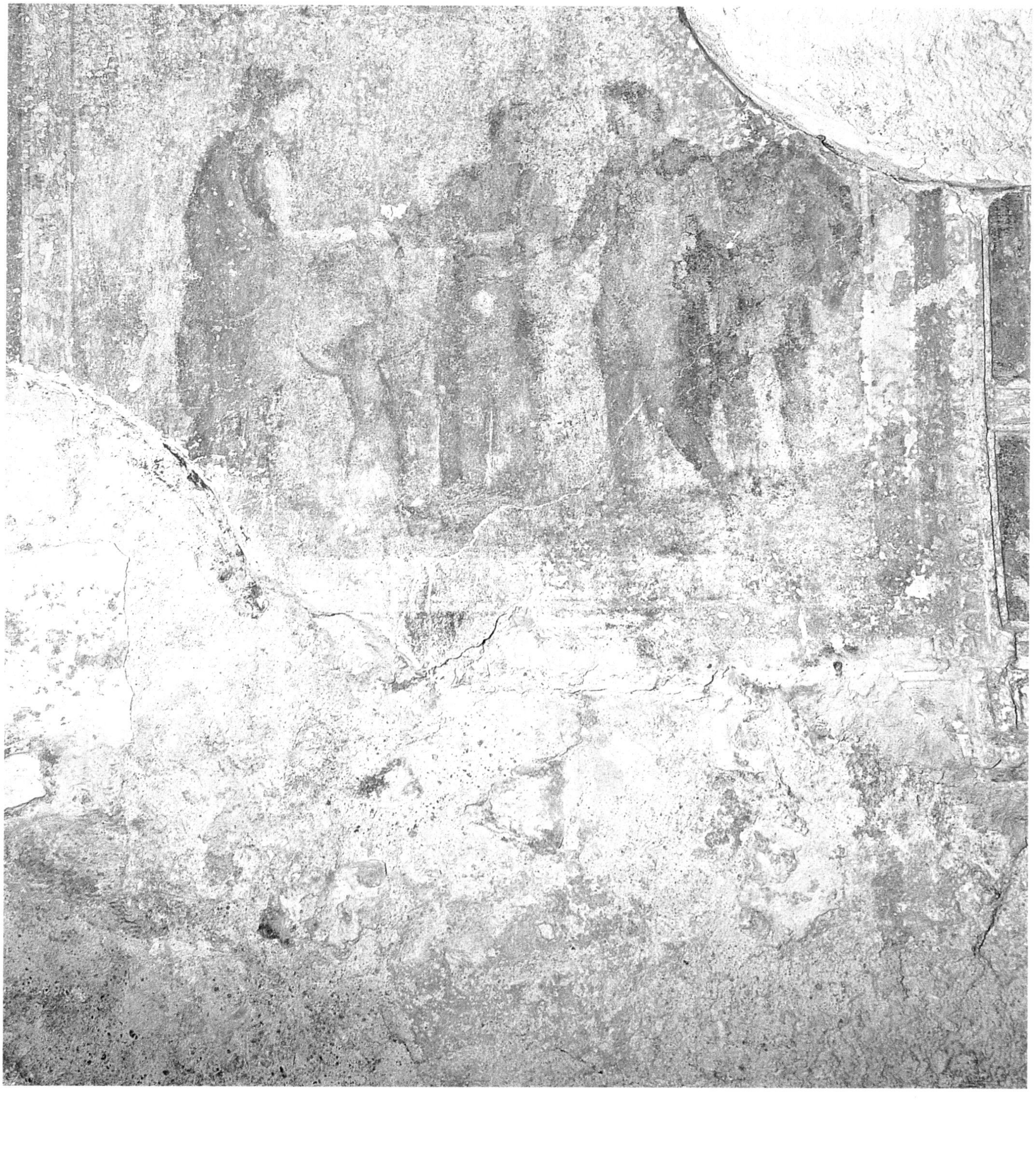

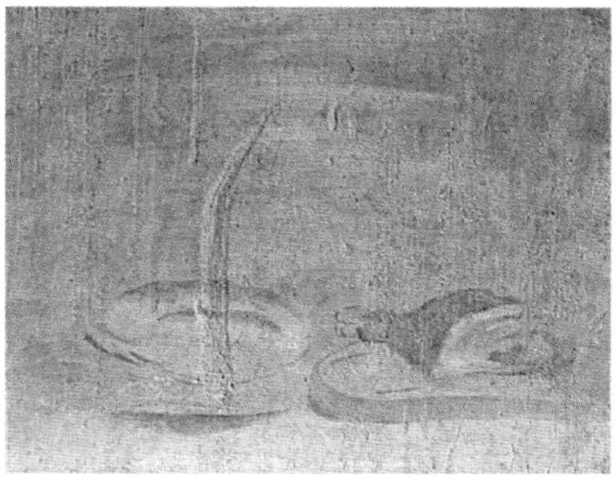

The corridor (79)

The corridor's function as a passageway explains the use of a simple and easily understood decorative system that conforms to Vitruvian rules about the decorative orders. Indeed, the entire wall decoration of the area is based on a simple linear architectural scheme, repeating on three registers (four on the lunettes) the motif of *aediculae* and schematic panels between *pinakes* (small panels with landscapes), held up by slender stems and festoons on a luminous white background. In the lower register, high *aediculae*, varying in the shape of their *tympana* (sometimes round, sometimes rectangular) upon the apexes of which perch animals, contain altars with masks beneath festoons. These *aediculae* alternate with wide frames bordered by elegant friezes, symmetrically repeated, in both vertical and horizontal planes. These reveal motifs of palmettes, spirals and animals finishing in plant-like volutes alternating with themselves or with subjects of animal form such as winged griffons heraldically placed and rows of herons with spread wings, sphinxes and spiral motifs alternated.

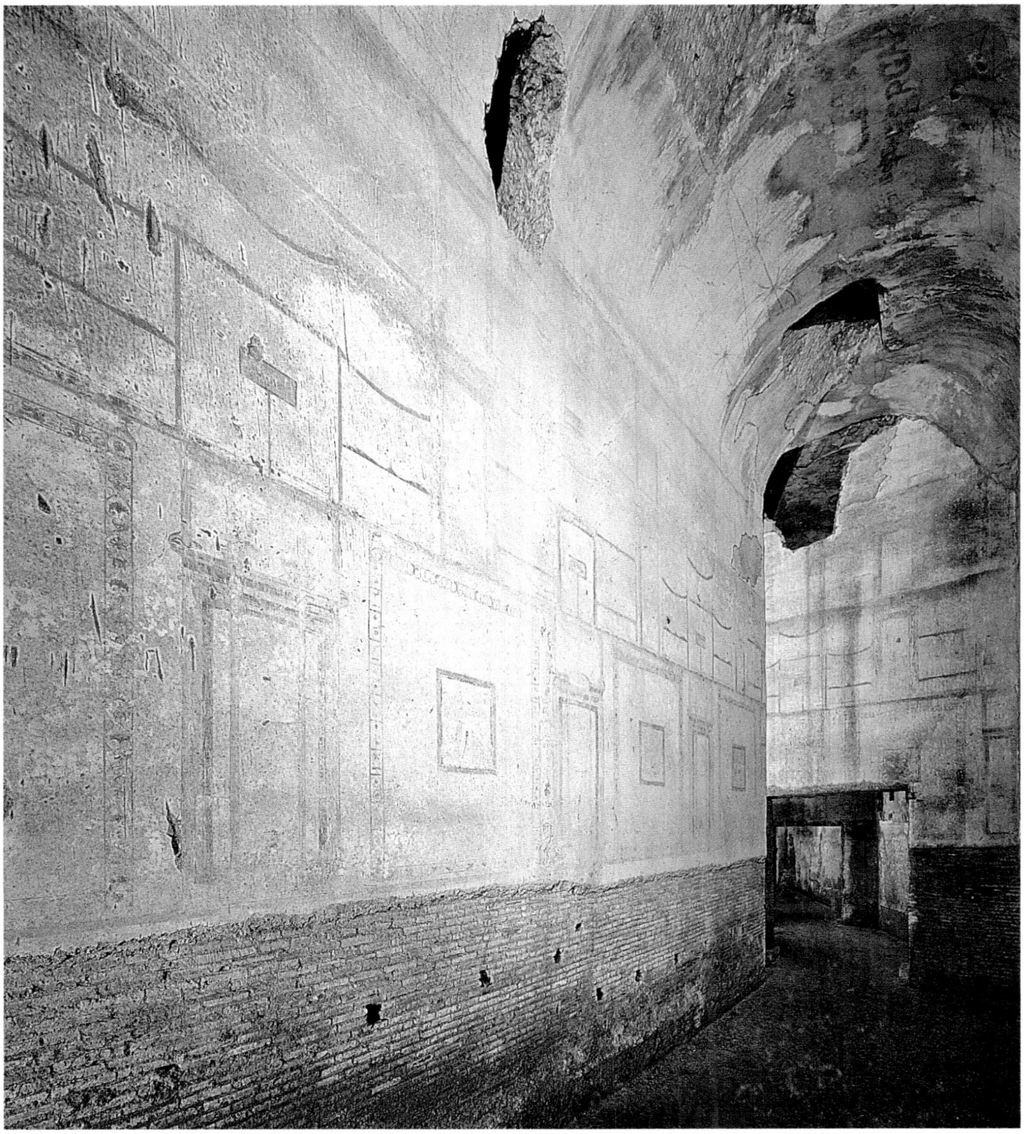

77. Corridor no. 79, architectural decoration organised into three and four (lunette) registers

78. Corridor no. 79, detail of architectural division of the wall

79. Corridor no. 79, architectural composition of the wall in three registers: in the lower register an aedicula and panels showing still lifes and landscapes (now lost)

While it lacks figured panels and decorative forms with minute details (more suitable for the decoration of rooms where observers might stop), nevertheless the corridor exhibits the characteristic elements of the decorative language of fourth style (although these were already present in the preceding styles): namely miniature landscapes and still lifes.

The still life of food on the south wall is depicted with a lively sense of nature. This is a particular figural motif (perhaps better adapted to a dining-room) which, in its thematic variety, goes beyond the typical repertoire seen in examples of Campanian painting.

This kind of decoration can be seen as the final type derived from the Hellenistic tradition. The literary sources are silent about it, with the exception of Pliny (*Natural History*, 35. 112) who cites the painter of food, *Peiraikos* (who lived in the 4th century and who was author of *minores picturae*), and Vitruvius (6. 7.4) who discusses the paintings depicting *xenia* (gifts of food offered to guests by the masters of houses). The *Domus Aurea* offers one of the very rare examples outside the Vesuvian context of this unusual type of decoration.

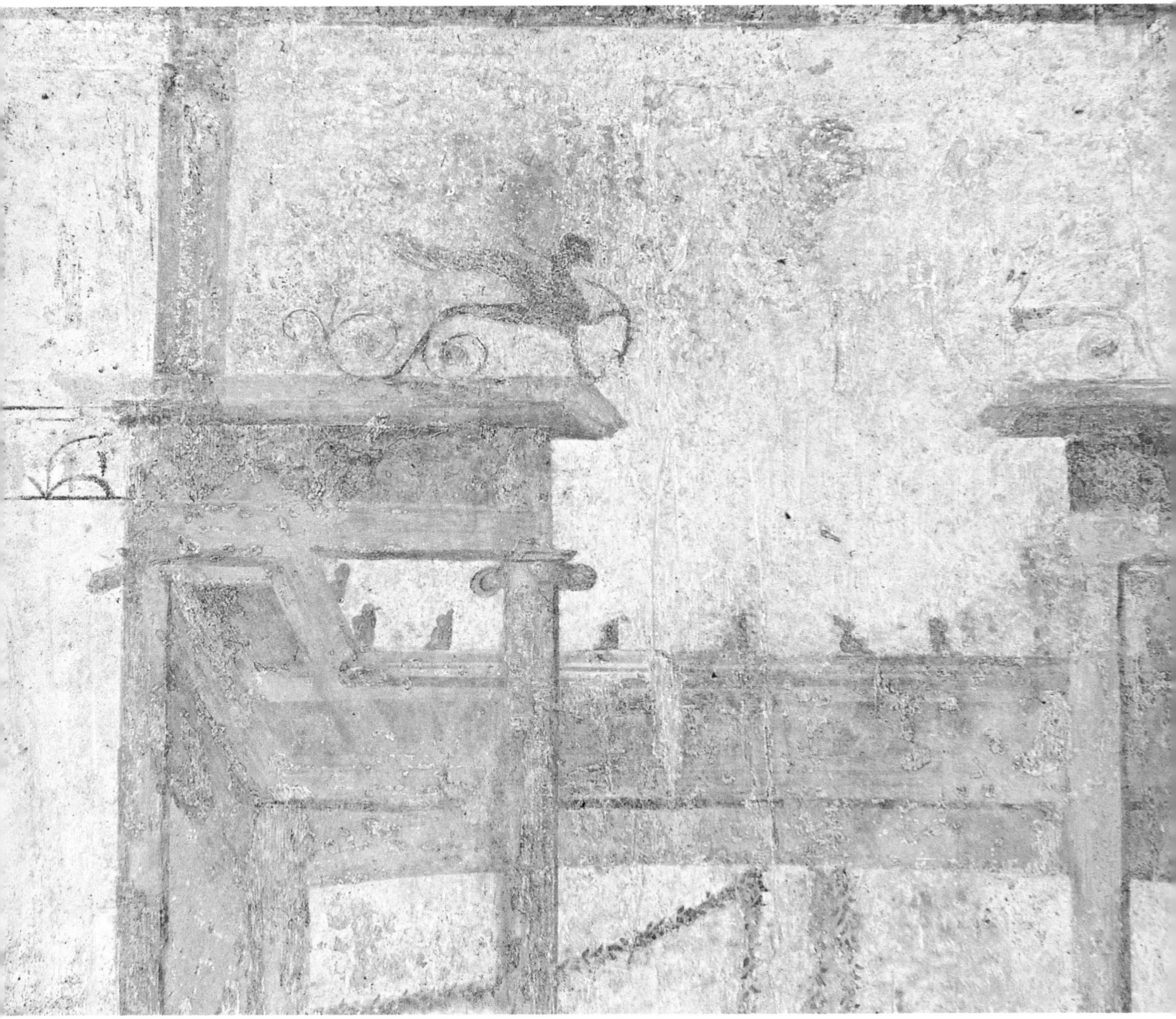

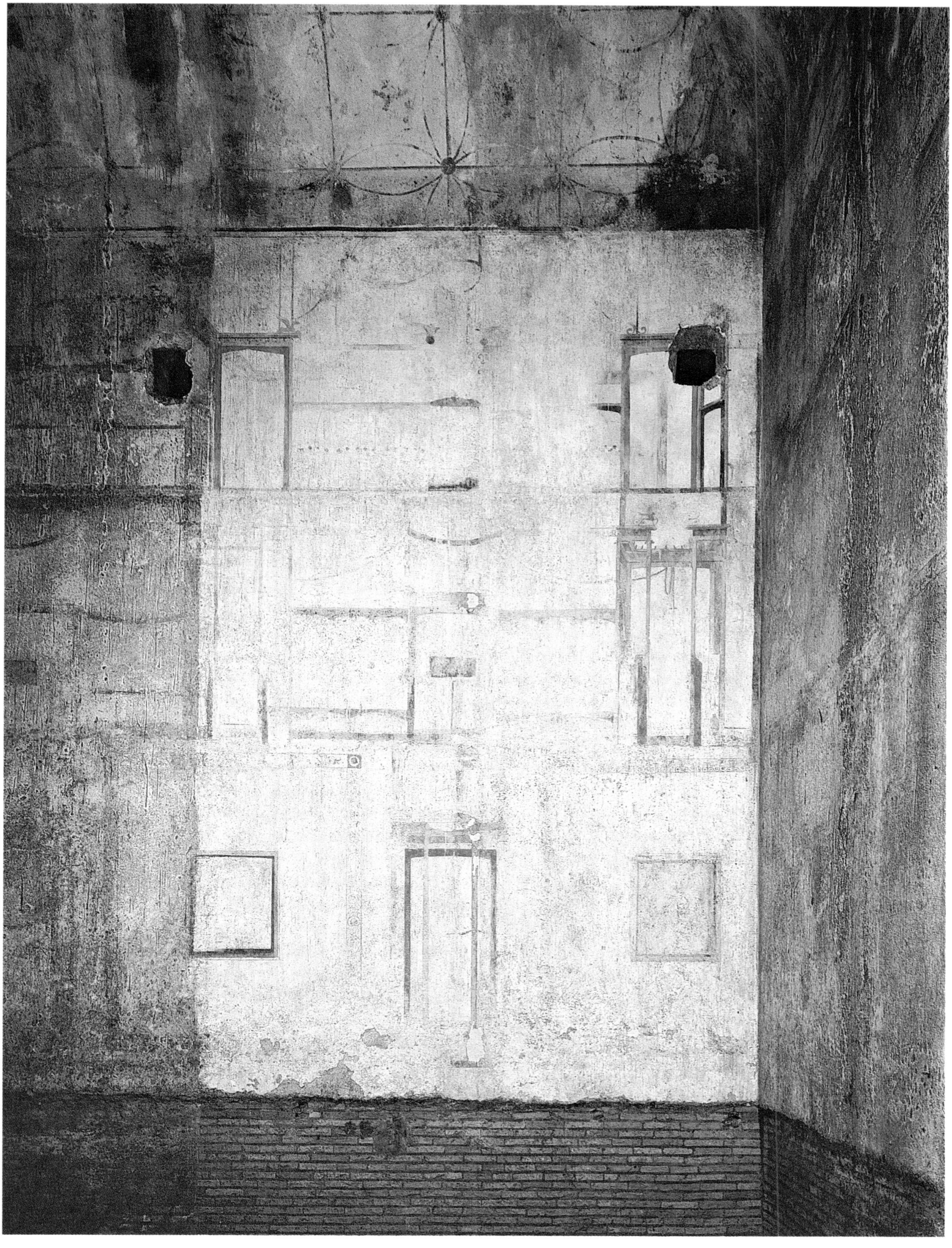

80. Corridor no. 79, south wall, detail of a still life with foodstuffs

81. Corridor no.79, detail of the lower register of the composition with aedicula and panels containing landscapes and still lifes

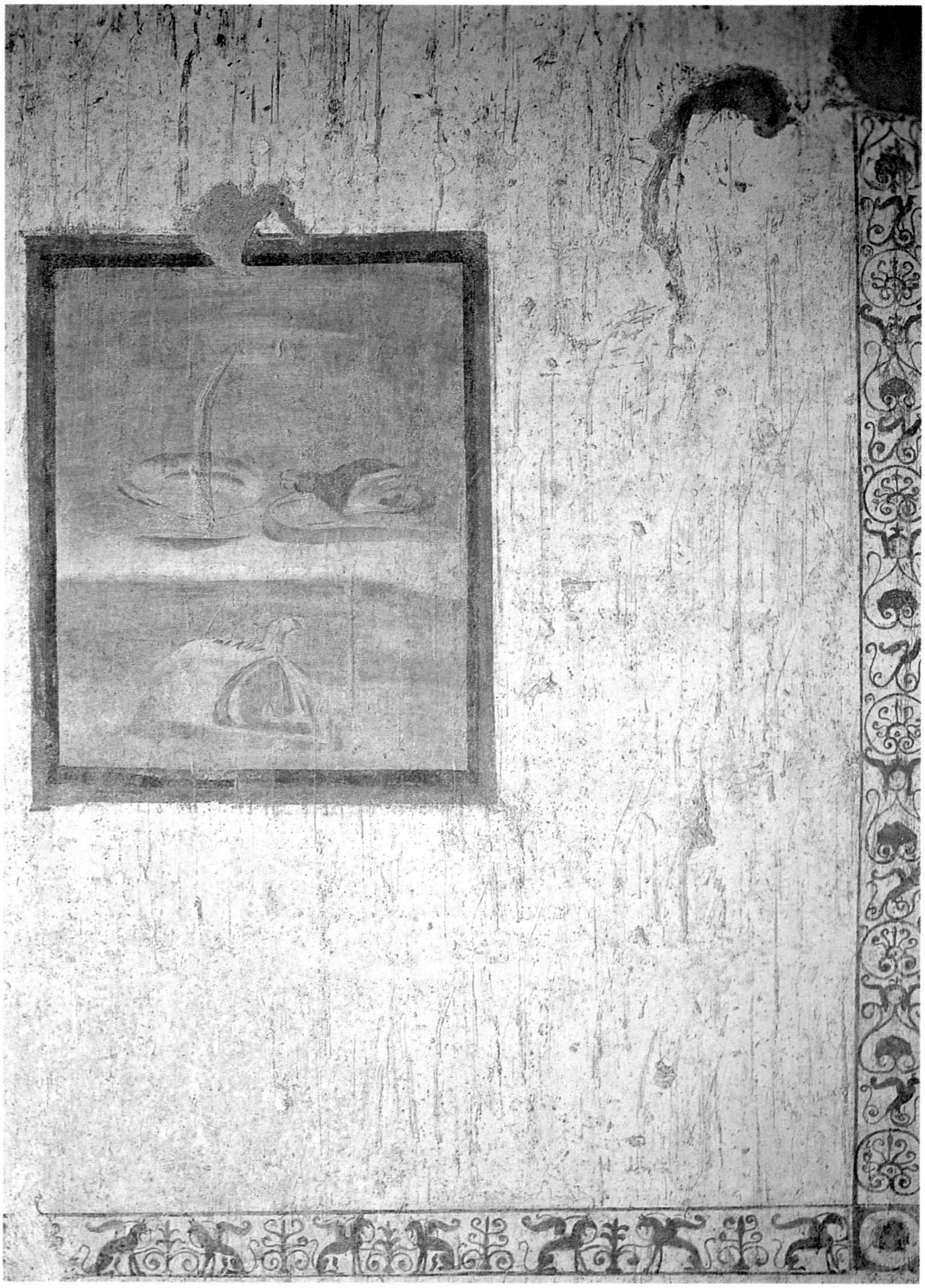

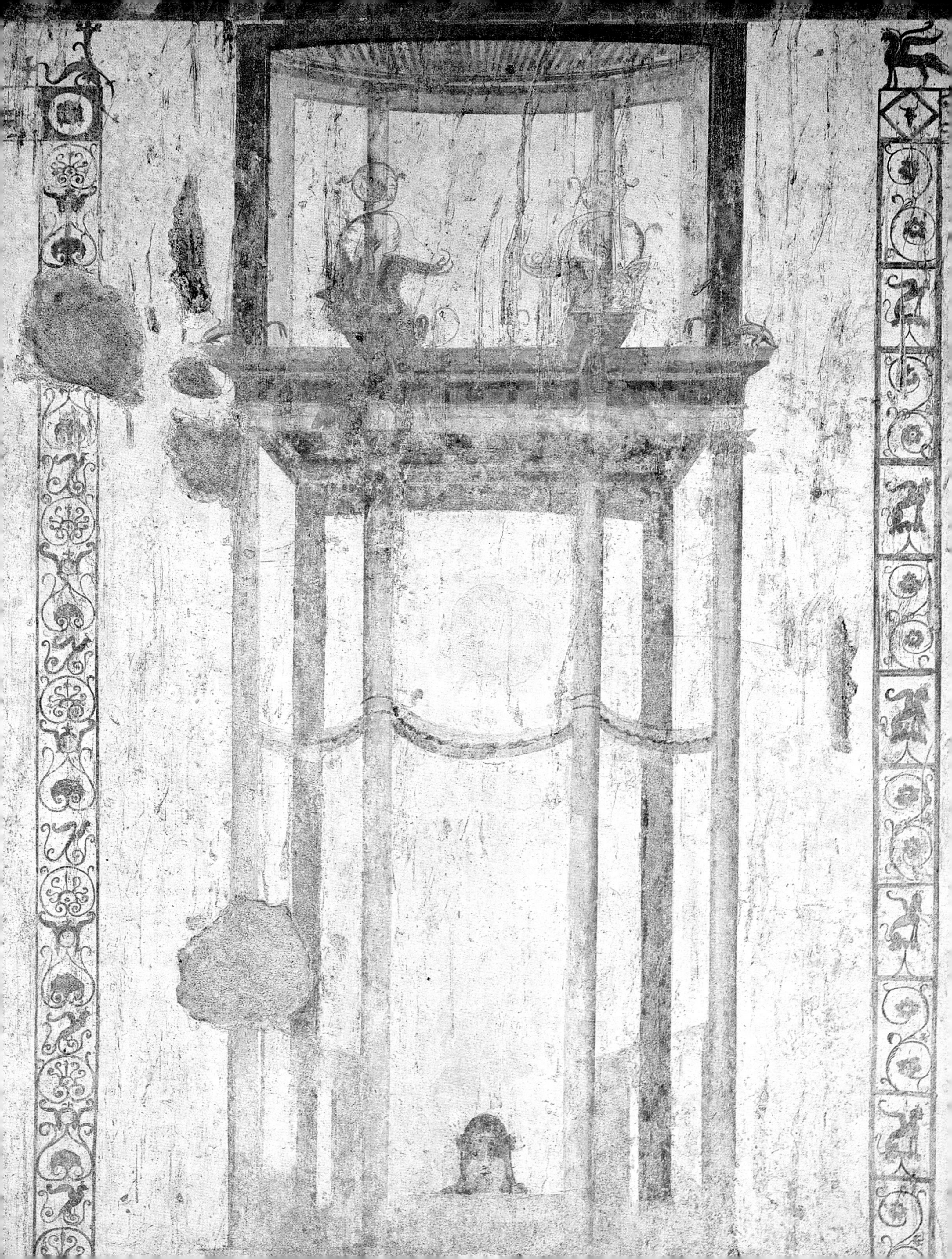

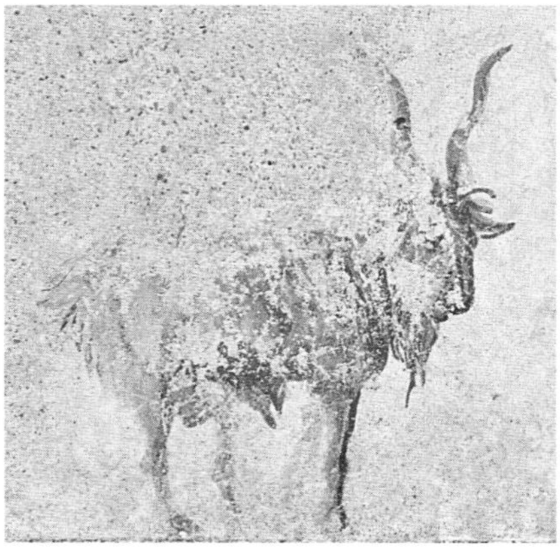

The cryptoporticus (92)

The decorative partitions of the vault of the large cryptoporticus 92 – which is an extension of the corridor n. 79 – and that of the cryptoporticus 142, which remains buried, are simple and repetitive. In addition, the architecture on the painting on the walls has nothing in common with the arrangements of illusionistic effects in the more important rooms of the east wing. There are no traces of the art of the Maestro who worked in the public sector of the *Domus*, where a different formal style can be seen in the fine and complex production in the imperial apartments.
Attribution of the decoration of this passageway and other rooms of less logistical importance to simple artisans is justified by the sketchy technique and outlined style of the motifs. These are mostly of animal form, and indistinctly cover the surface of the wolf's mouths as they do the surface of the arch which divides the cryptoporticus (and thus its decoration), and the ornamental character of the whole.
In the early 1900s, the draftsman, Cartocci, carried out a complete restoration drawing of the vault of cryptoporticus 92. This demonstrates an adherence to ornamentation in the form of tapestries and cloth drapery in its eastern part. The western part is adorned by panels whose surfaces are subdivided into red and blue rhomboids and square, similar to mosaic floors. These contain human and animal figures or are entirely embroidered with arabesque motifs. Slender architecture connected by festoons occupies the yellow band of colour that links the walls along with human figures terminating in petals, plant-like

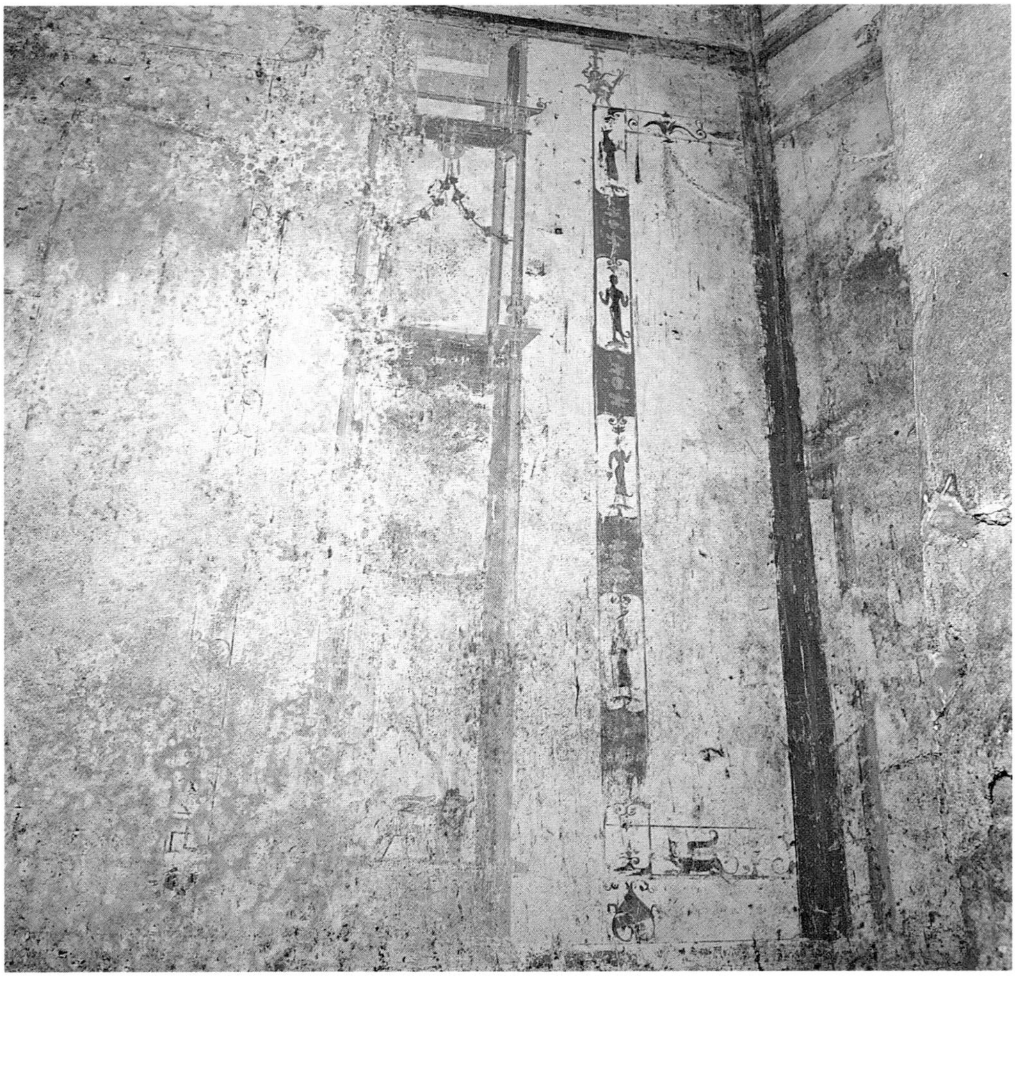

82. Cryptoporticus no. 92, wall decoration with architectural pavilions and panels with a border of Egyptianising figures, including Anubis

83. Cryptoporticus no. 92, 'wolf's mouth', festoon motifs and small 'grotesques' set opposite one another, surrounding a panel with a griffon

84. Cryptoporticus no. 92, decoration of the arch dividing the corridor

candle-sticks and fantasy animals. This architecture recurs amongst the themes employed by the artists as early as the school of Ghirlandaio, and was amongst the subjects chosen by Raphael and Giovanni da Udine to transfer to their painted work in the Vatican. This evidence, along with many signatures which 16th artists left on the decoration of this vault, attests to the frequency with which the vault was visited and of the fame of which the extensive 'grotto' enjoyed in the 15th-17th centuries.

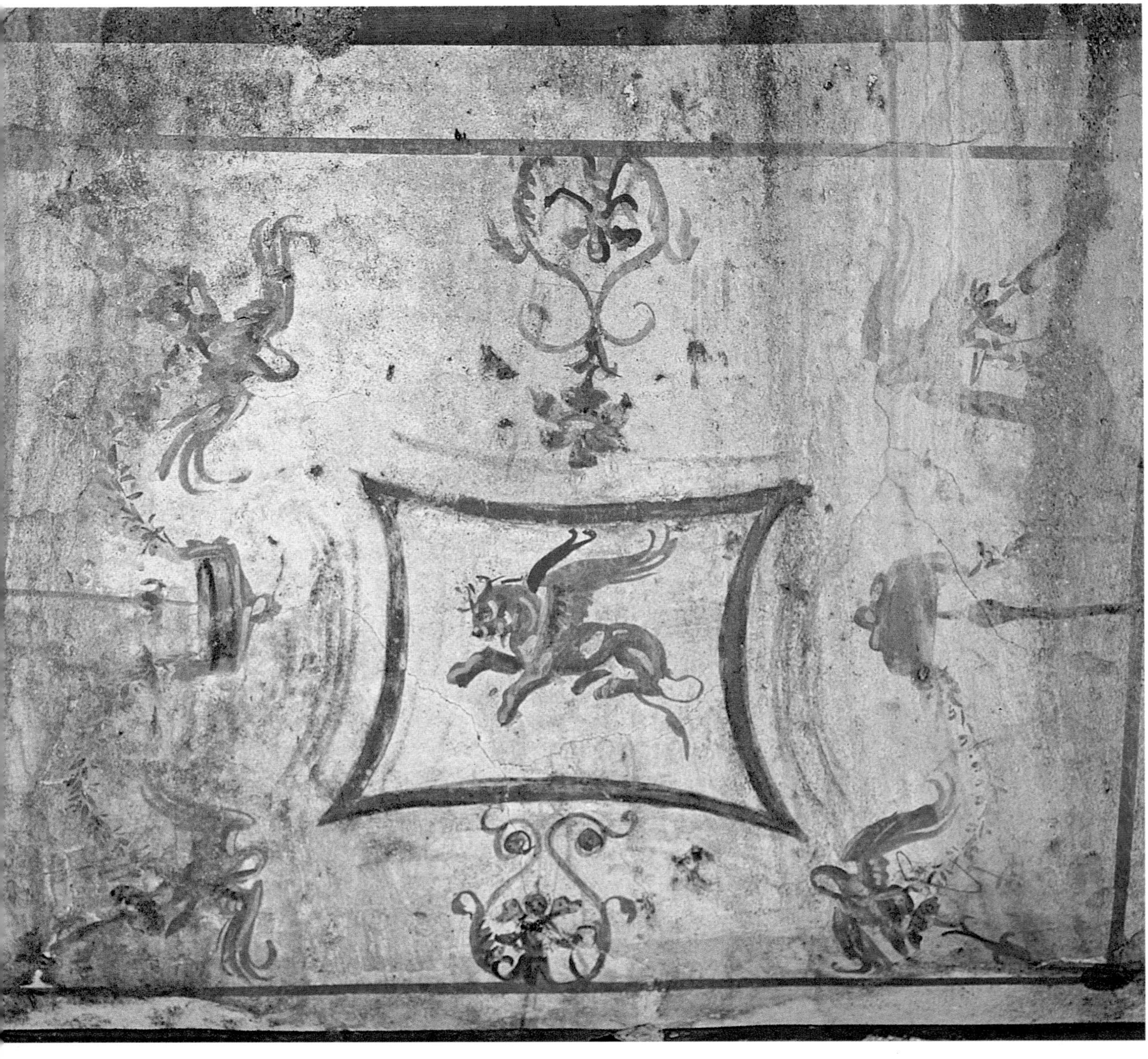

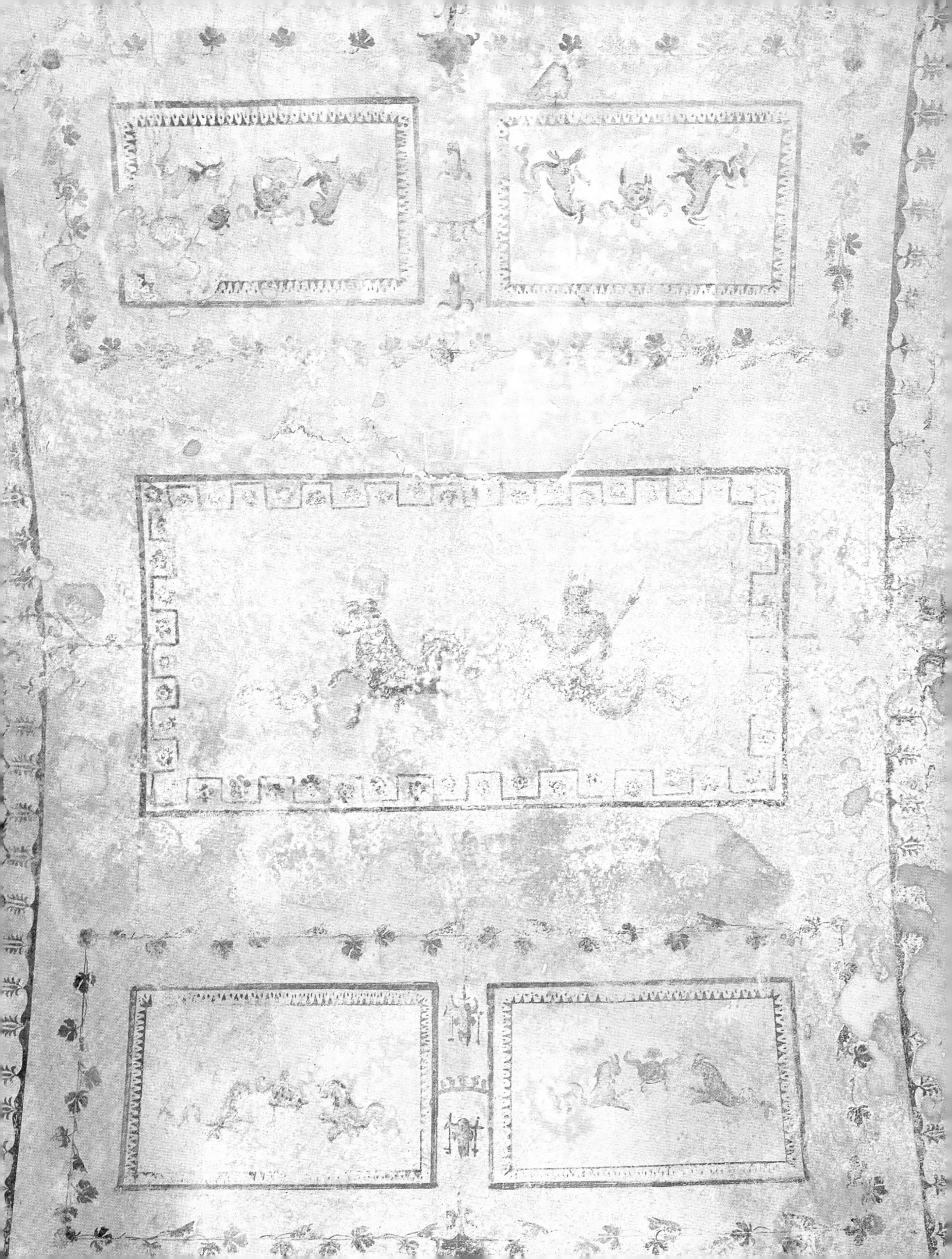

85. Cryptoporticus no. 92, decoration of the arch dividing the corridor, detail with various animal motifs

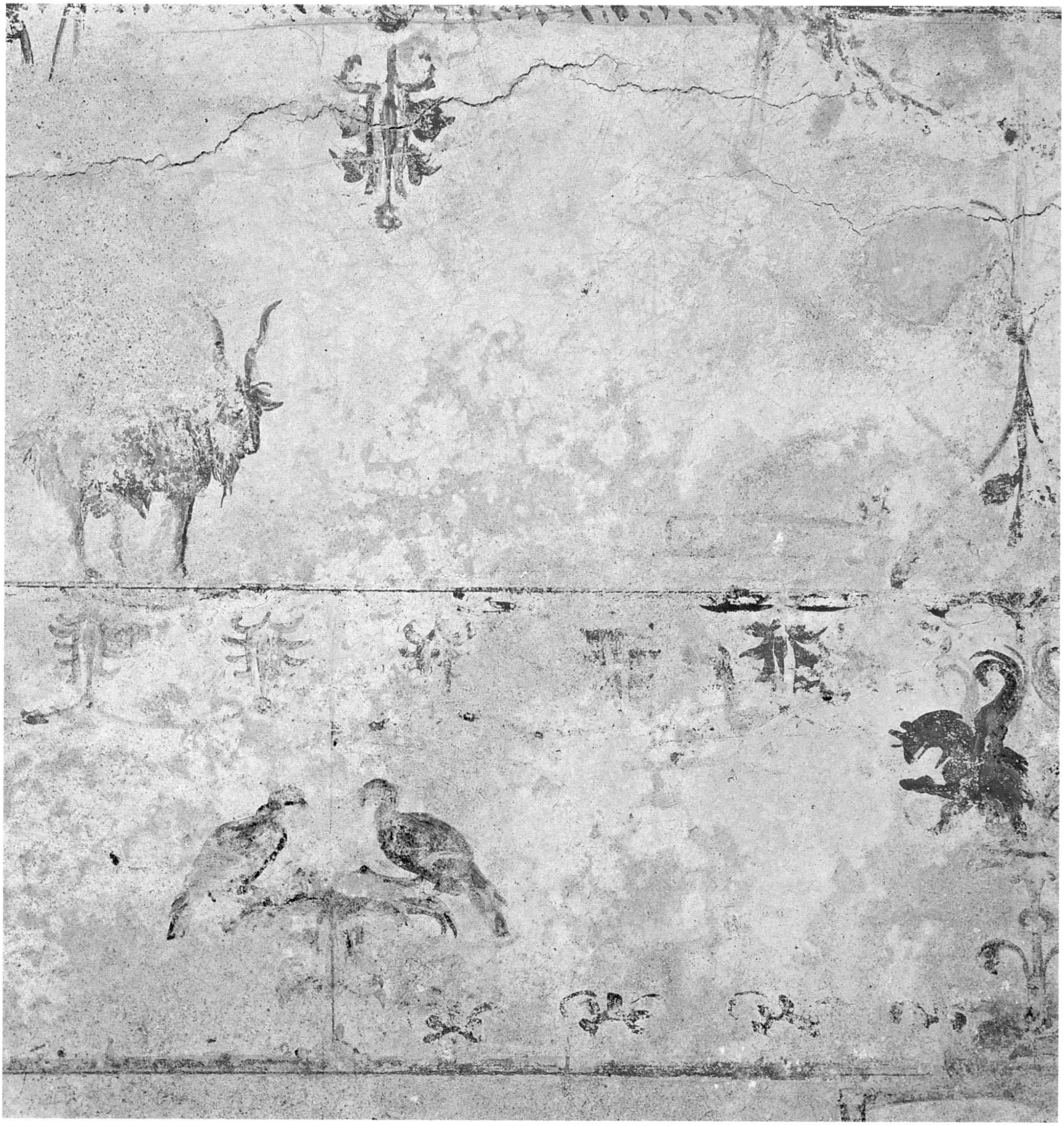

86–87. Cryptoporticus no. 92, eastern section, composition of decoration of the central part of the vault in the style of embroidered furnishings, watercolour by Cartocci (Weege 1913)

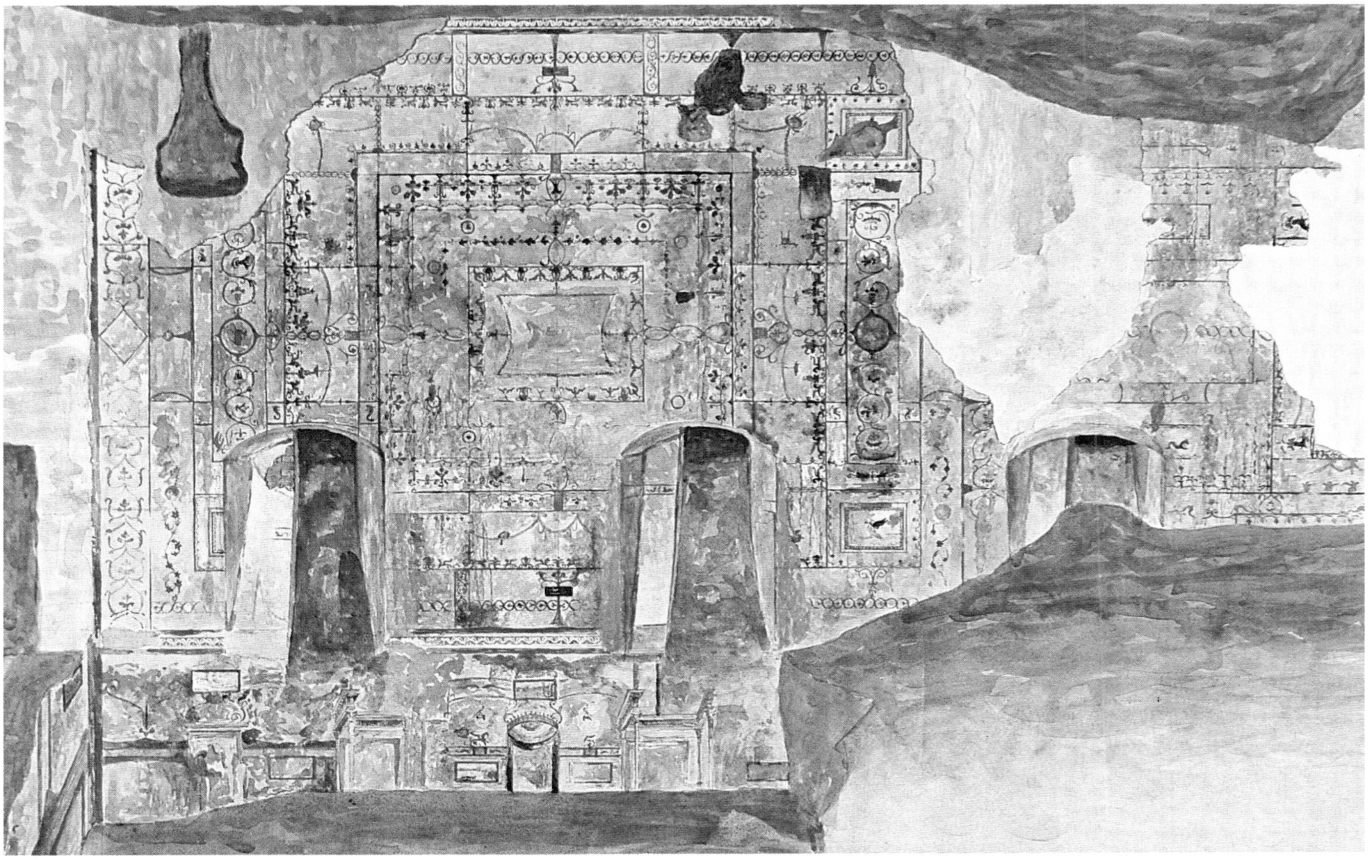

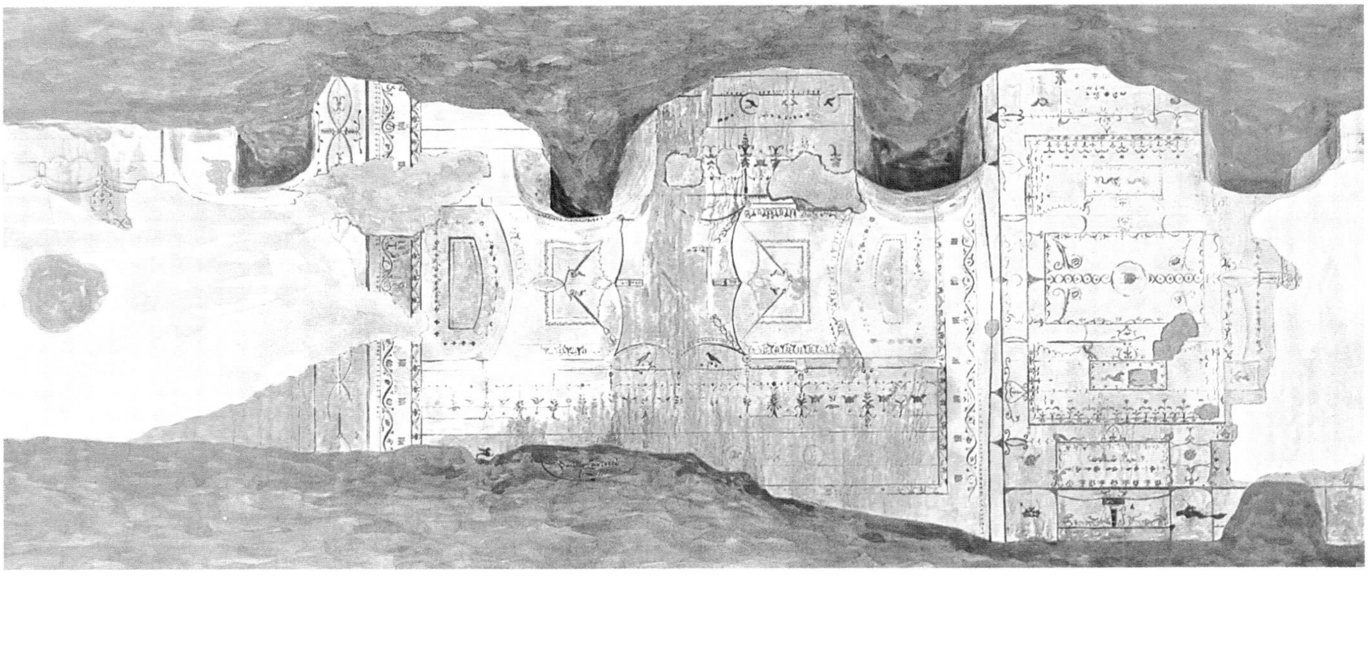

88–89. Cryptoporticus no. 92, eastern section, decoration of the vault, condition today

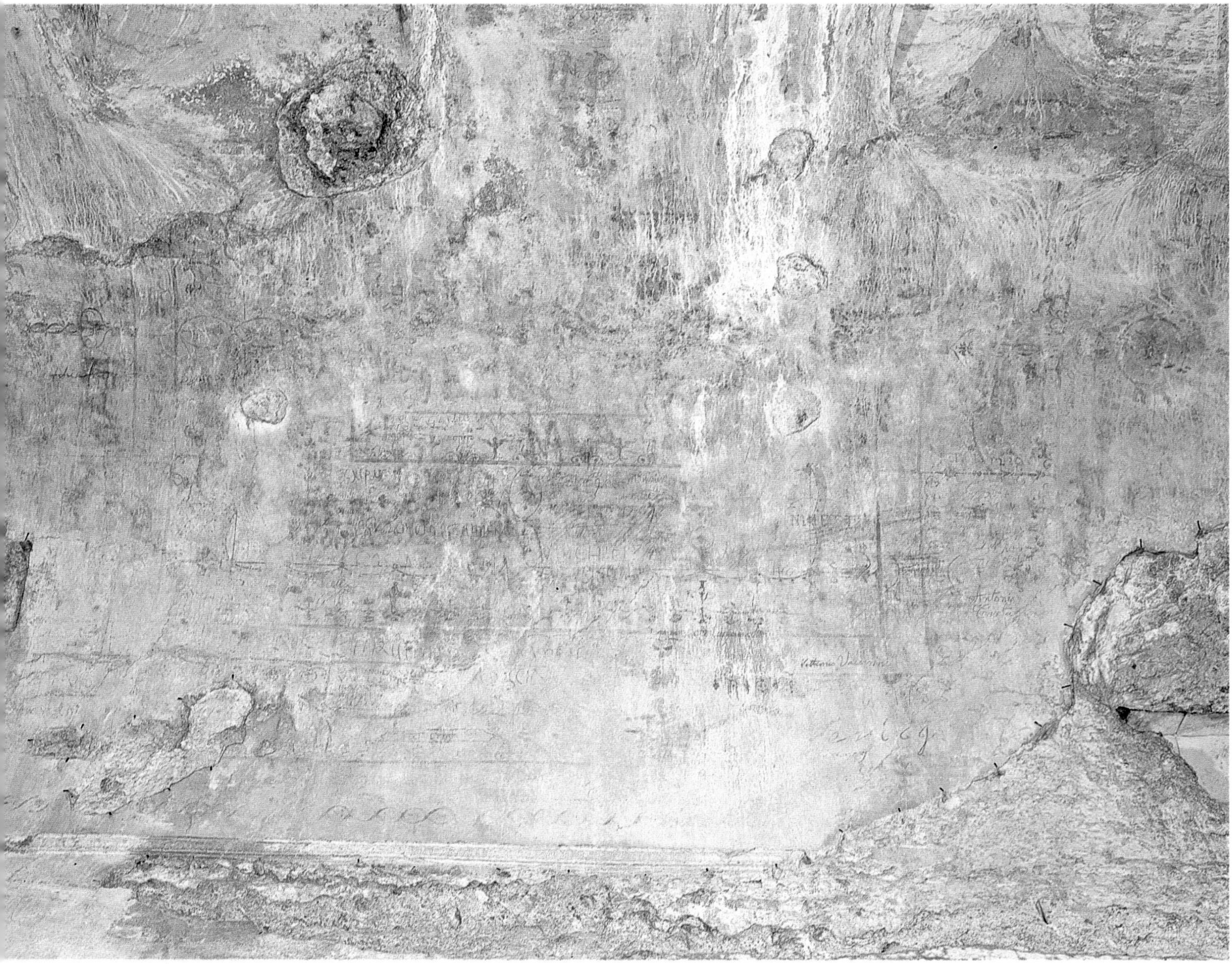

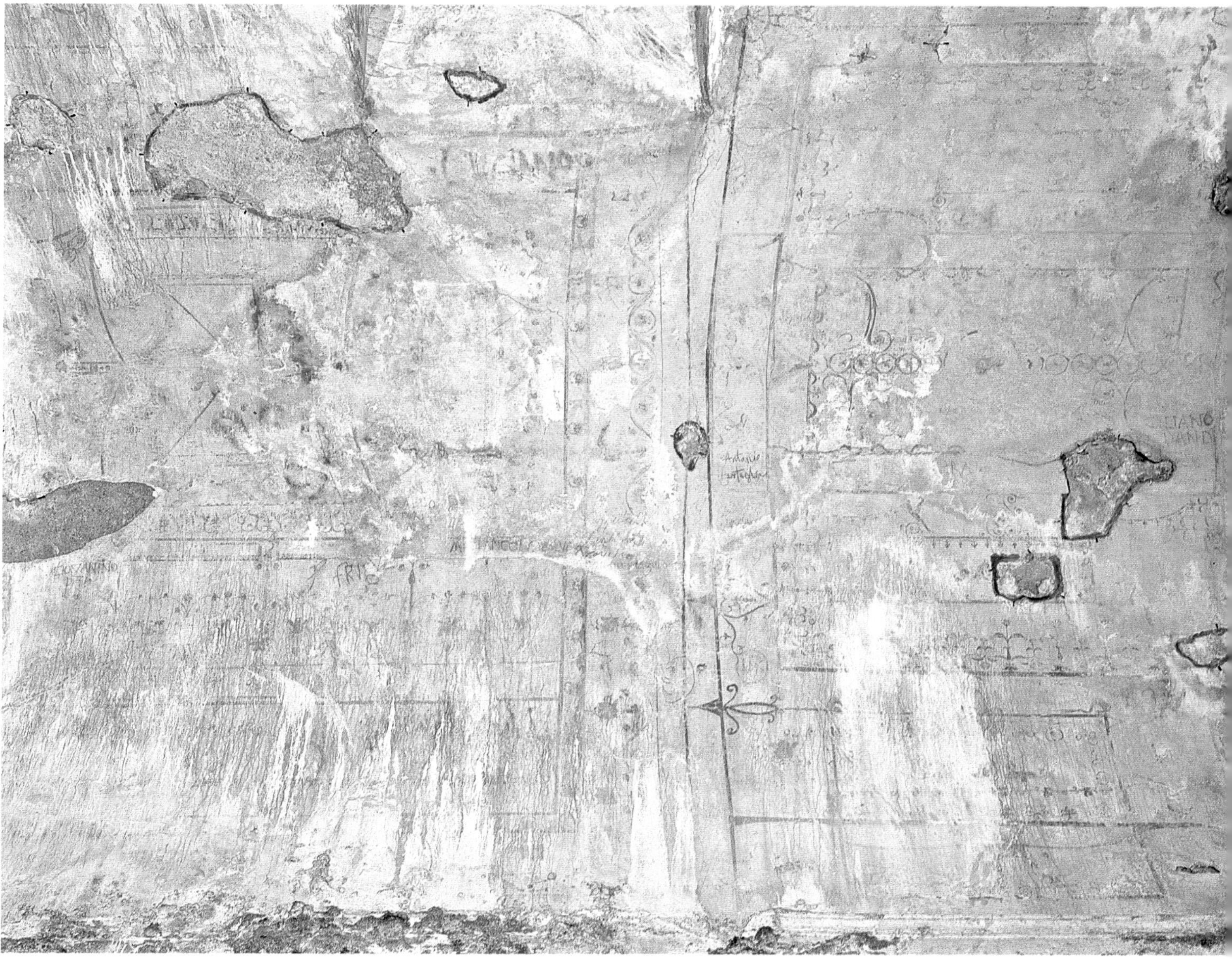

90. *Cryptoporticus no. 92, western section, centre of the vault with 'carpet' decoration interwoven with rhomboid and square motifs, watercolour by Cartocci (Weege 1913)*

91. *Cryptoporticus no. 92, western section, centre of the vault with 'carpet' decoraton, watercolour by Cartocci (Weege 1913)*

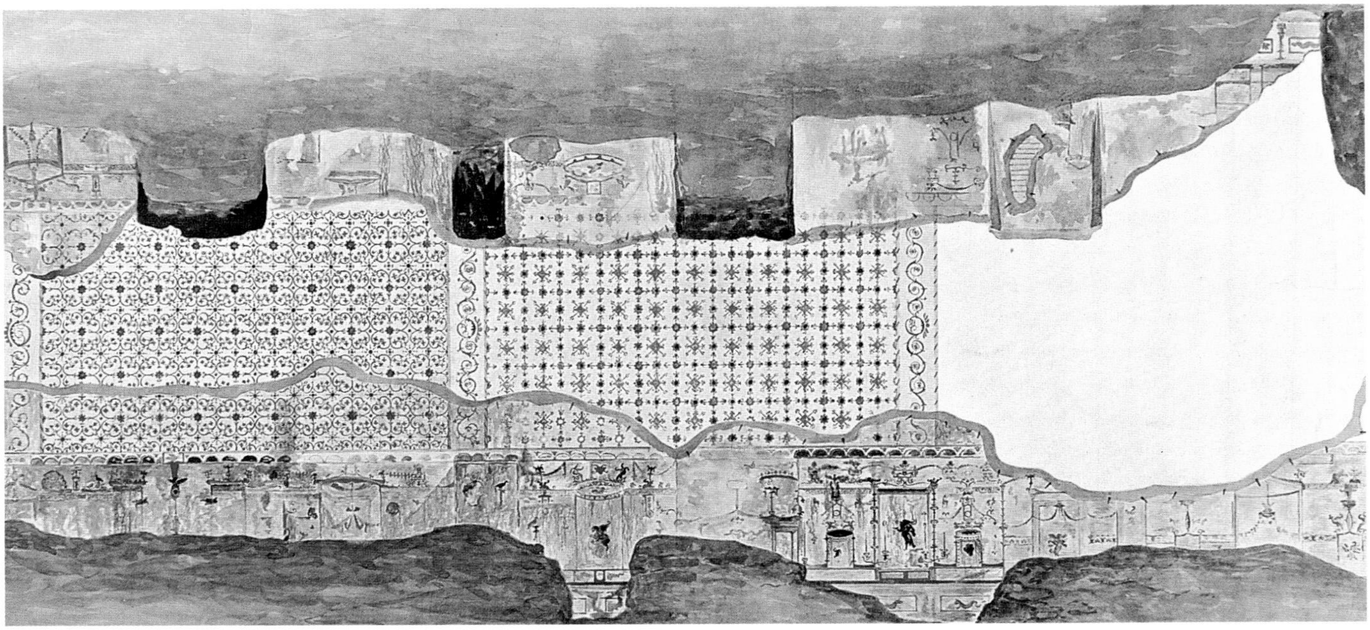

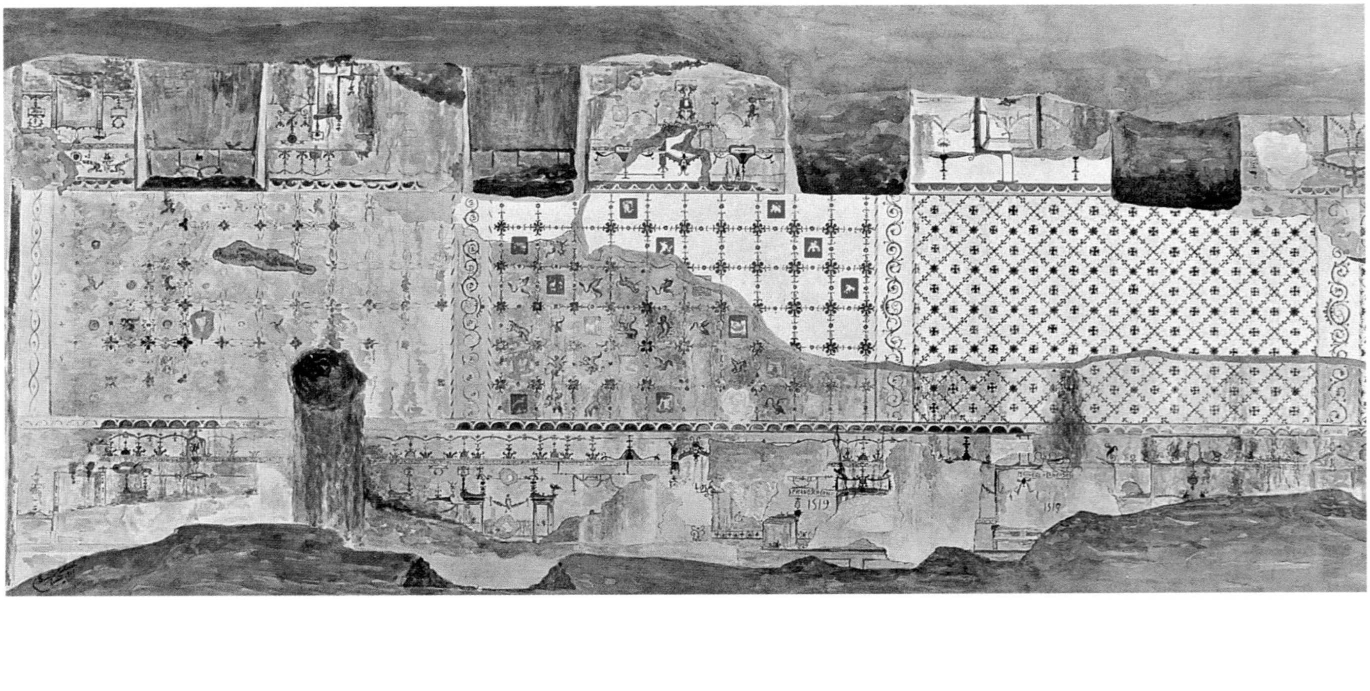

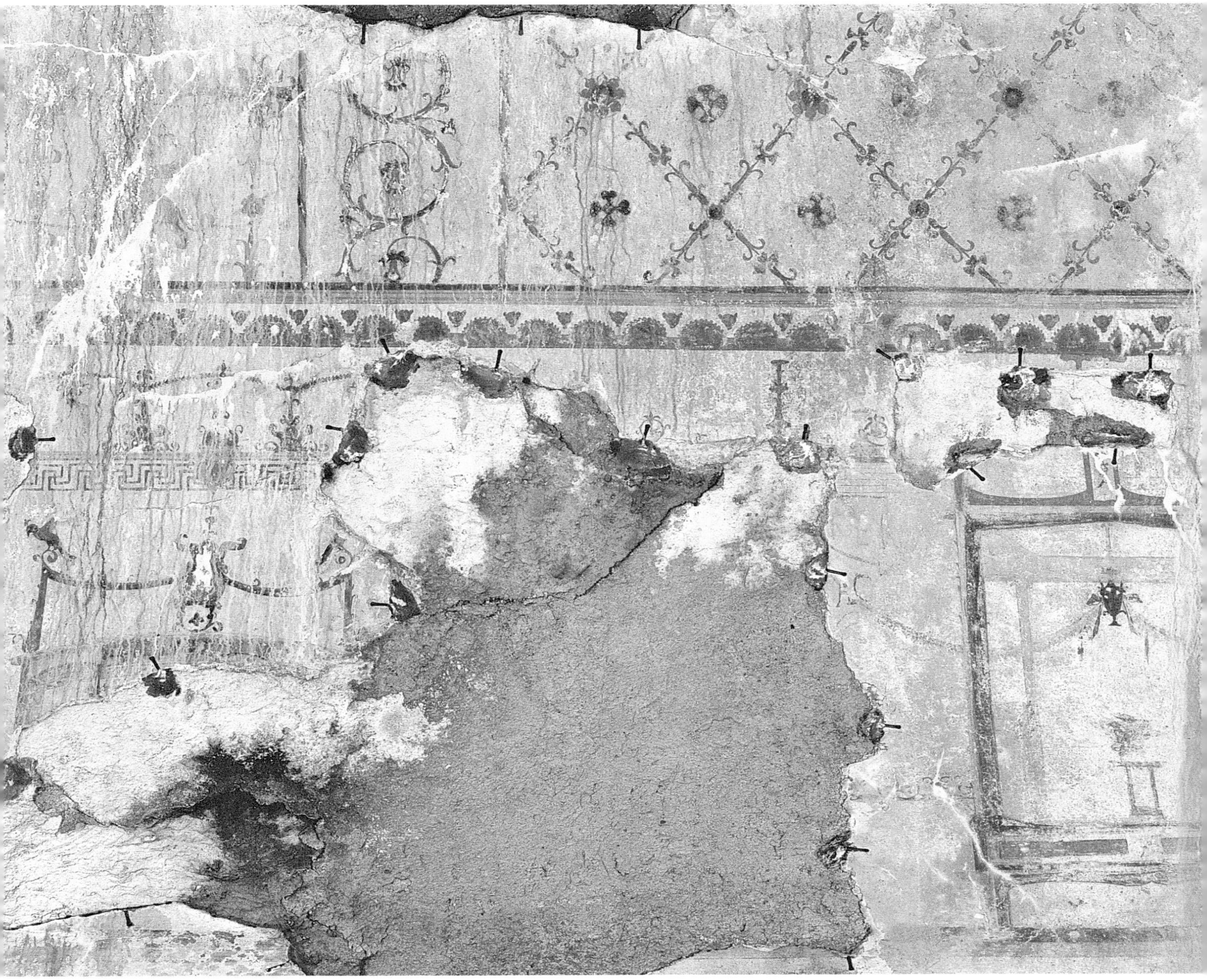

92. Cryptoporticus no. 92, western section, decoration of the vault, condition today

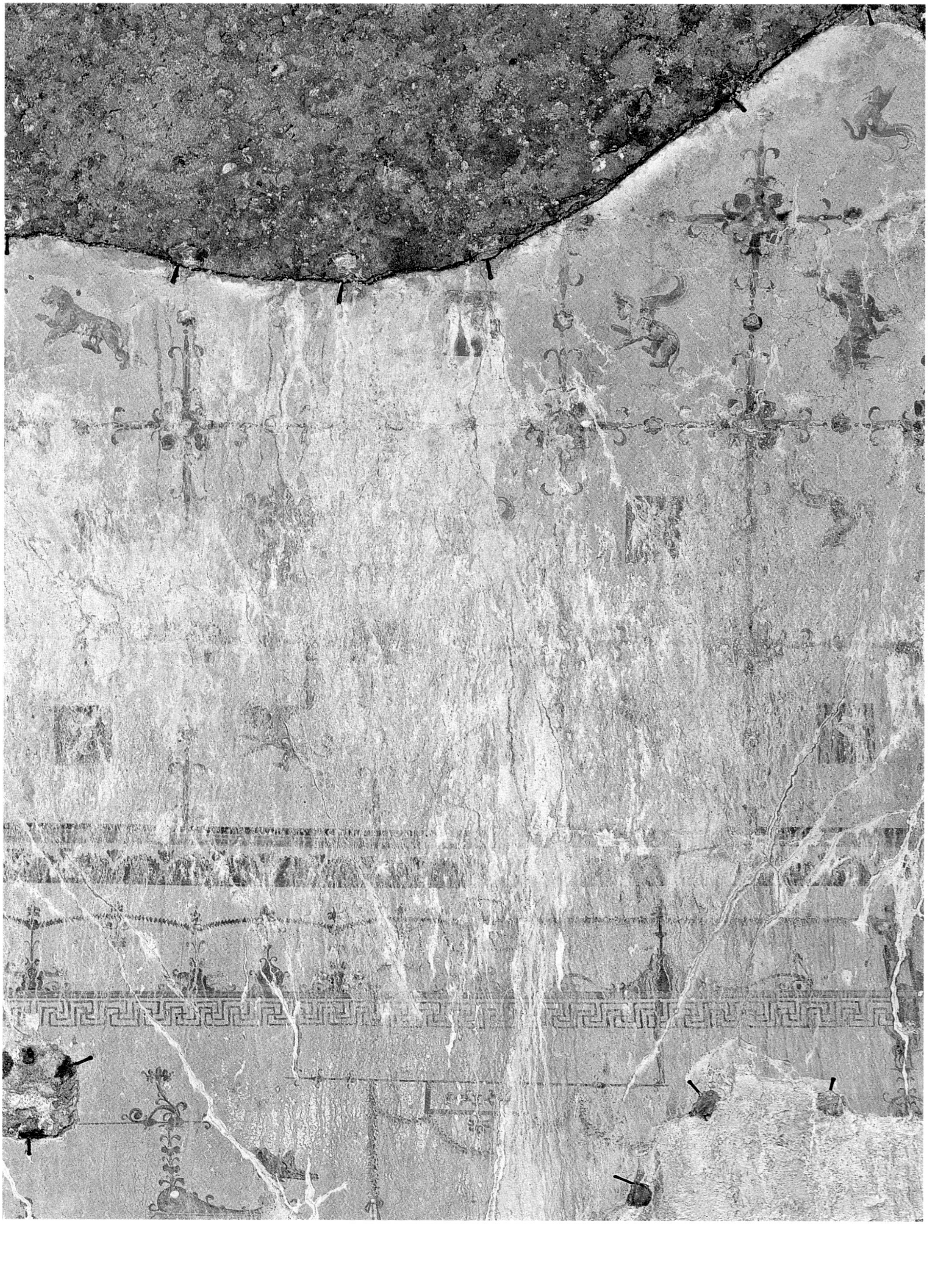

93. Cryptoporticus no. 92, western section, decoration of the vault, condition today

94. Cryptoporticus no. 92, vault, architecture with festoons and 'grotesque' elements in band beneath the 'carpet' decoration

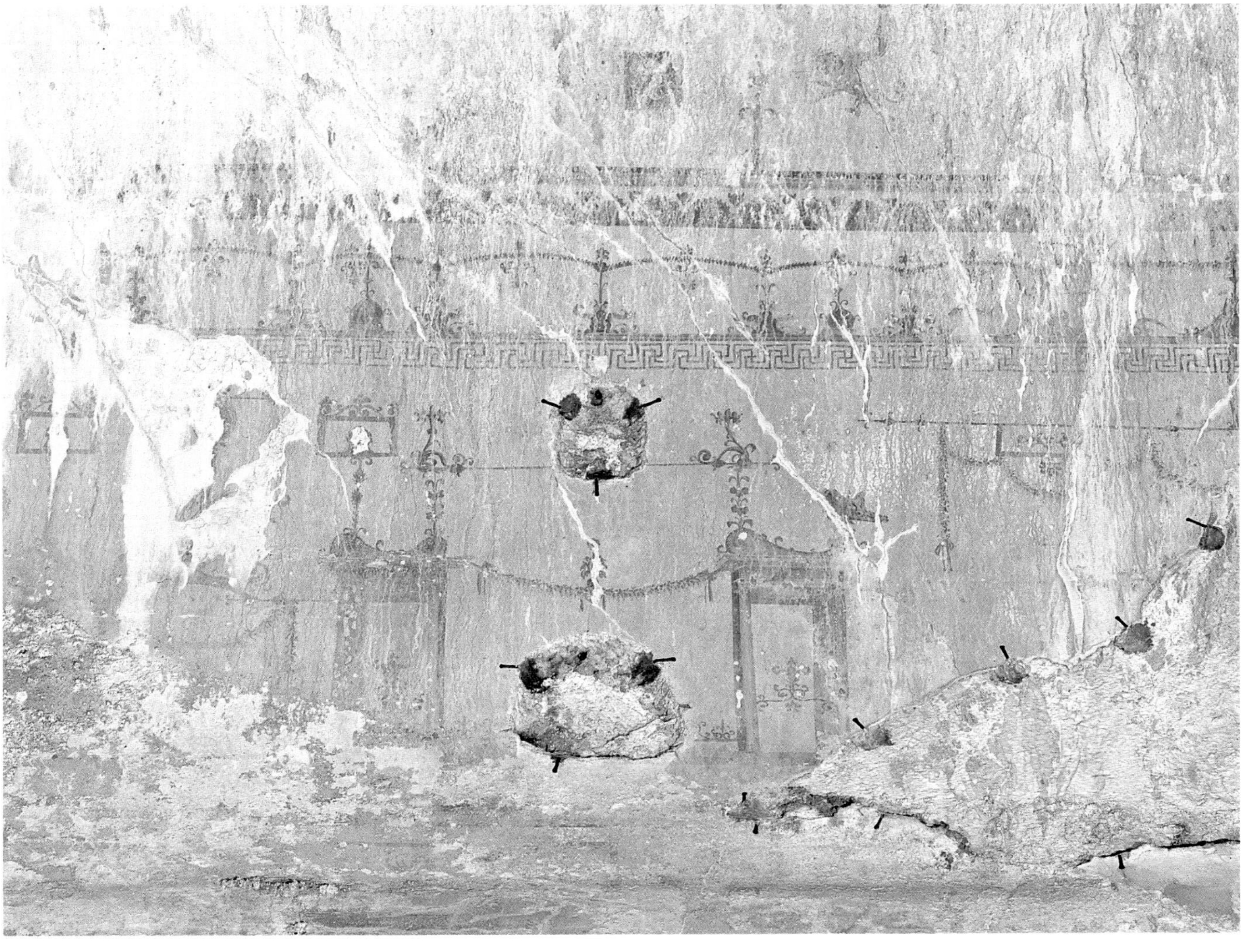

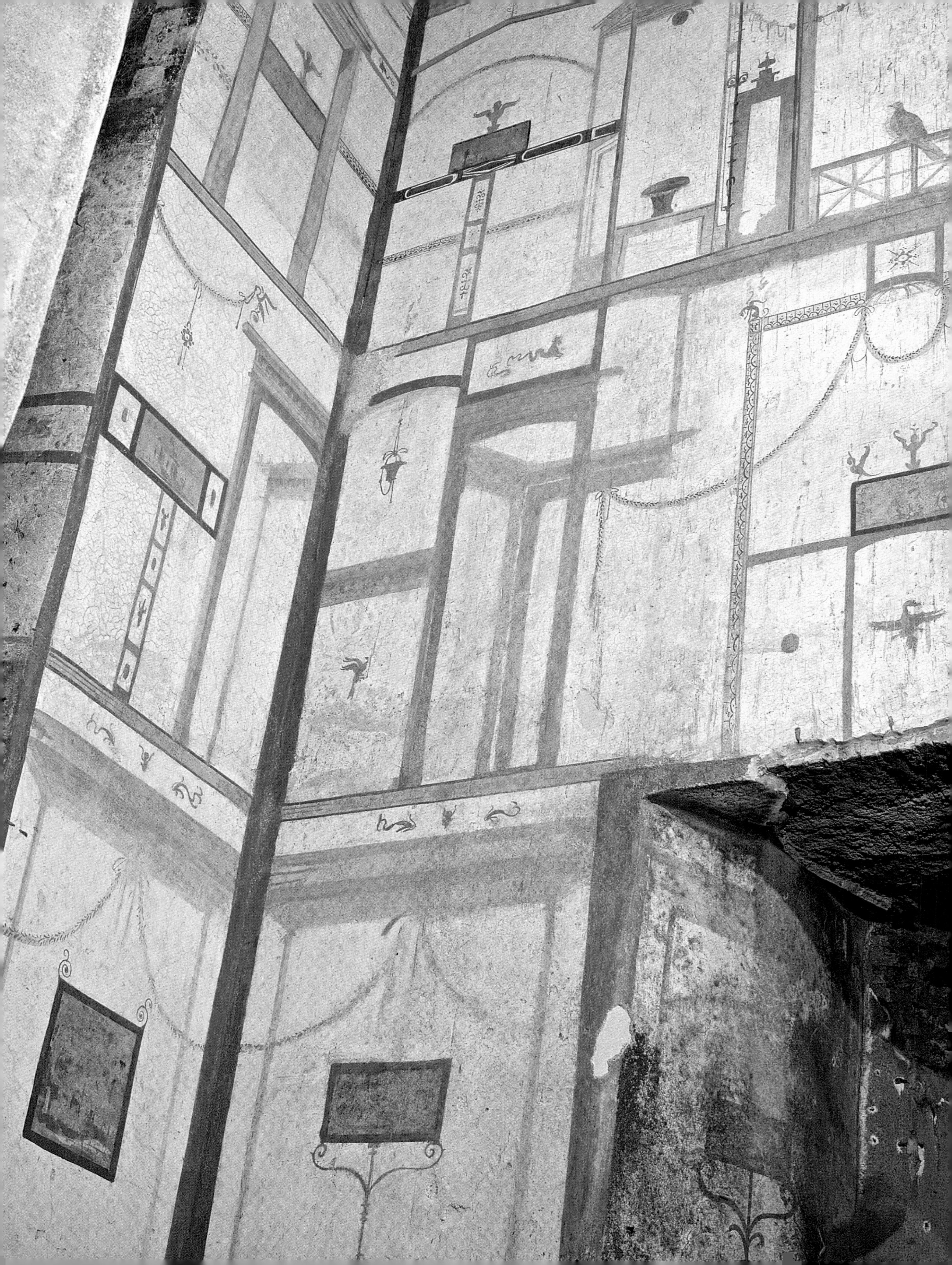

95. Cryptoporticus no. 92, architectural decoration of the walls

96. Cryptoporticus no. 92, architectural decoration of the walls, detail

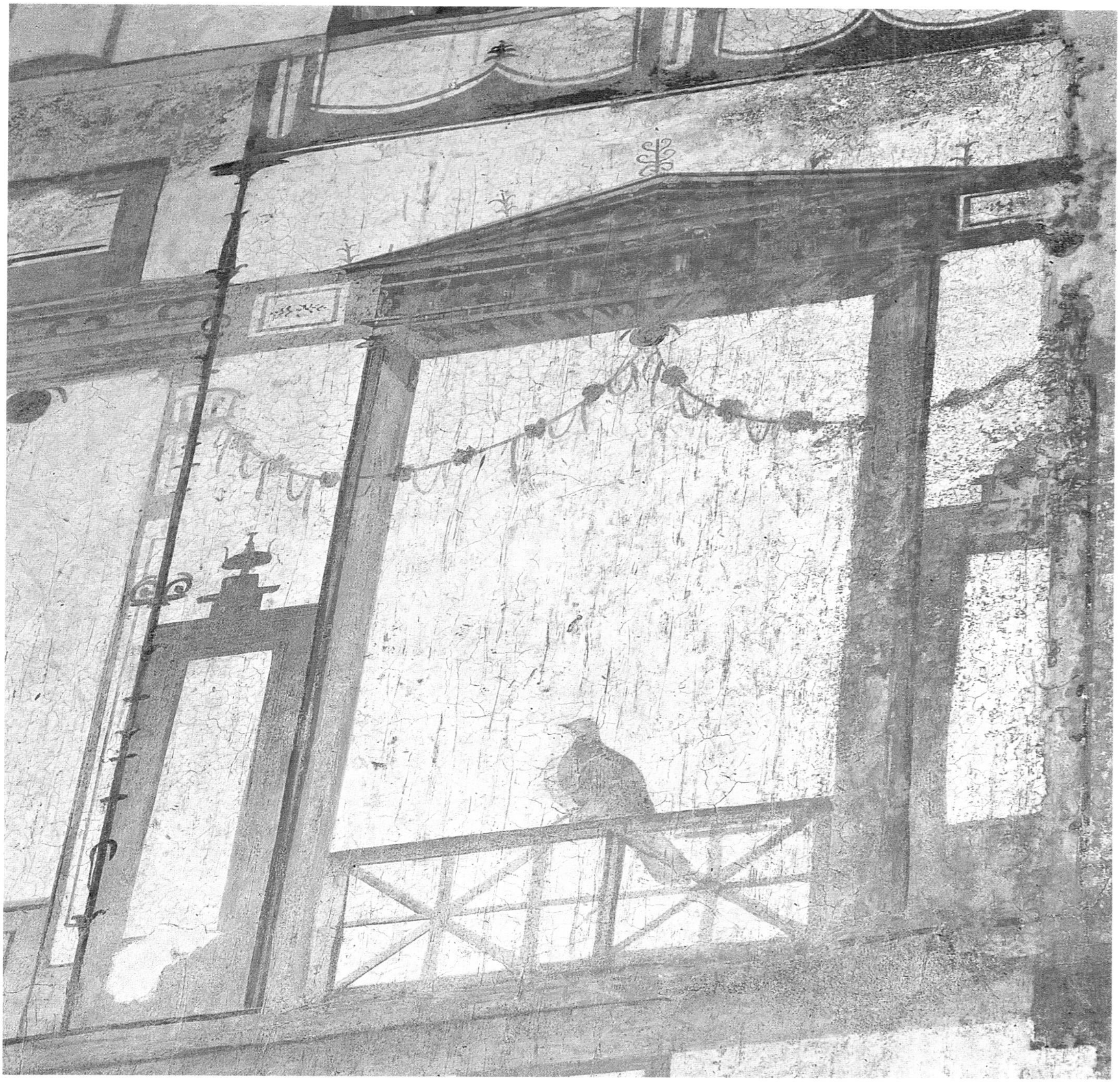

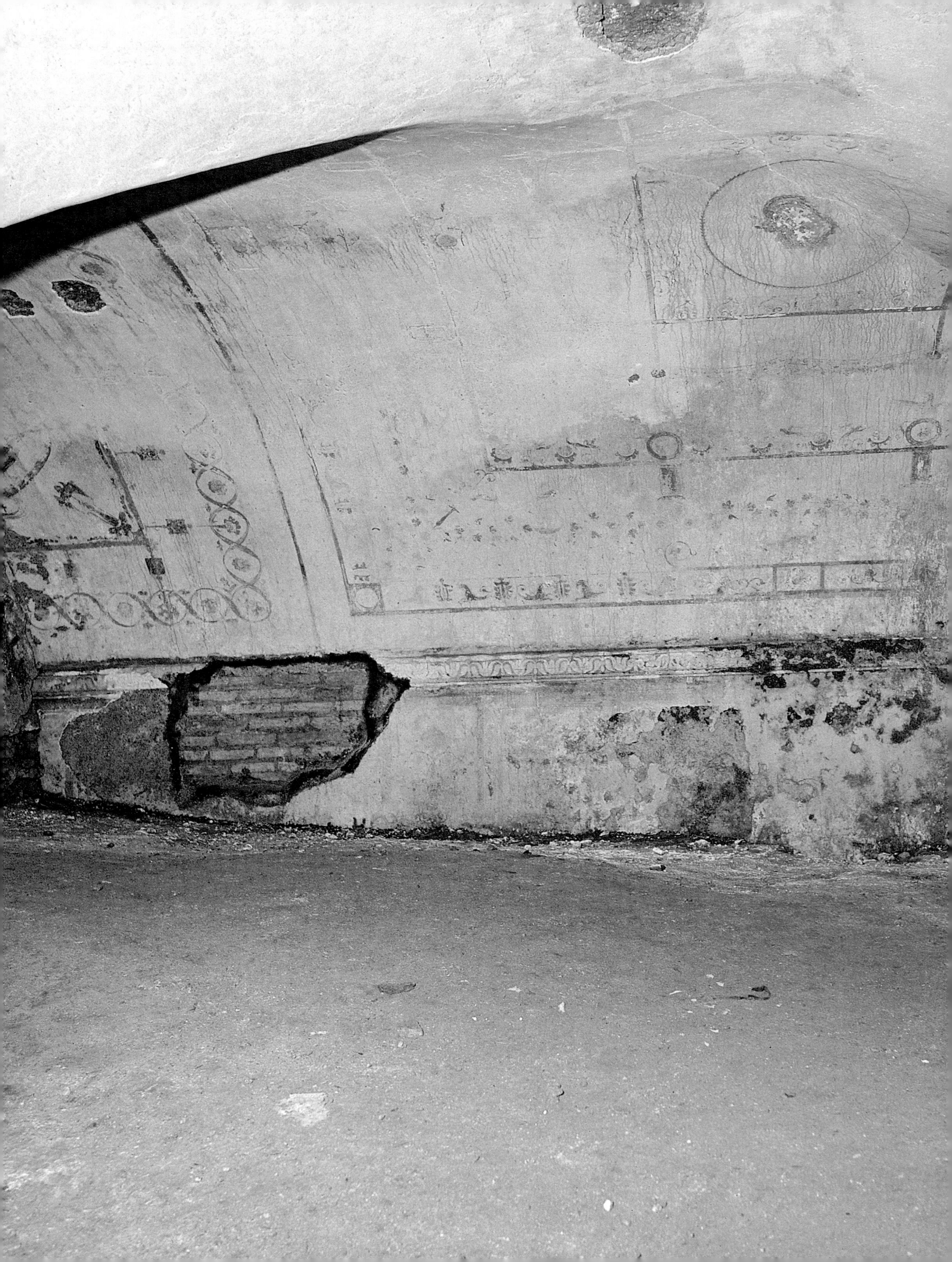

97–98. Cryptoporticus no. 142, decoration of the vault, detail

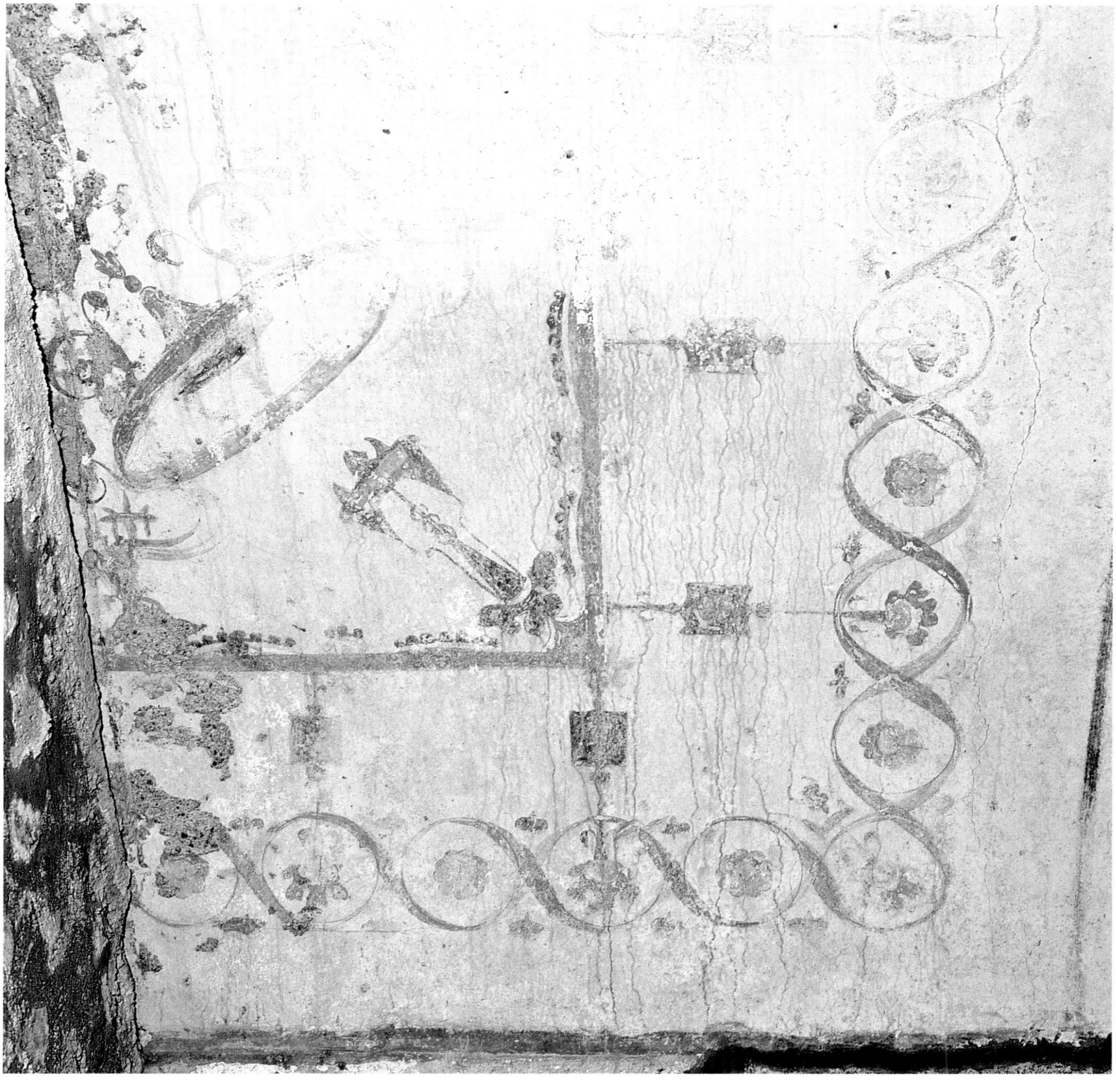

99–100. Cryptoporticus no. 142, decoration of the vault, detail

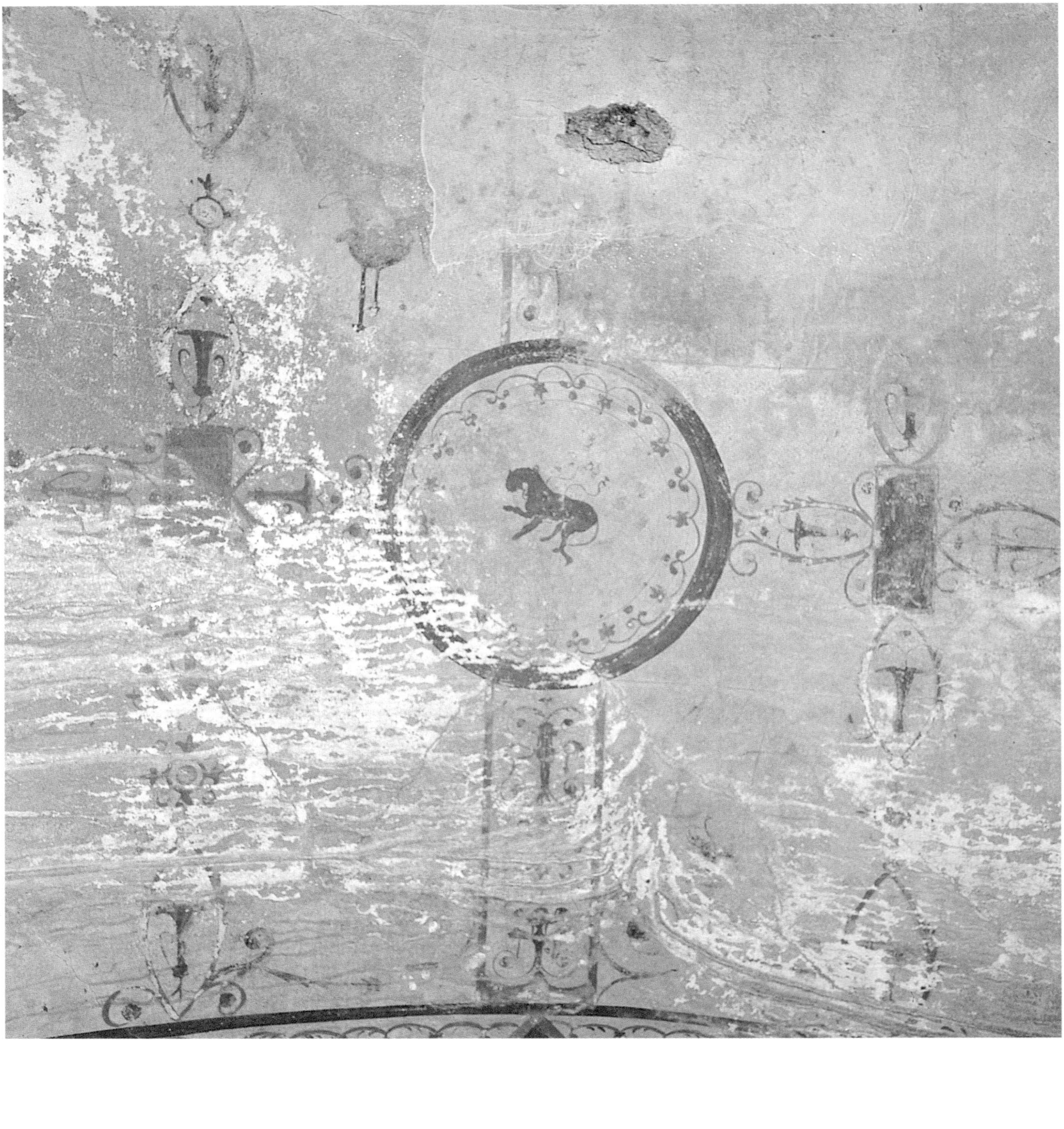

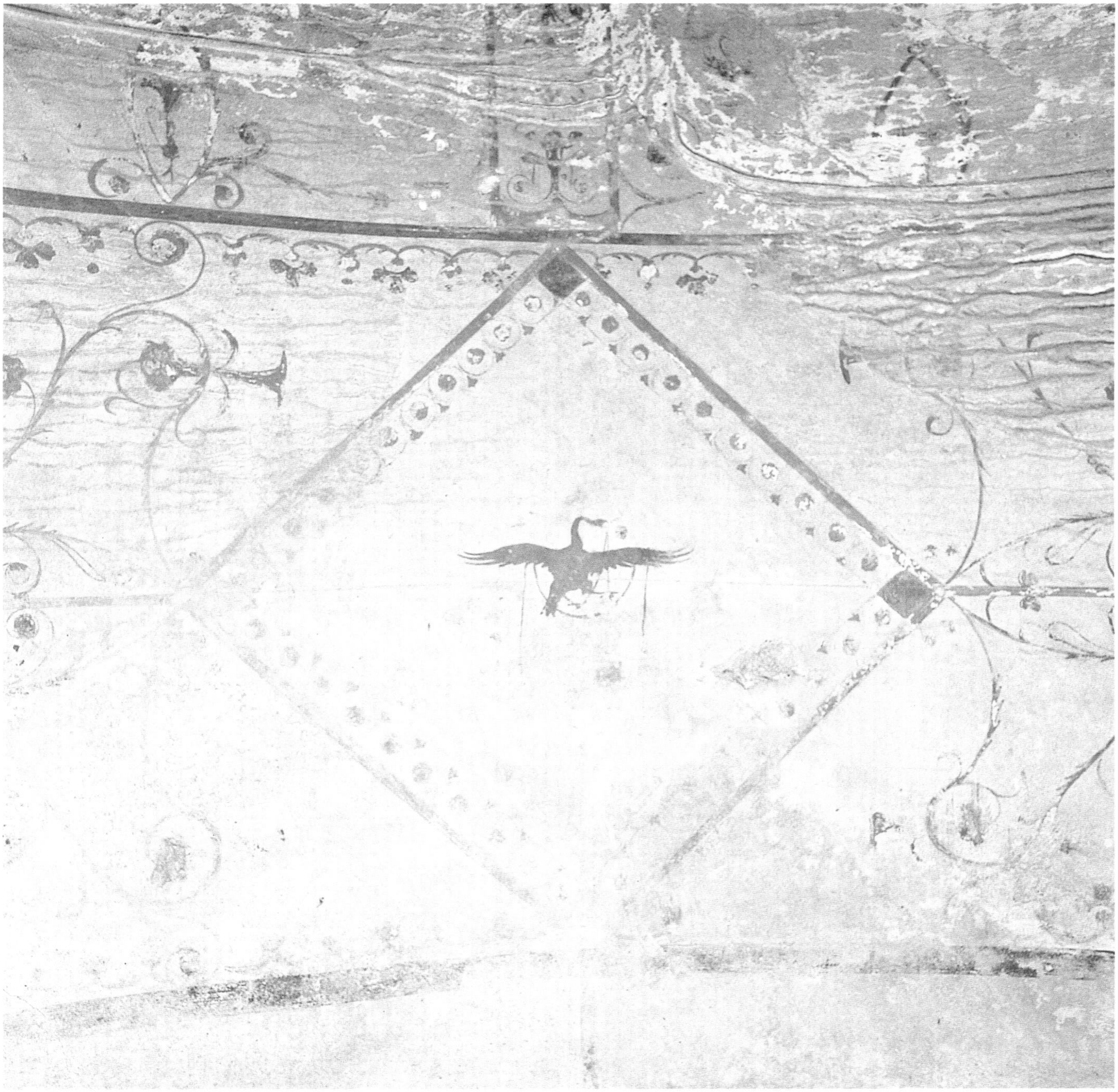

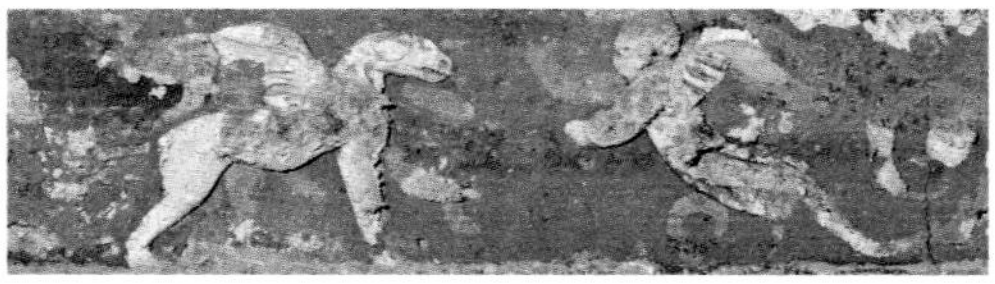

Secondary rooms of the eastern wing

The use of marble *crustae* up to the imposts of the vaults (generally associated with the use of stucco and to high quality painting decorating the highest parts of the walls) is evidence of the importance of a room. Wall veneers limited to the socle come with a mainly painted decoration taking the form of a single broad decorative surface, almost always lacking stucco refinements, as in the case of room 70 situated to the south of the *nymphaeum* of Polyphemus.

Although it cannot be included amongst the most elegant examples of large wall schemes transmitted by the 18th century copiers, this decoration covers the entire wall with an arrangement of rich architecture with wide illustionistic openings. It is a characteristic example of the fourth style, which derived from the *scaenarum frontes* or theatre stage-sets - panels and painted cloth with palaces facades with columns and pilasters and statues which, according to Vitruvius (5. 6. 9), came to be used in theatrical representations, mostly tragic, or else recall real porticoes existing in the *postscaenia* of theatres.

In this painting, spatial illusion can be seen in the openings looking onto backgrounds and scenes of porticoes, where the perspective is highlighted by figures looking out from balustrades. The detail of the architecture, covered in part by *parapetasmata*,

101. Room no. 70, 'stage set' decoration with curtains stretched between the architectural elements

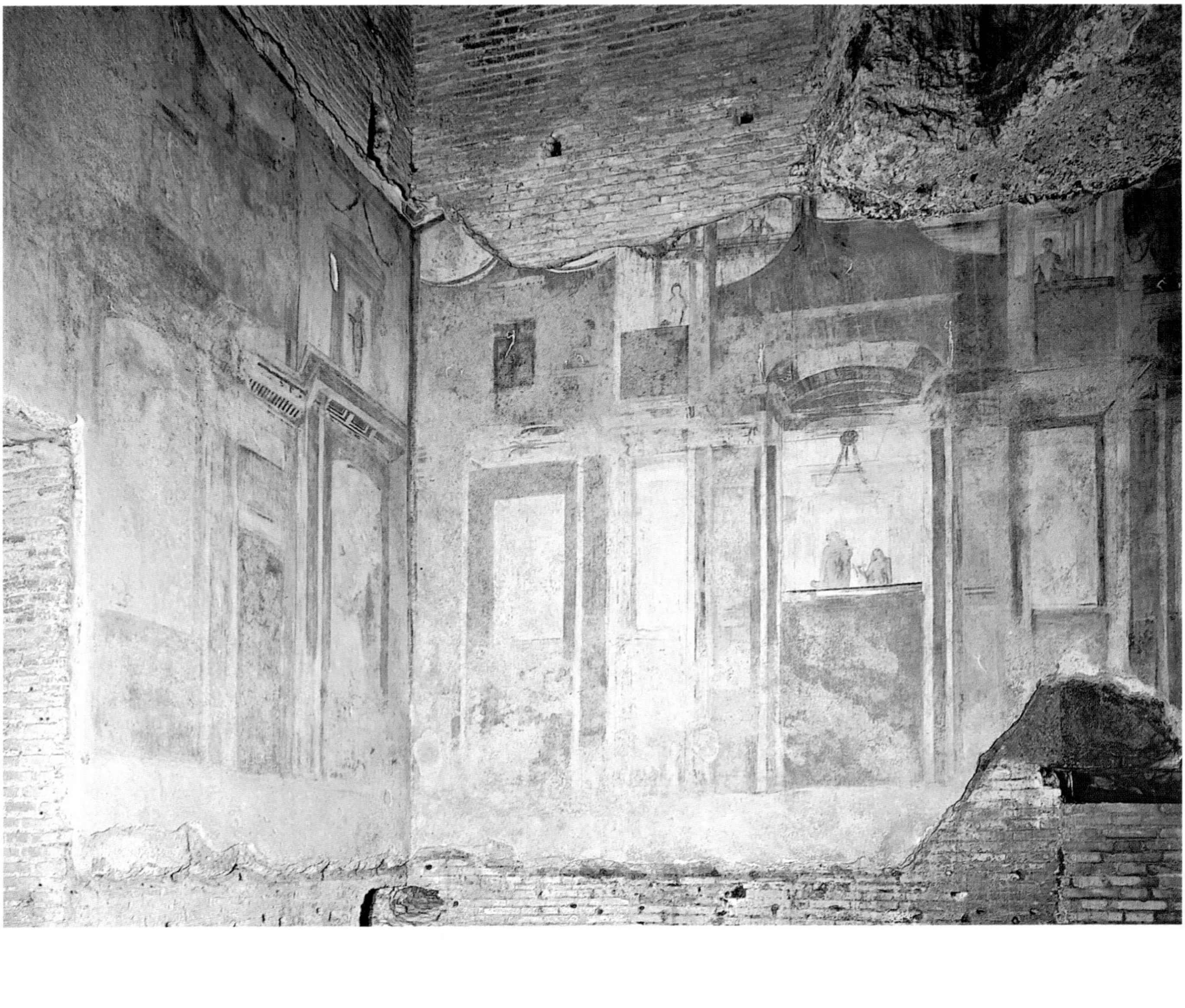

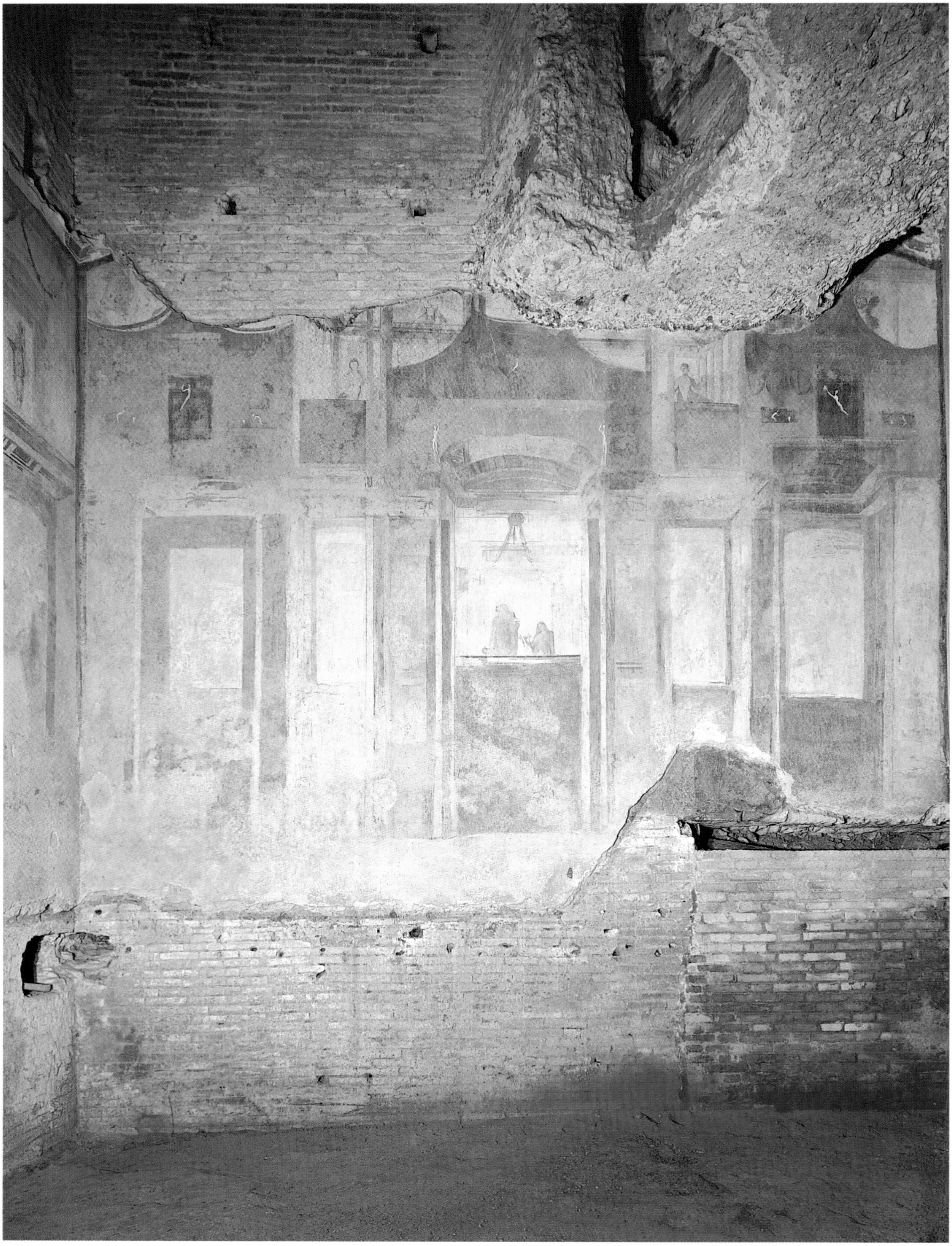

stretched veils, perhaps constitutes here a variant of the *scaenarum frontes*, analogous to that suggested recently for similar Pompeian examples of Neronian date (Peters). The compact solidity of the painted architecture is neither permeated by a sense of unreality nor overloaded, and seems to distance itself from the characteristics of Neronian illusionism in order to take on those of the Flavian era.

A monumental stage-set arrangement covers the walls of rooms 131 and 42. Human figures are added to the complex architecture on the first floor and on different levels. Elaborate friezes in polychrome stucco with small figures in varied poses, and erotes and fantasy animals frame the painted surface, or, together with the moulded architecture in relief, enrich the architectonic partitions. The extension of the painted decoration along the entire wall, with a total absence of marble veneering, indicates the secondary and service-oriented function of the rooms. The level of their decoration is mediocre, though it is quite effective in some parts, such as the long corridors. The decorative scheme presented is always that of a stage-set, in some cases rendered in an extremely schematic manner, far from the elaborate stage-sets organised on two or three registers depicted in the remaining rooms of the *Domus*.

In room 114, the so-called 'room of the masks', the decoration develops in more zones. The principal register reveals an architectural vista with a central *aedicula* looking out into backgrounds, with festoons disappearing behind the structures closer to the foreground. This all shows that they derive from *scaenarum frontes*. In the first register a band divided into squares and rectangles, containing large masks amongst plant-like spirals and pairs of tritons and hippocamps, tops off the base decoration of *aediculae* and festoons. These alternate with panels adorned with decorative borders and contain landscape scenes within them. A simple architectural arrangement, which recalls the *scaenarum frontes* of the register below, develops in the zone where the lunettes are.

This decorative typology, which shows a simplified architectural arrangement and from which the emphasis on spatial illusion is often completely eliminated, characterises, even in forms which differ slightly from each other, a group of passages, corridors and secondary rooms of the east wing, all situated behind the pavilion. Even in room 86 the decorative parti-

102. Room no. 70, north wall, 'stage set' view with porta regia *and* hospitalia

103. Room no. 70, east wall, 'stage set' view between stretched curtains

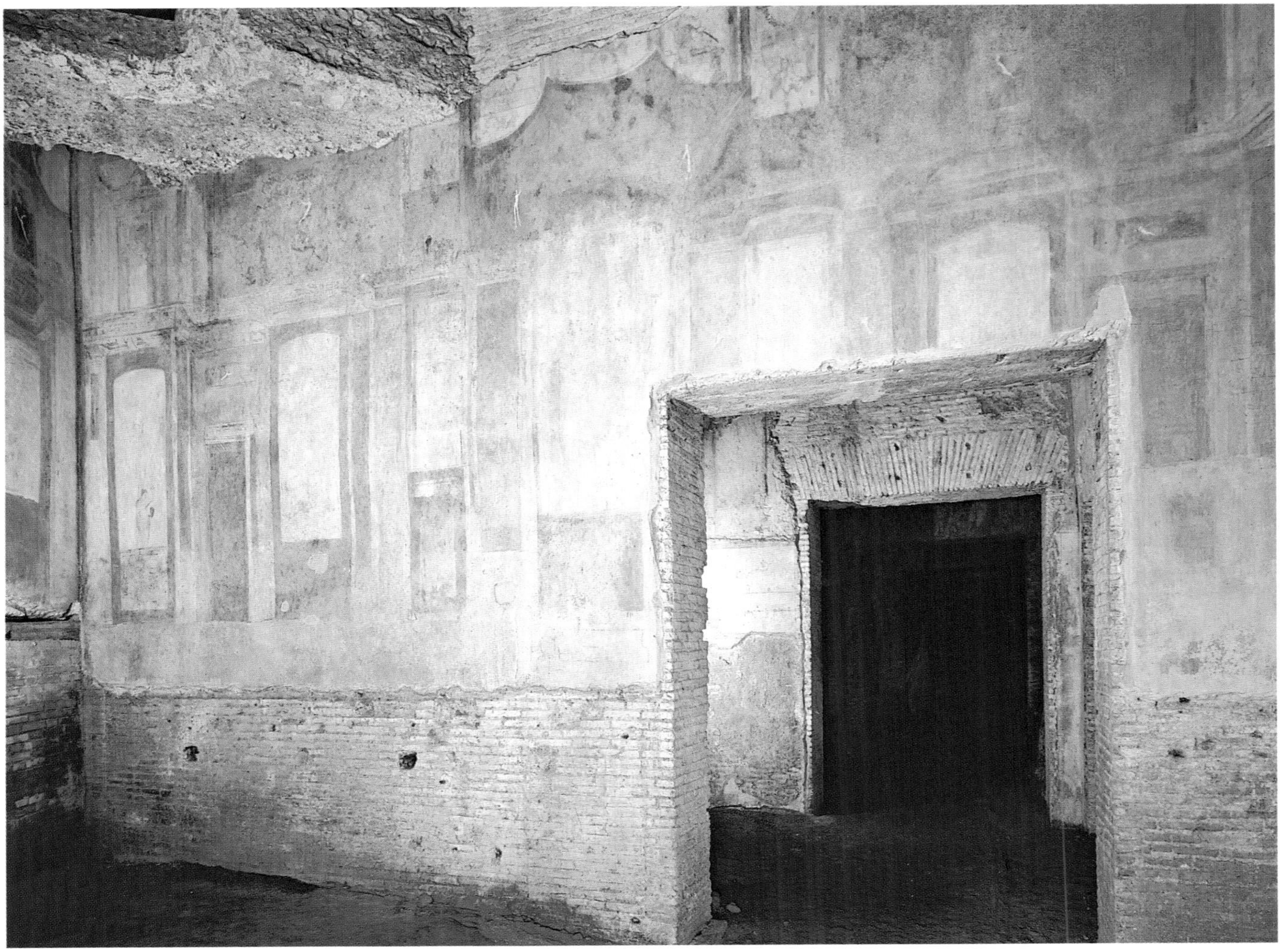

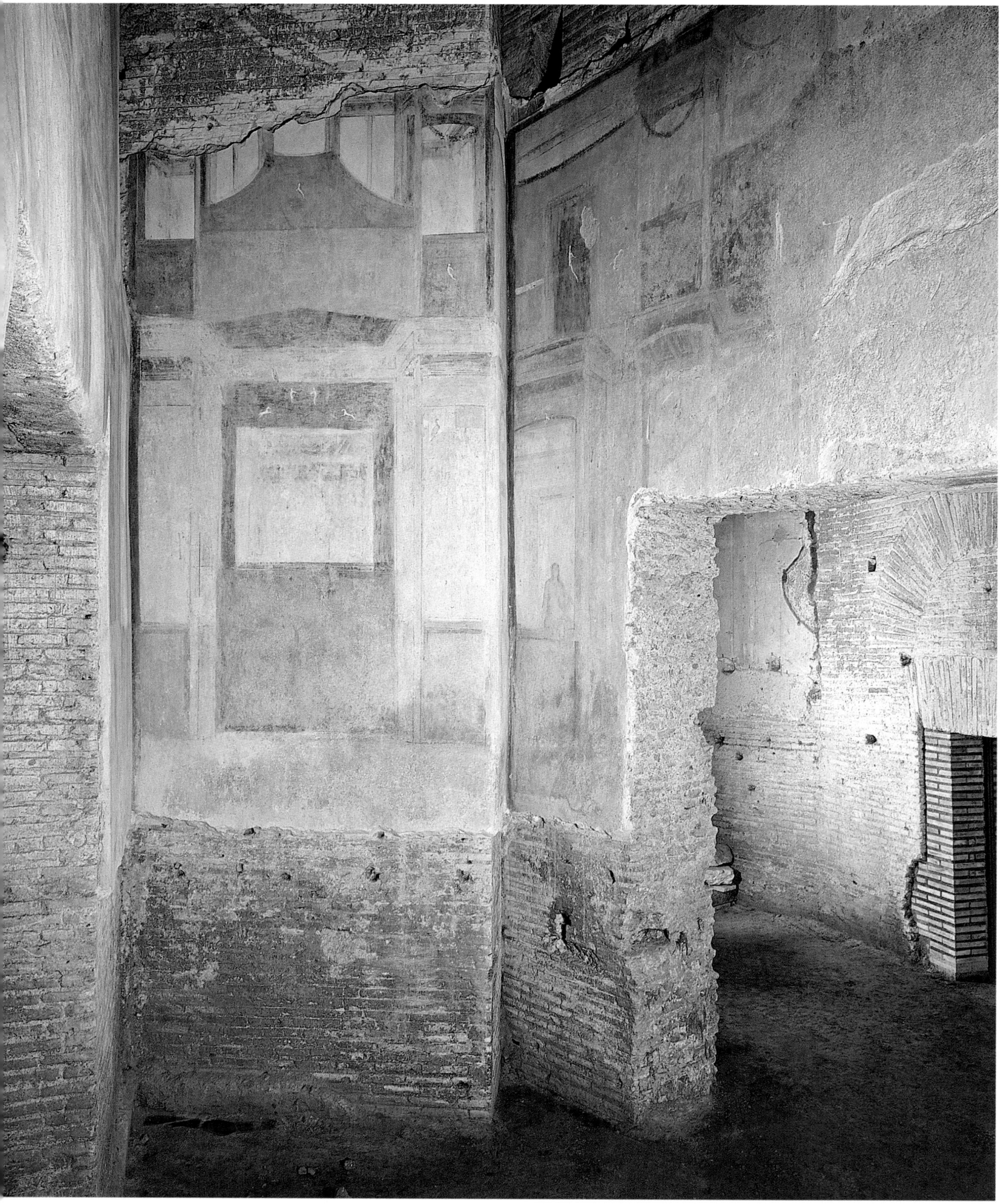

tion develops on three registers. One difference is encountered in the decoration of the small panels containing landscape scenes between the columns of obliquely set *aediculae*, while in the upper register the architectural paintings rendered with dark lines on a white background are enlivened simply by ornamental motifs and small landscapes.

A further overall scheme for the arrangement of the architectural partitions of a *scaenae frons* can be seen in room 94, north of the octagonal room. A simplified architectural scheme, rendered by linear and unrealistic lines, is laid out on the walls in three registers. The arrangement is enlivened by slender festoons and by griffons, centaurs and feminine figures finishing in spiral tendrils. Hovering, isolated on the white background, these bring to mind their origin in the so-called third style.

Within several of these arrangements are inserted landscape panels that are preserved in the *Domus* in great numbers. These are a characteristic element of the fourth style. Sometimes they alternate with still lifes in small panels on slender supports set in the field of the walls in the long corridors; sometimes they adorn the inside of the openings of fake windows (86); and sometimes, with strong illusionistic effect, they open a window in a wall which is otherwise closed (114). Rendered in an outline style, with simple strokes, they differ from the general pattern of idyllo-sacred landscapes of the second Pompeian style in their depiction of more realistic panoramas (even if always idealised), views of cities and of ports, also animated by human figures. A genre, typically Hellenistic and very much in fashion at the time, is defined by Pliny (*Natural History* 35. 116) as 'containing beautiful vistas and of little expense' (with reference to panel paintings) and by him attributed to *Ludius,* a painter of the Augustan age.

104. Room no. 70, south corner, 'stage set' view, detail

105. Room no. 70, west wall, 'stage set' view between stretched curtains

on the following pages:

106. Room no. 70, south corner, 'stage set' view, detail

107. Room no. 70, 'stage set' view with architectural elements depicted in sharp relief, detail

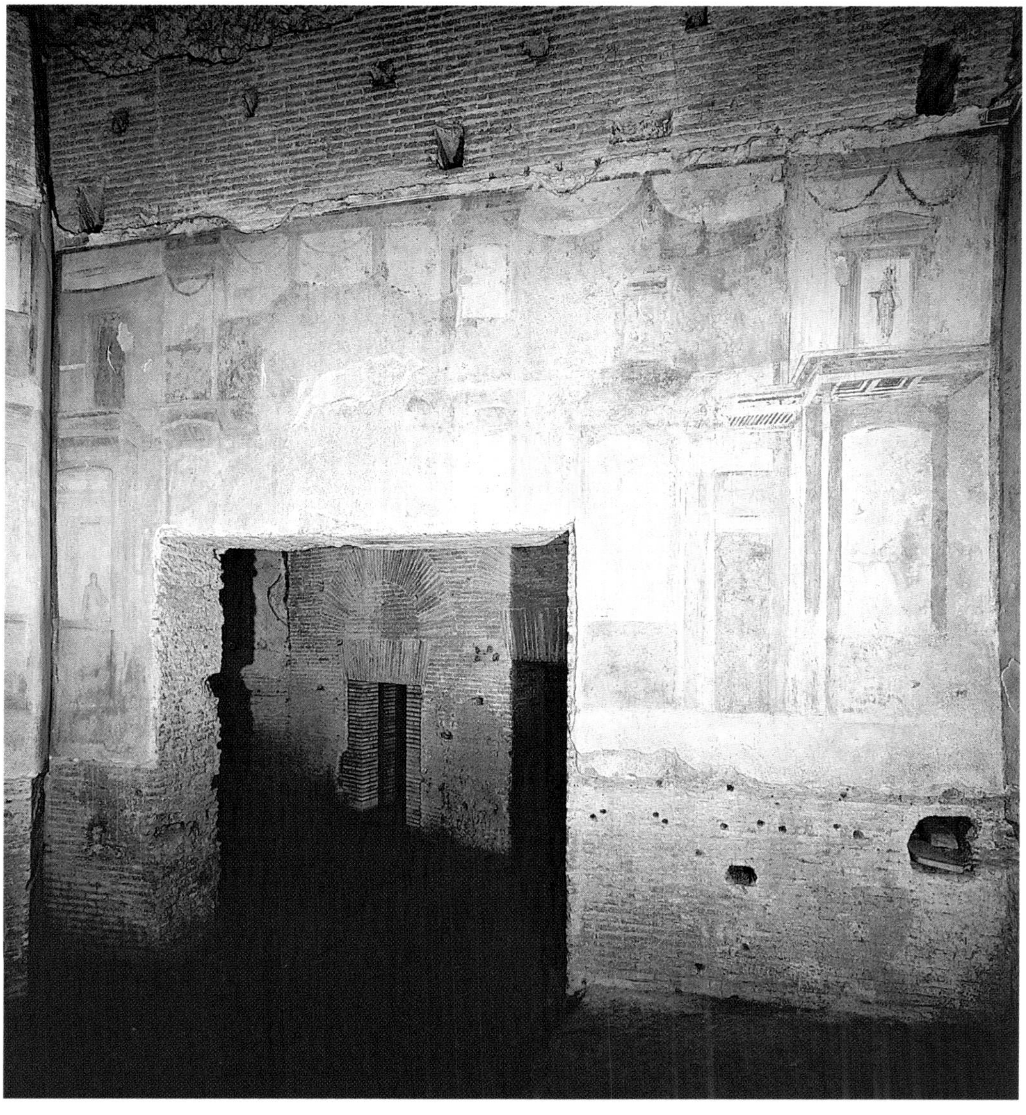

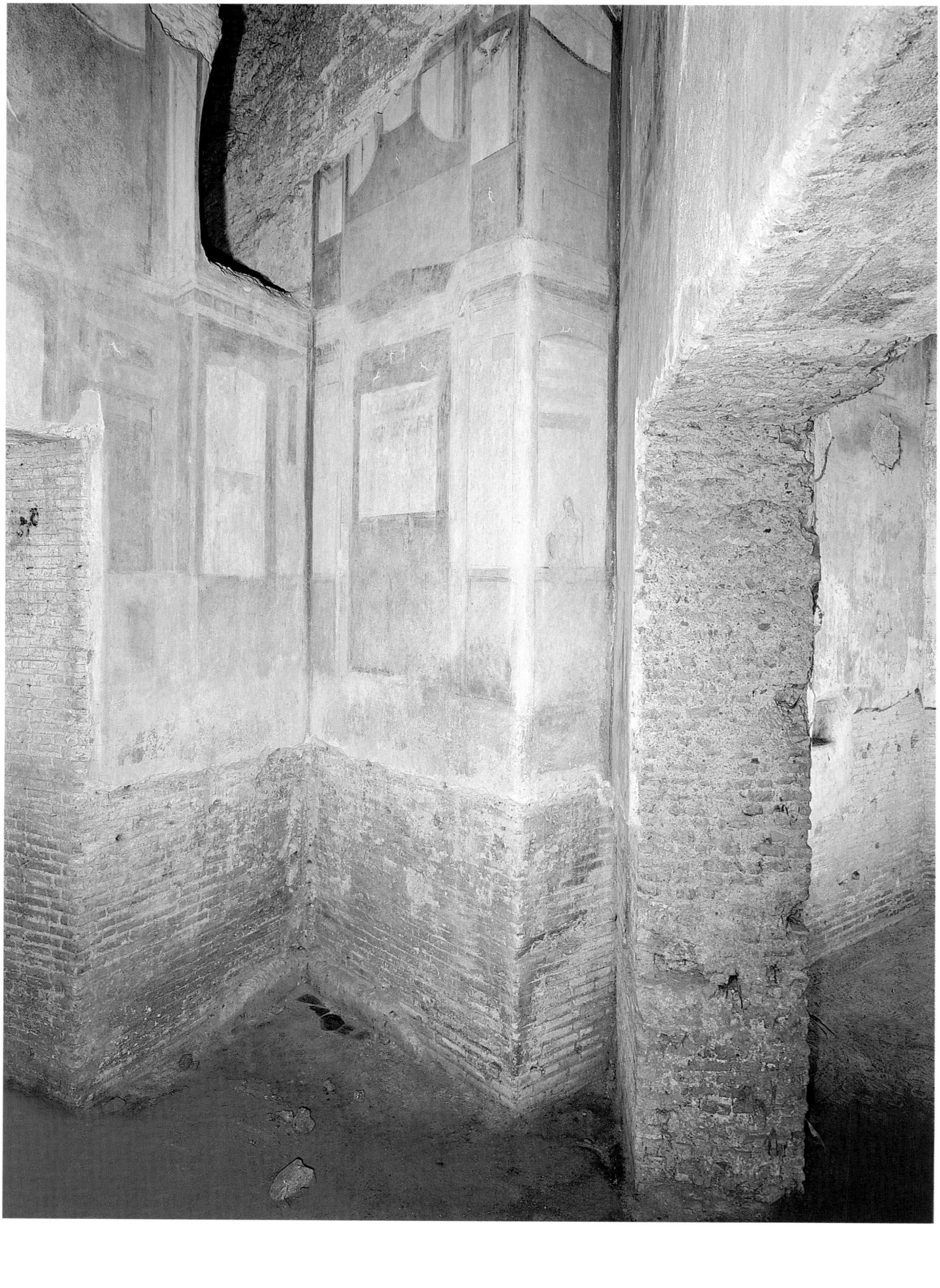

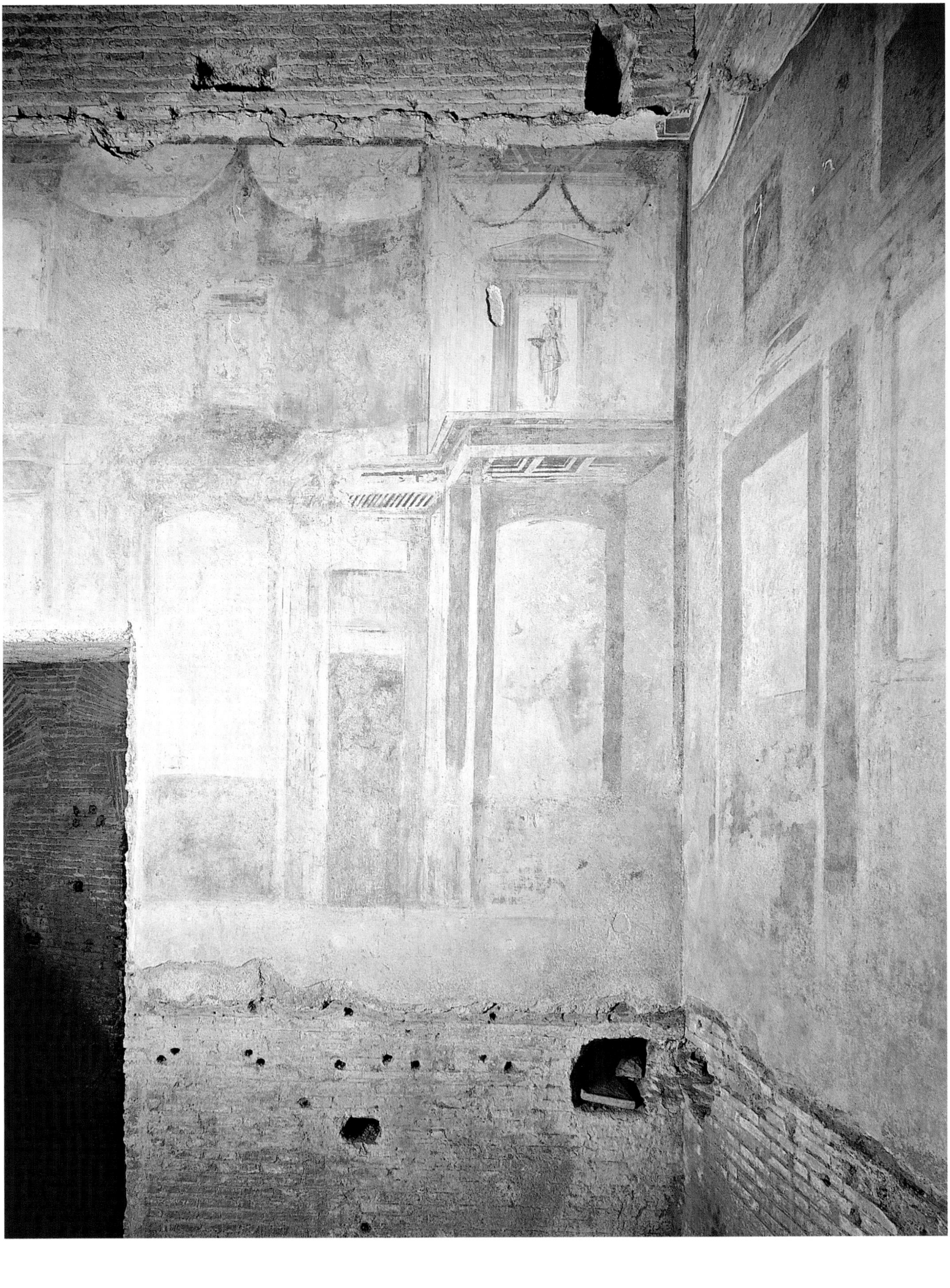

108. Room no. 70, 'stage set' view with curtains and ceilings with openings, rendered in perspective in sharp relief

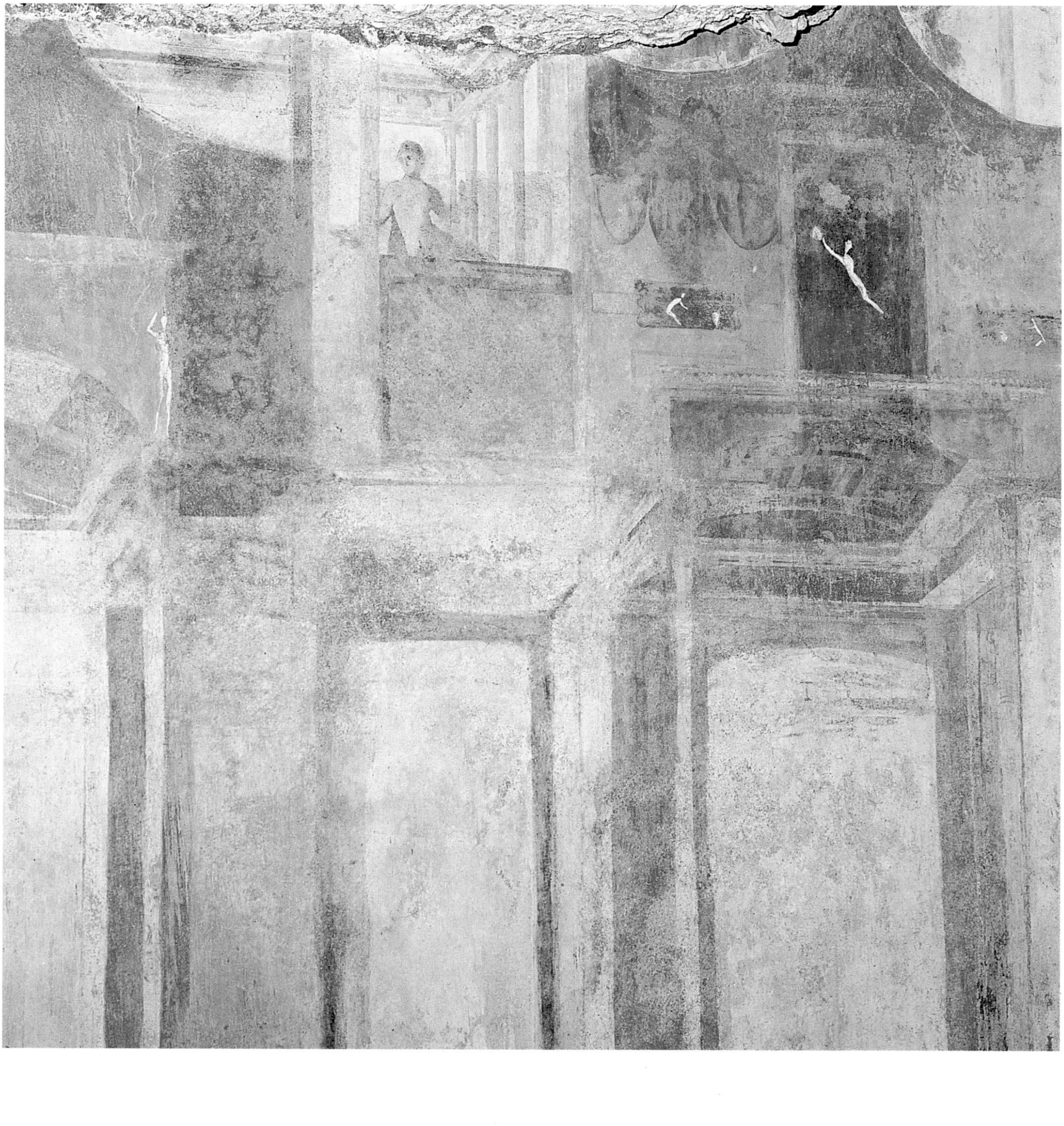

109. Room no. 70, 'stage set' view, detail with figure making an offering inside an aedicula

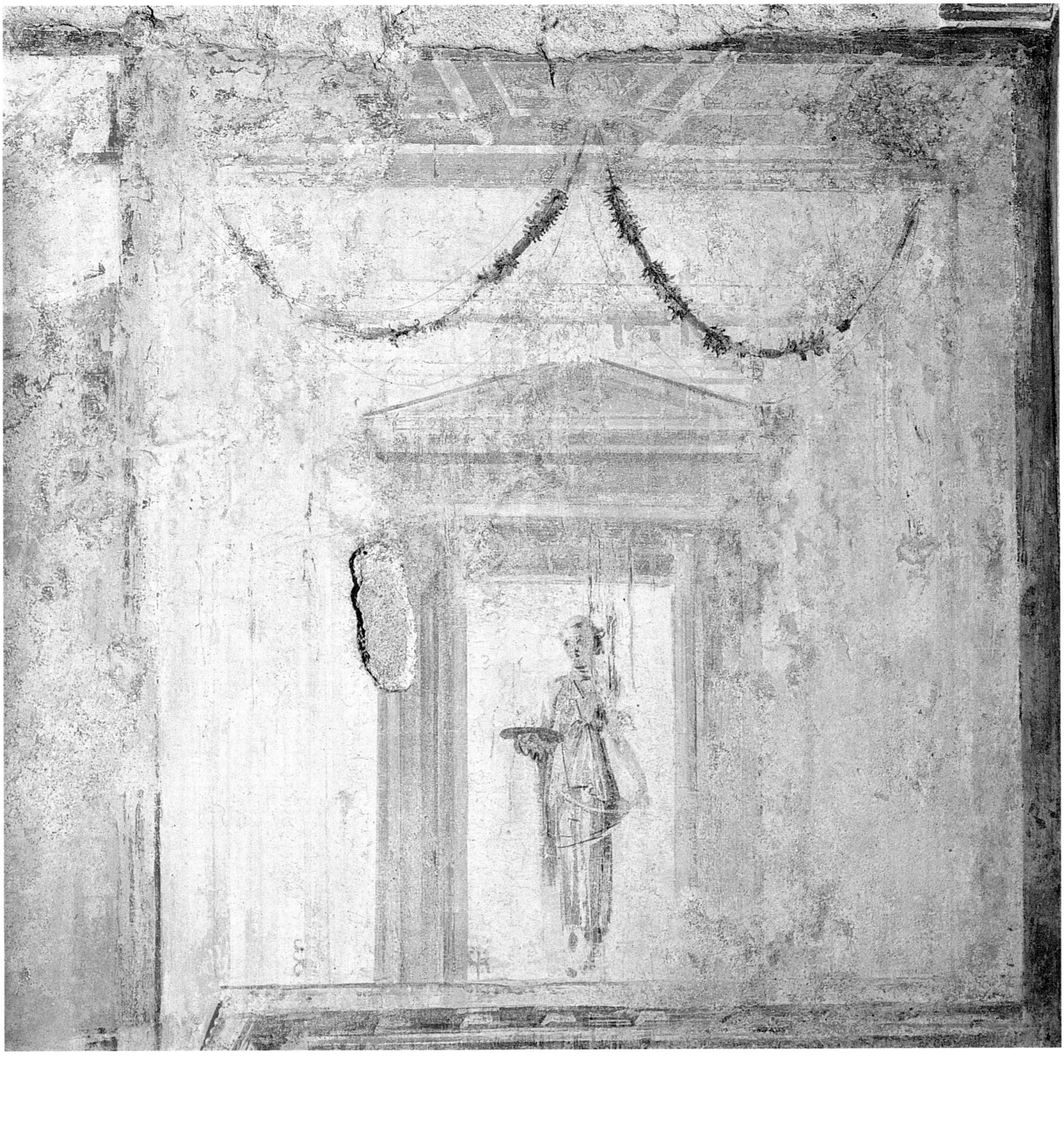

110. Room no. 70, 'stage set' view, figures between the architectural views, detail

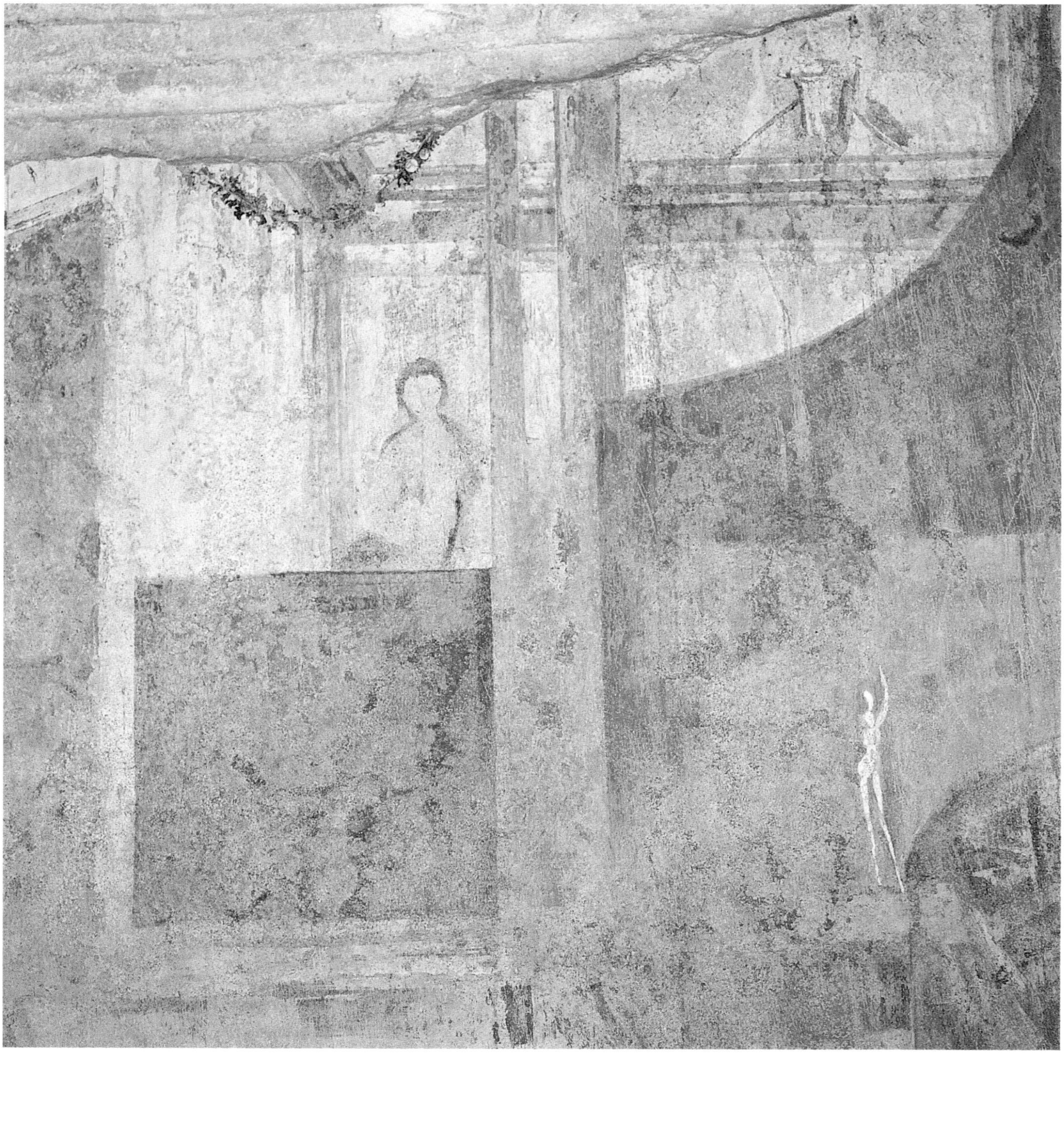

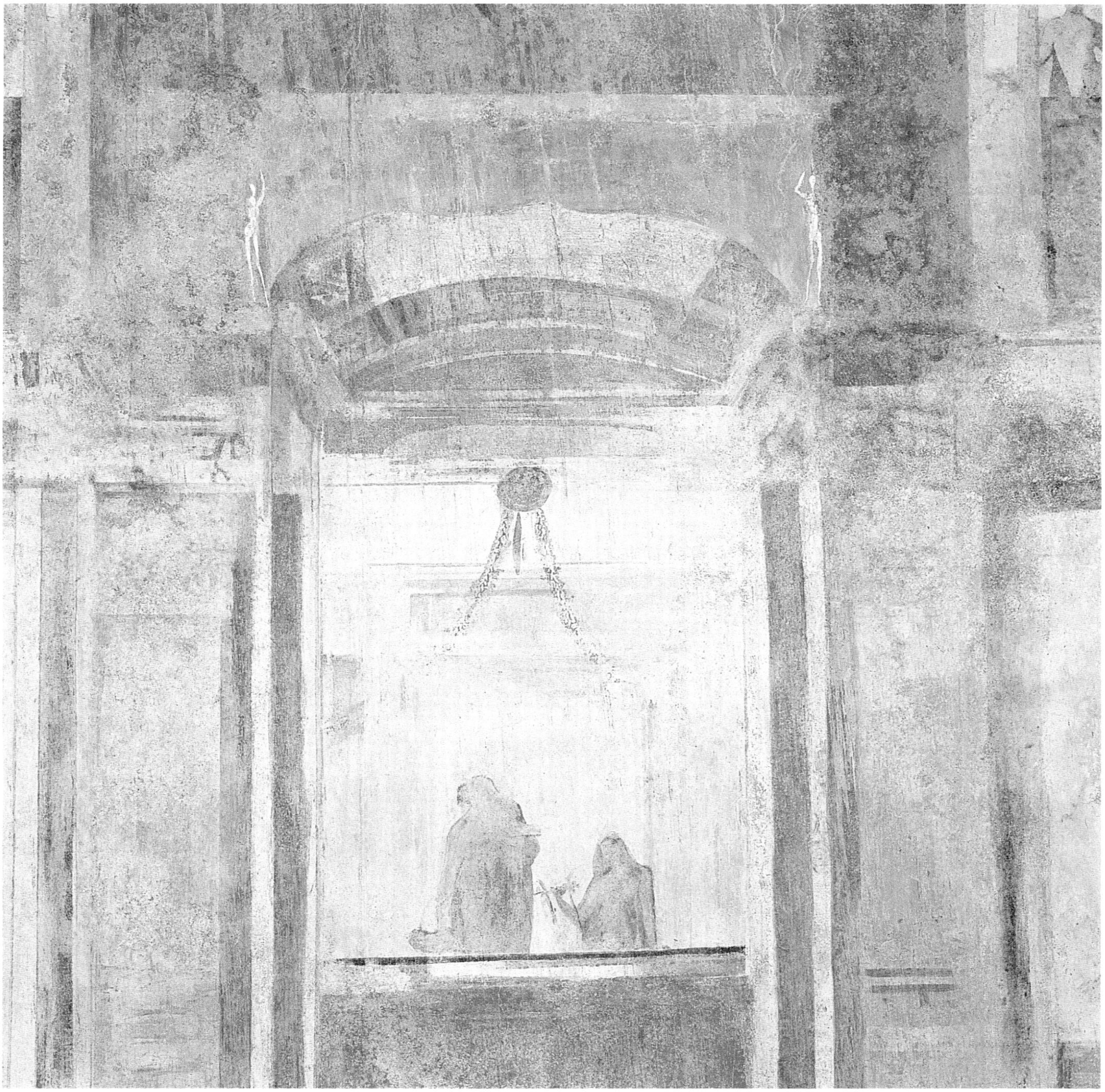

111. Room no. 70, 'stage set' view, porta regia *with figures and architectural views, detail*

112. *Corridor no. 131, architectural vista with depiction of spatial depth and figures placed on many levels*

113. *Corridor no.131, decorative scheme with elaborate architecture and figures set on many levels*

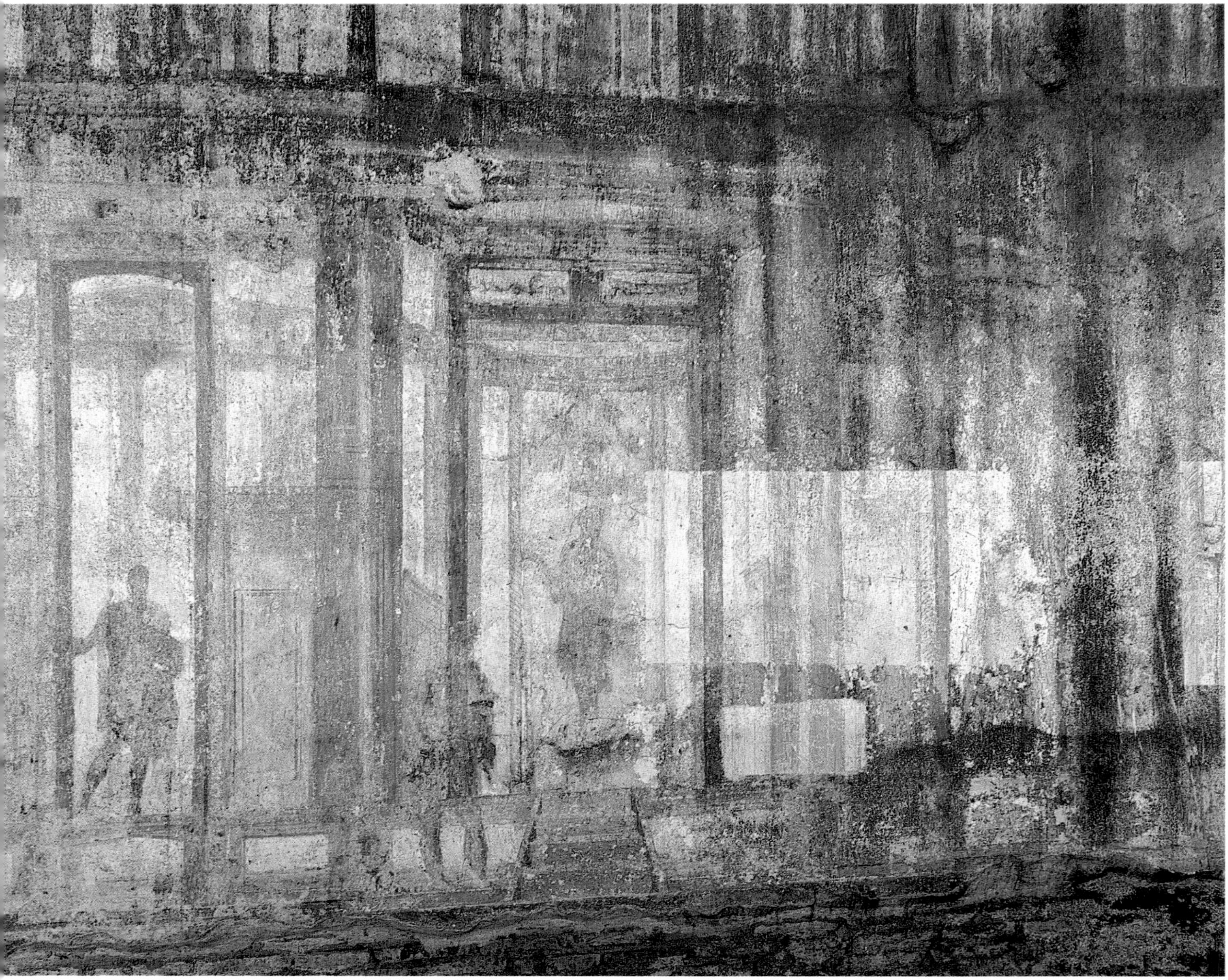

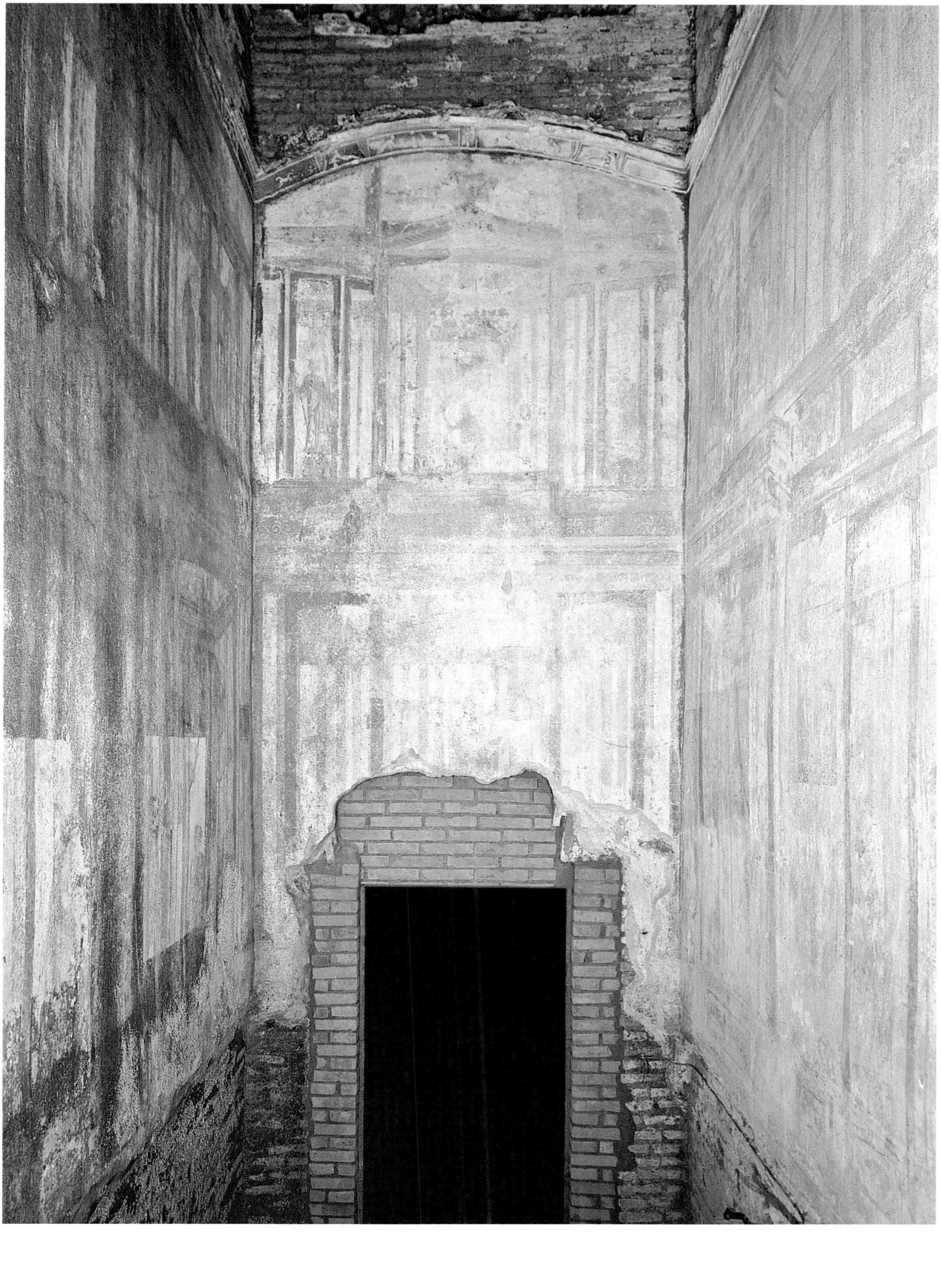

114. Corridor no. 131, architectural vista opening onto structures with architraves and with spiral columns, detail

115. Corridor no. 131, architectural vista with standing and sitting figures

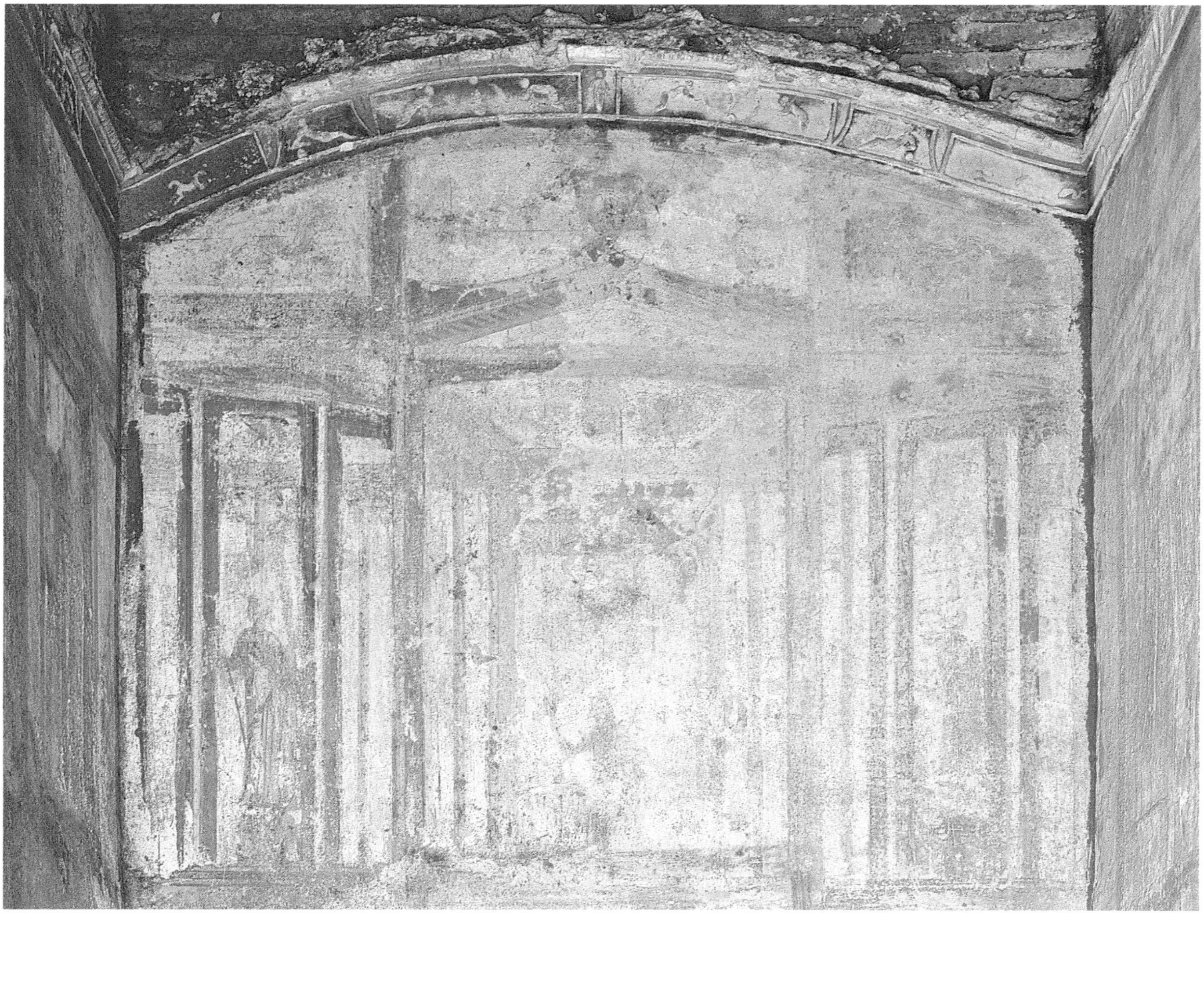

116. Corridor no. 131, Erotes and griffons in the stucco and painted frieze framing the architectural vistas, detail

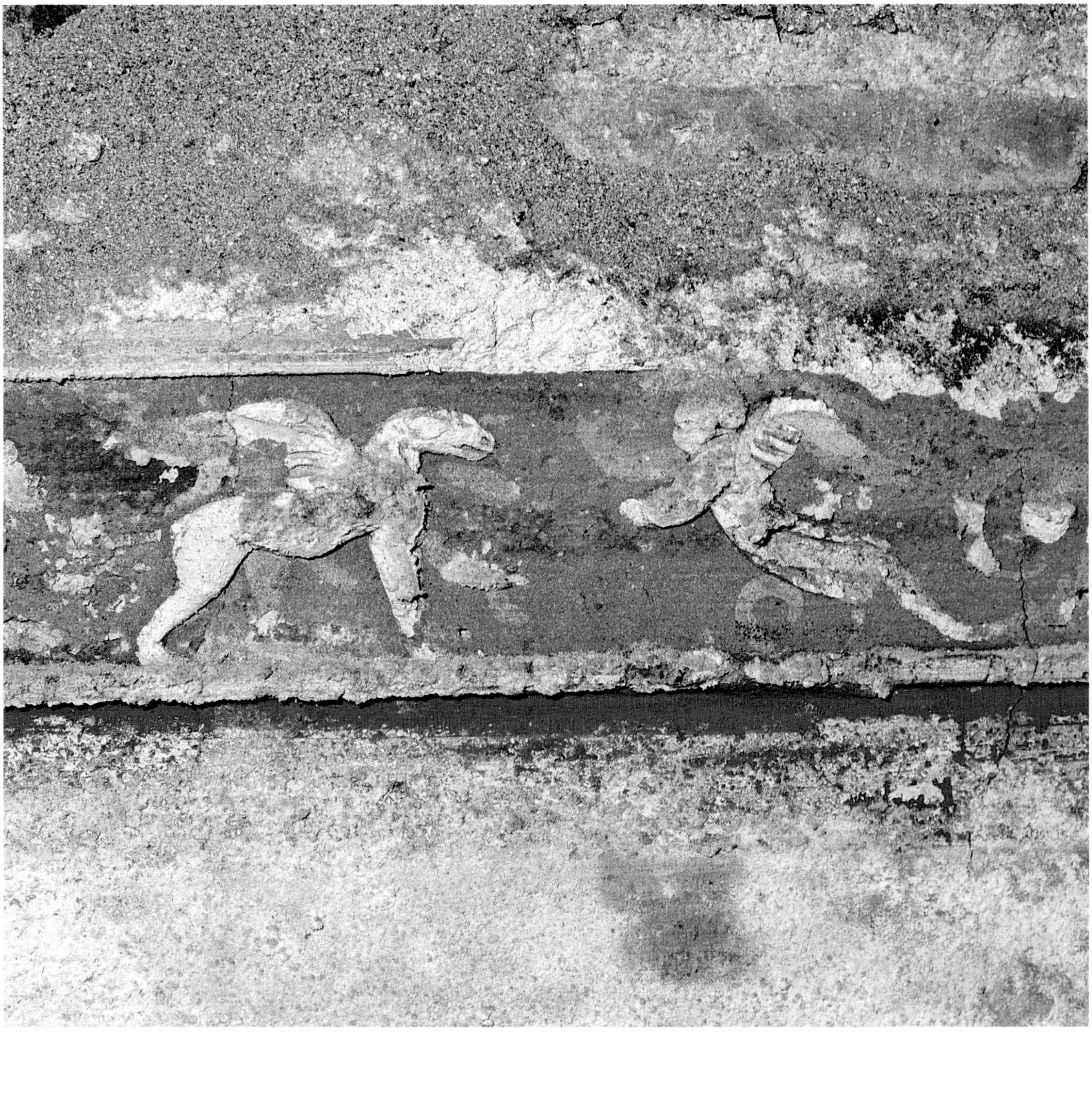

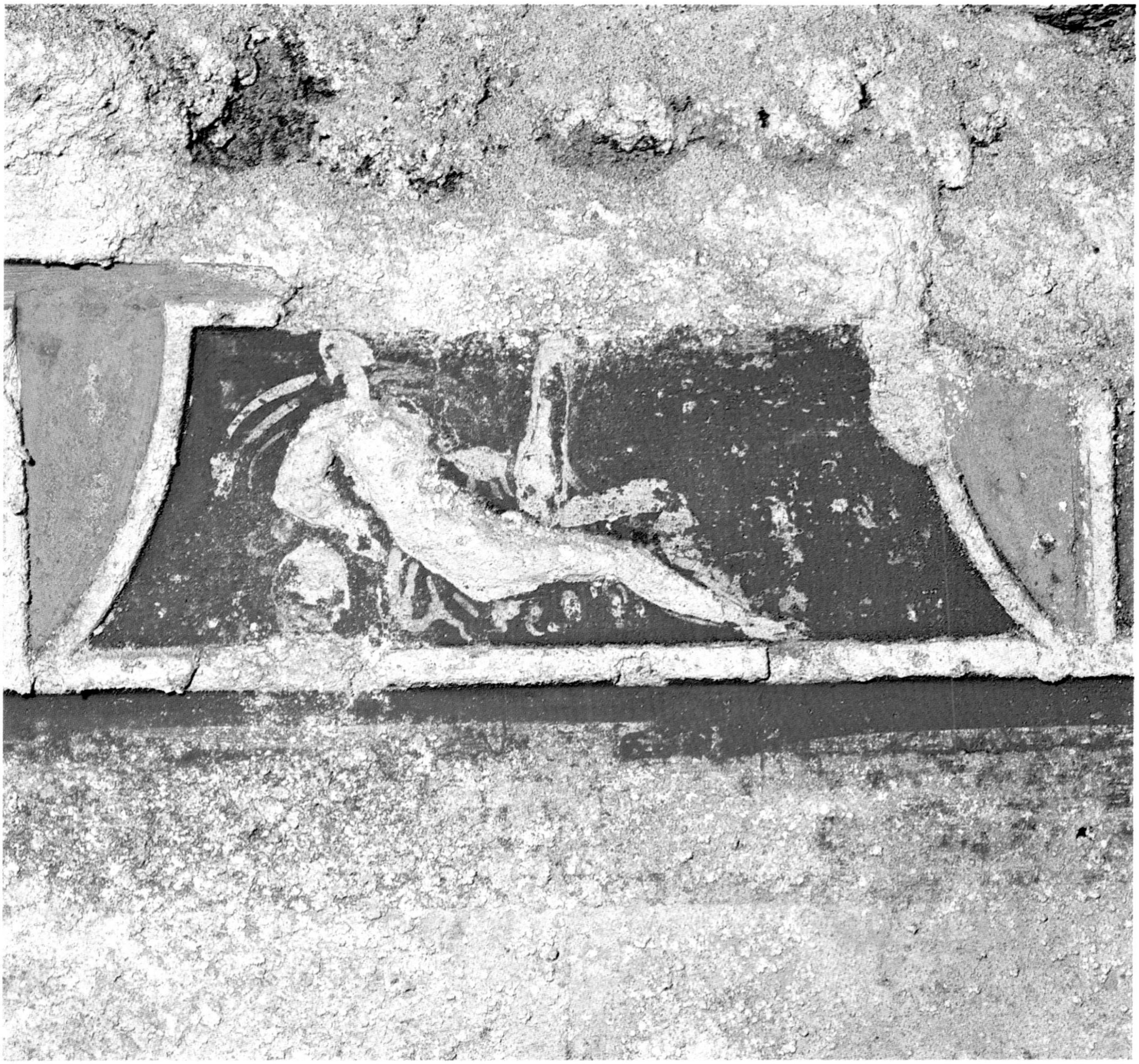

117. Corridor no. 131, reclining female figure in the stucco and painted frieze framing the architectural vistas

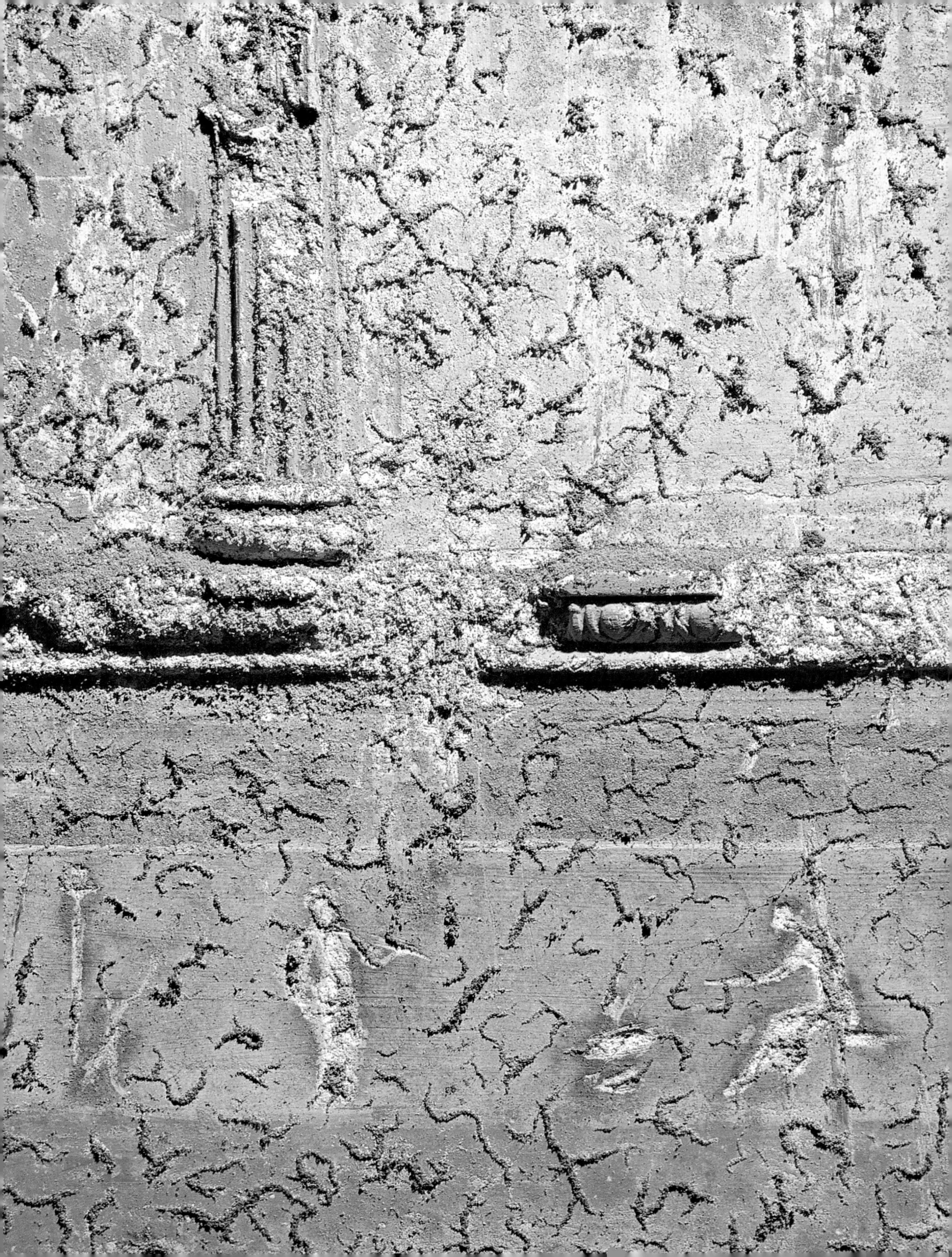

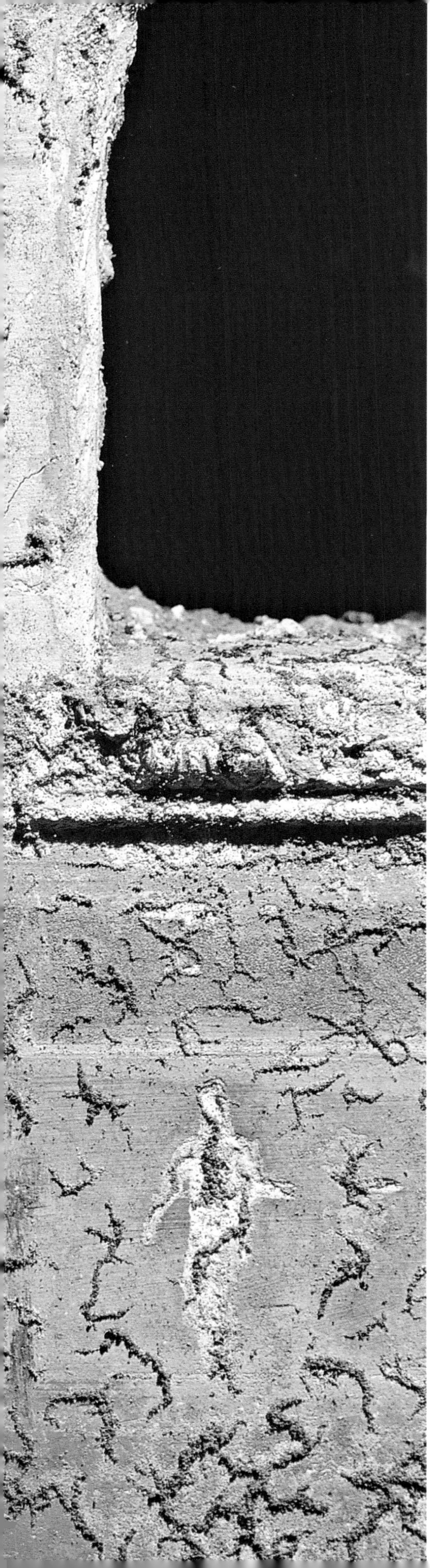

118. Room no. 42, frieze with small stucco figures on blue background. The small columns of the architectural scene can be seen rising from the frieze.

119. Room no. 42, vault, with marine thiasos

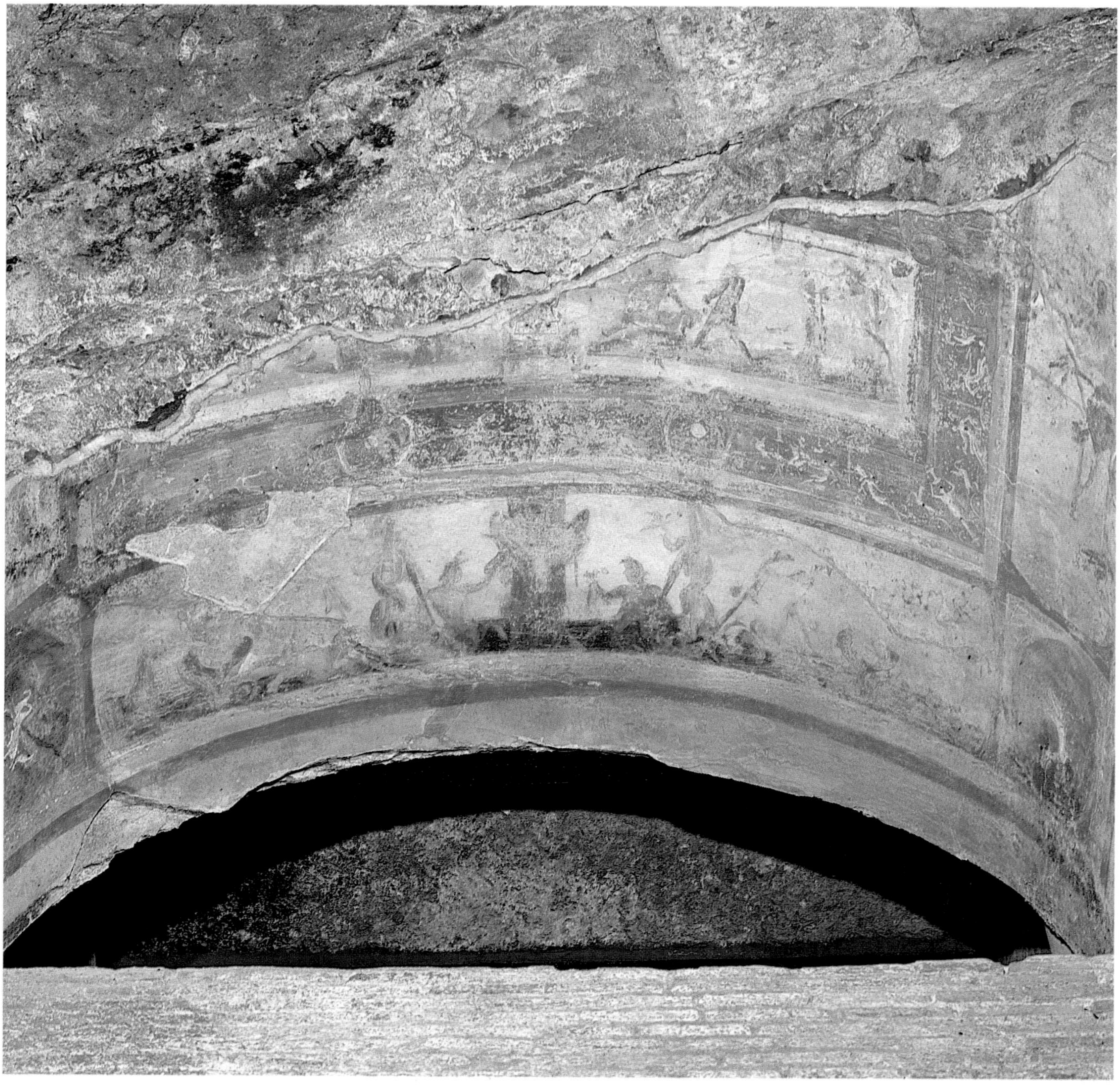

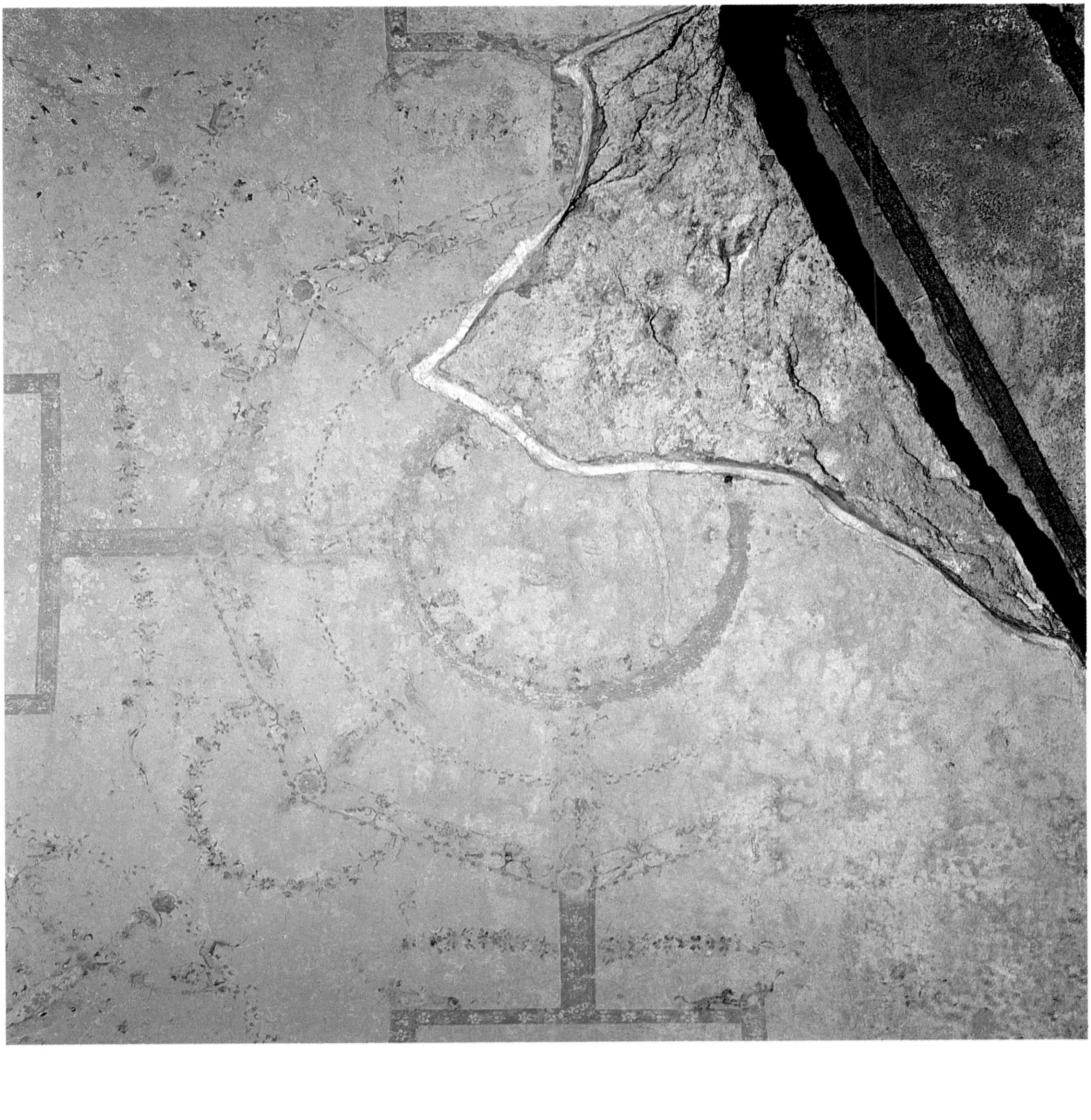

120. Room no. 42, yellow ground vault with remains of gold leaf belonging to a second decorative phase of the room

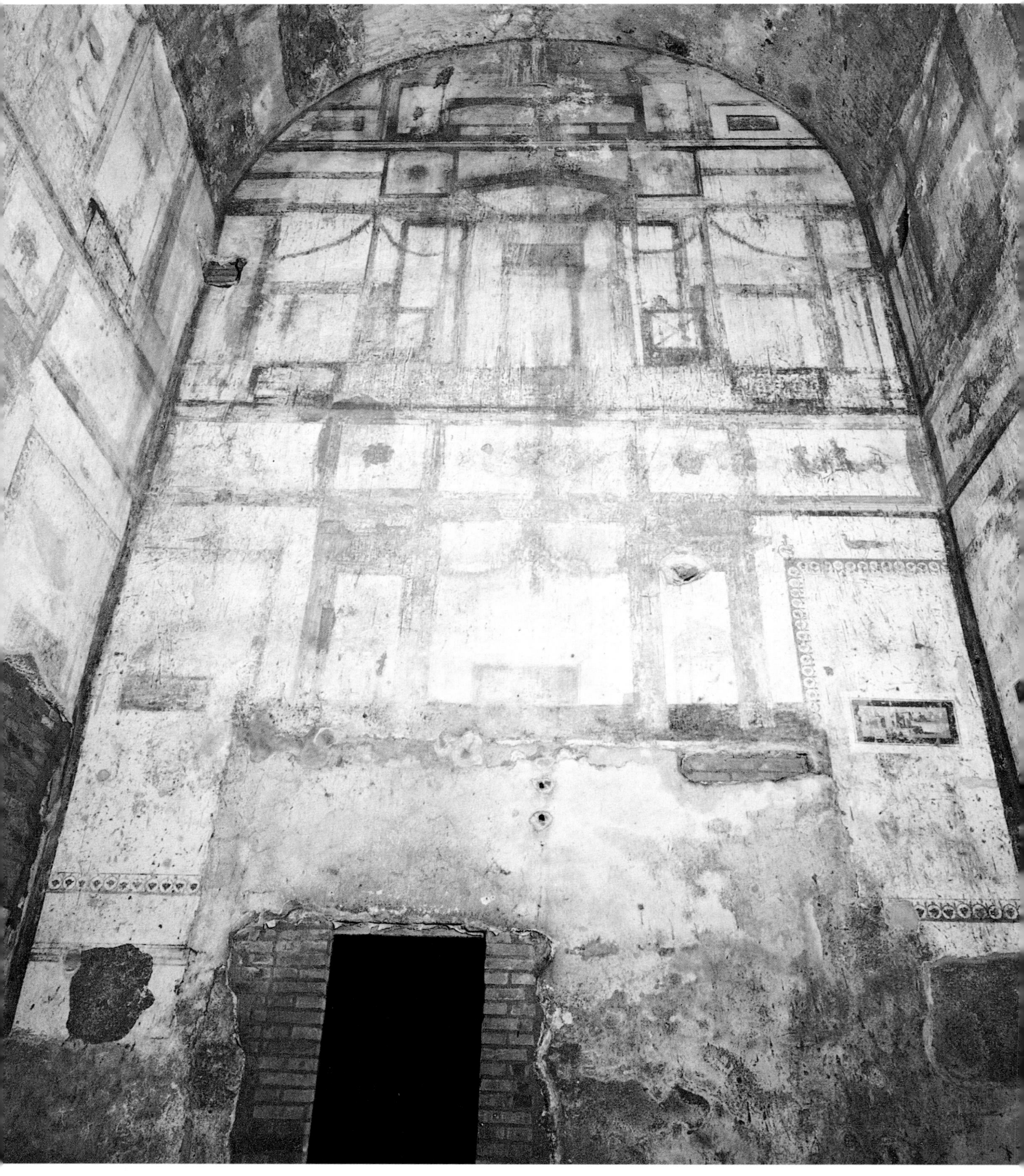

121. Room of the masks, architectural decoration on multiple registers

122. Room of the masks, western wall, lower register with aedicula between festoon decorations, depictions of architectural pavilions in the background, and landscape panel in the centre

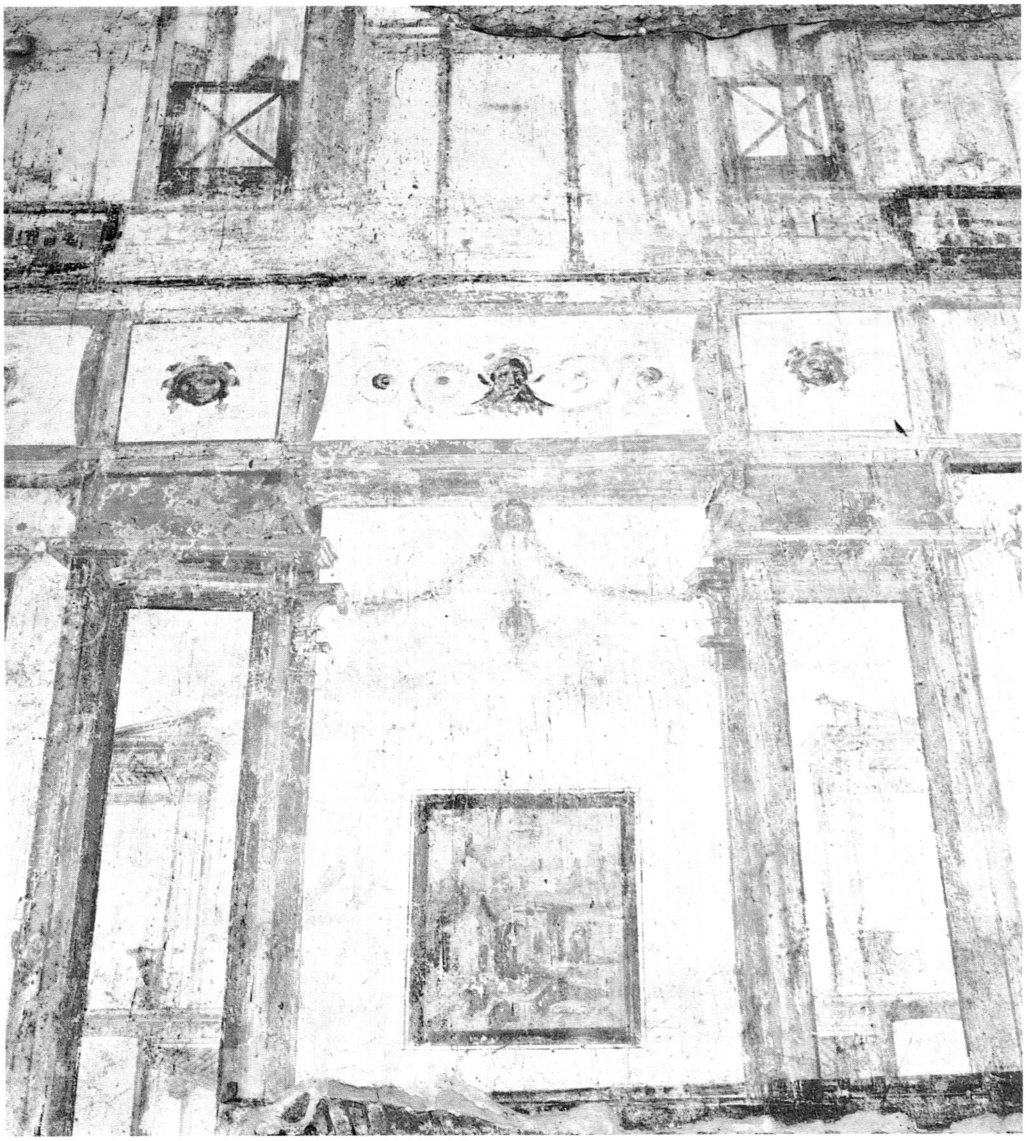

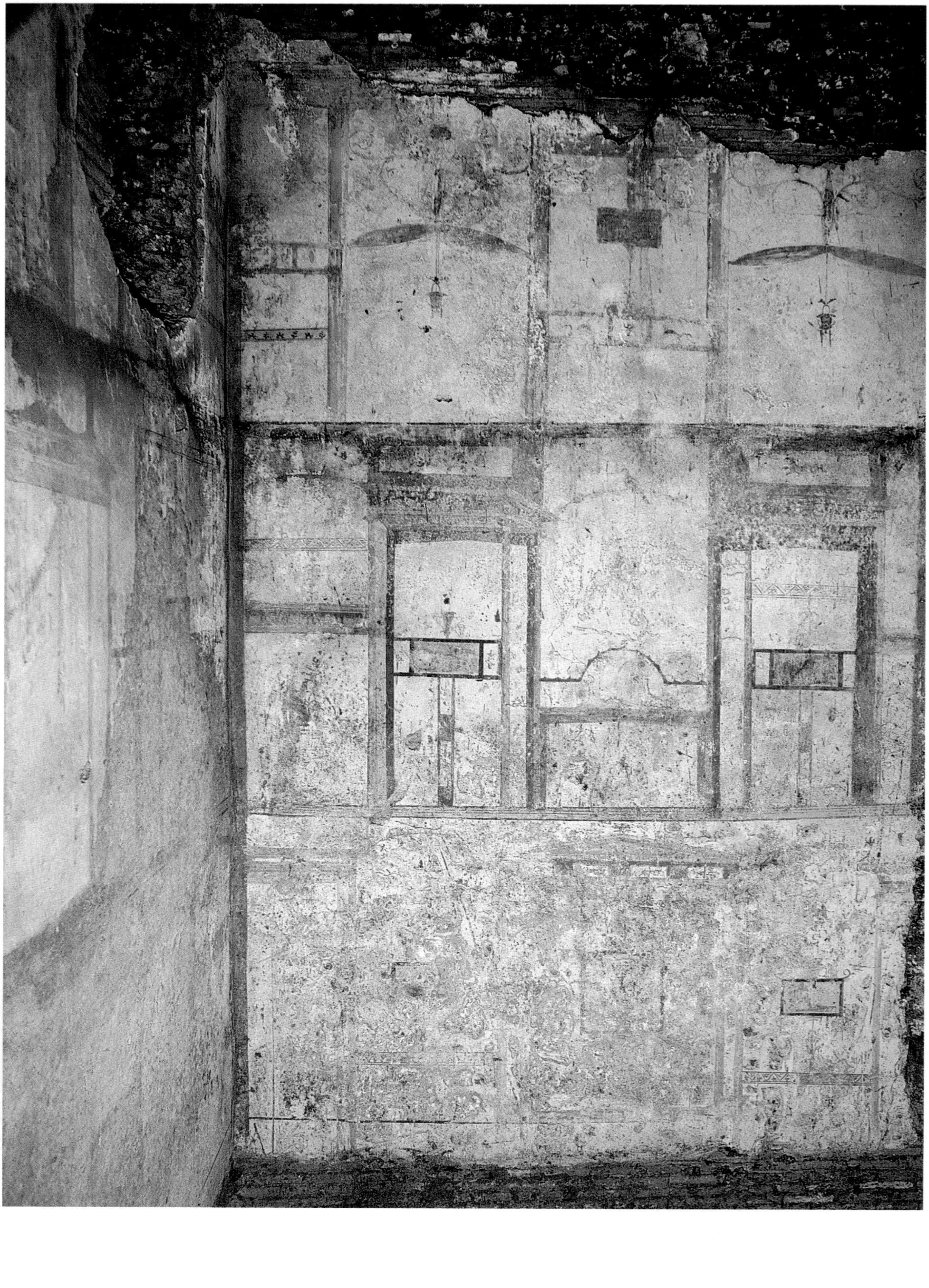

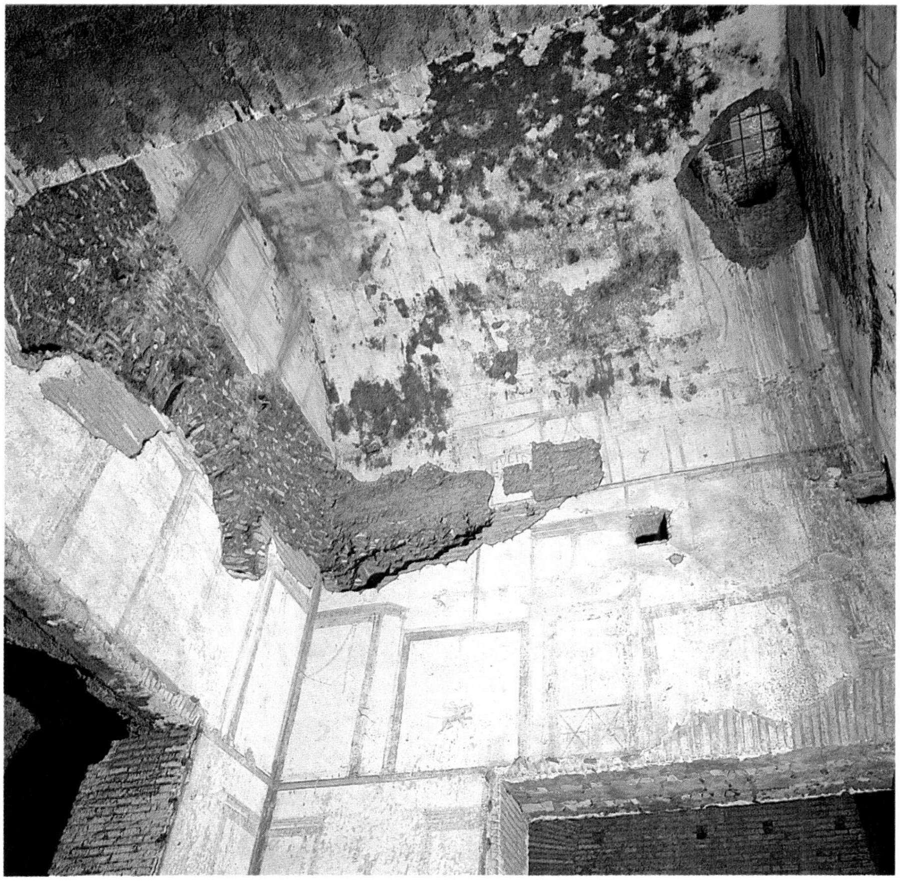

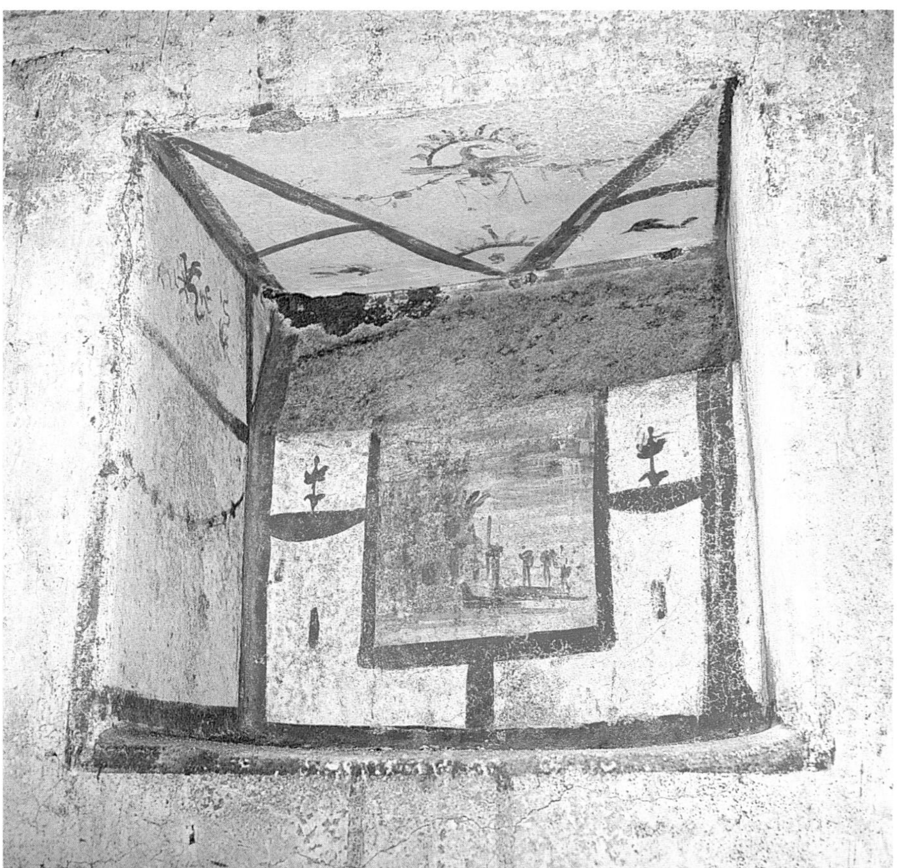

123. Room no. 86, architectural decoration on three levels with small landscape panels

124. Room no. 94, linear style architectural decoration on white background

125. Room no. 85, small panel with lake-side landscape, enlivened by roughly sketched figures

126. Room of the masks, small panel with lake-side landscape

127. Room of the masks, small panel with lake-side landscape

128. Room of the masks, small panel with harbour landscape

129. Room of the masks, small panel with scenic composition in natural landscape

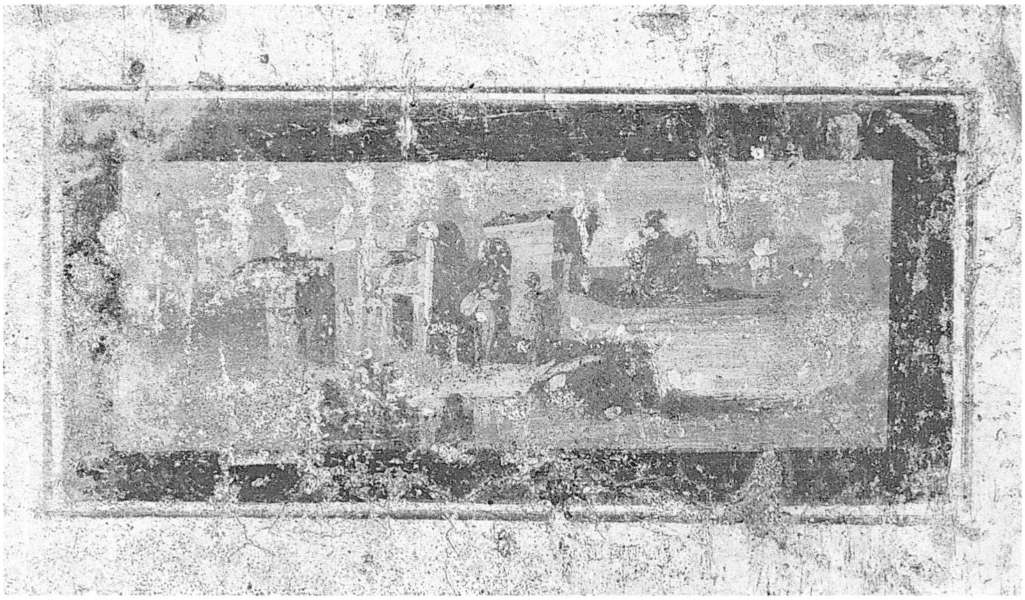

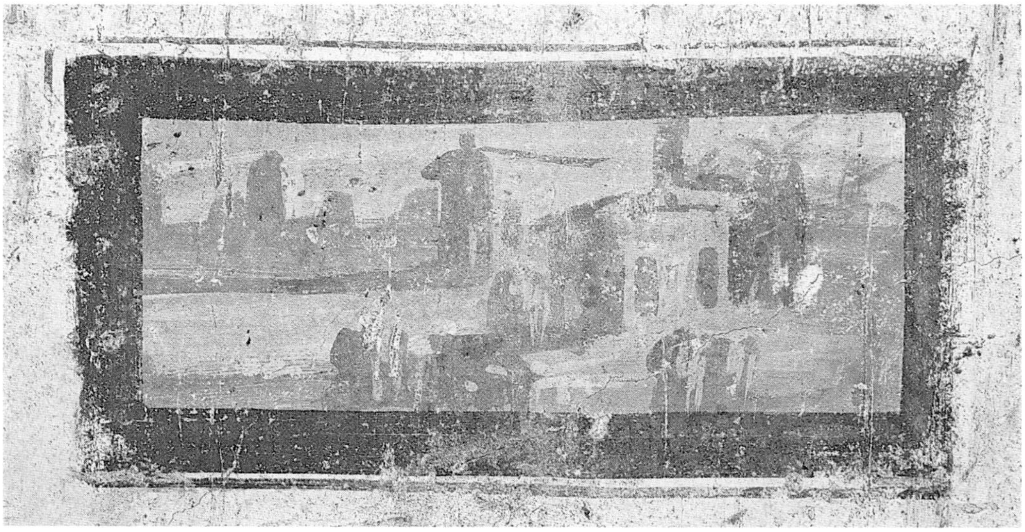

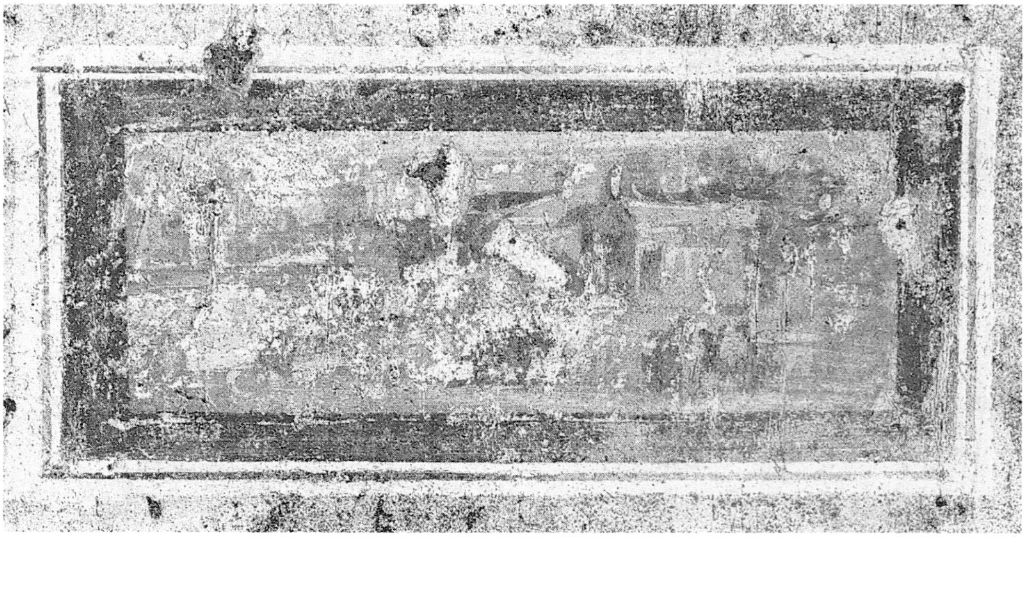

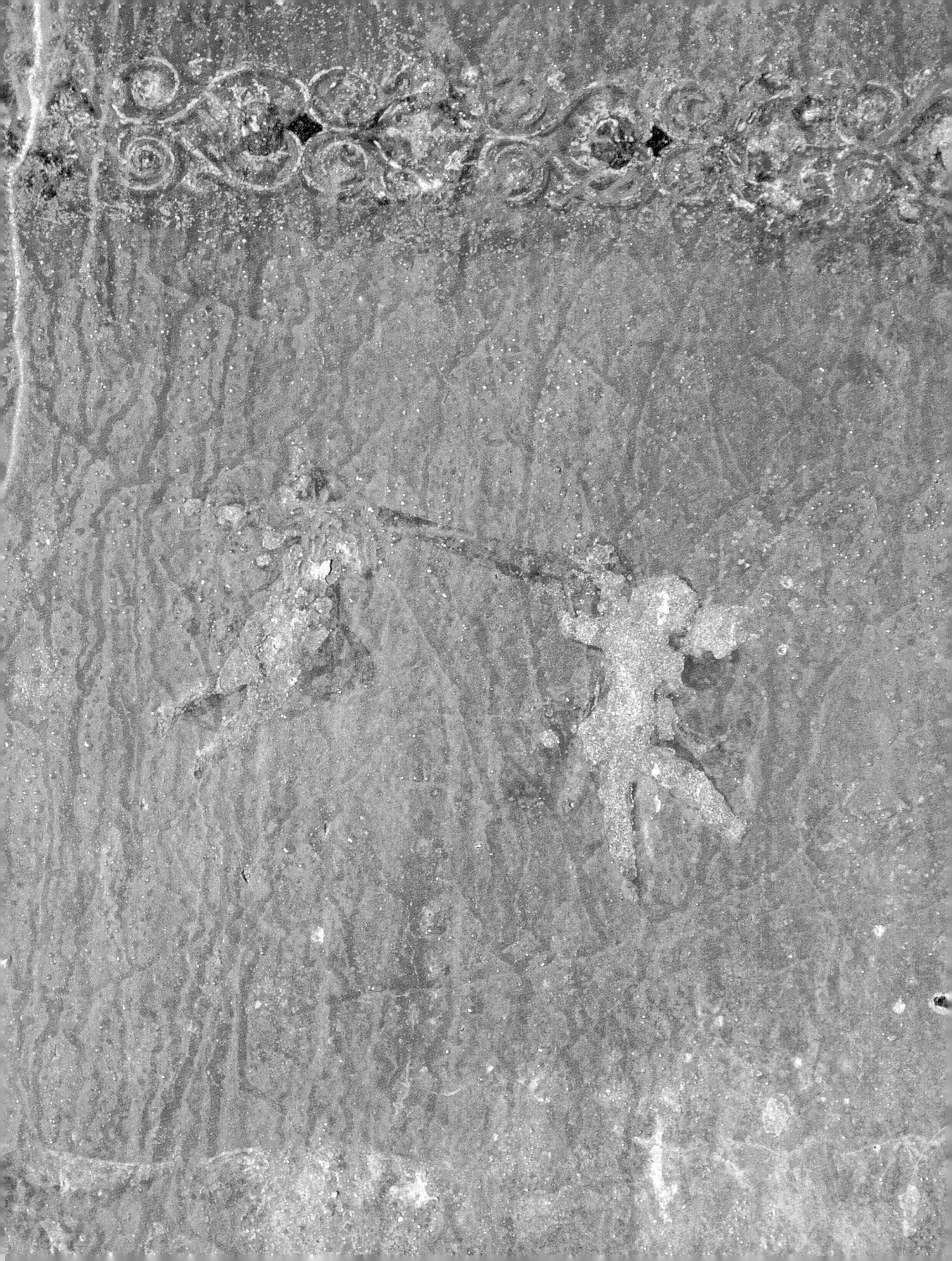

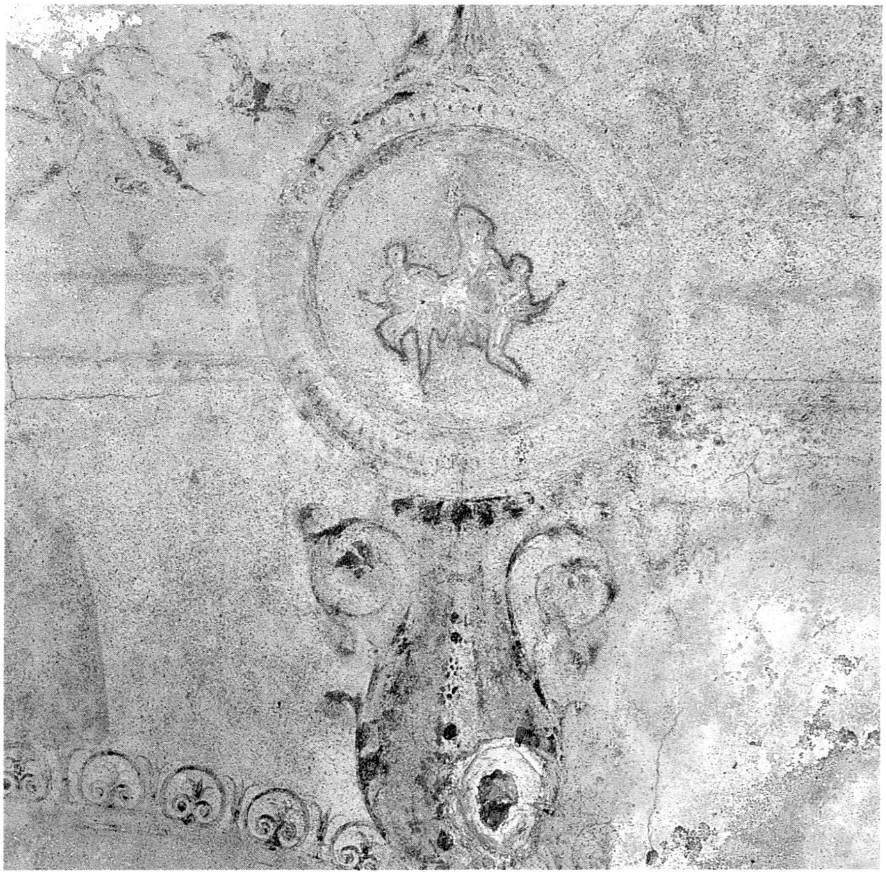

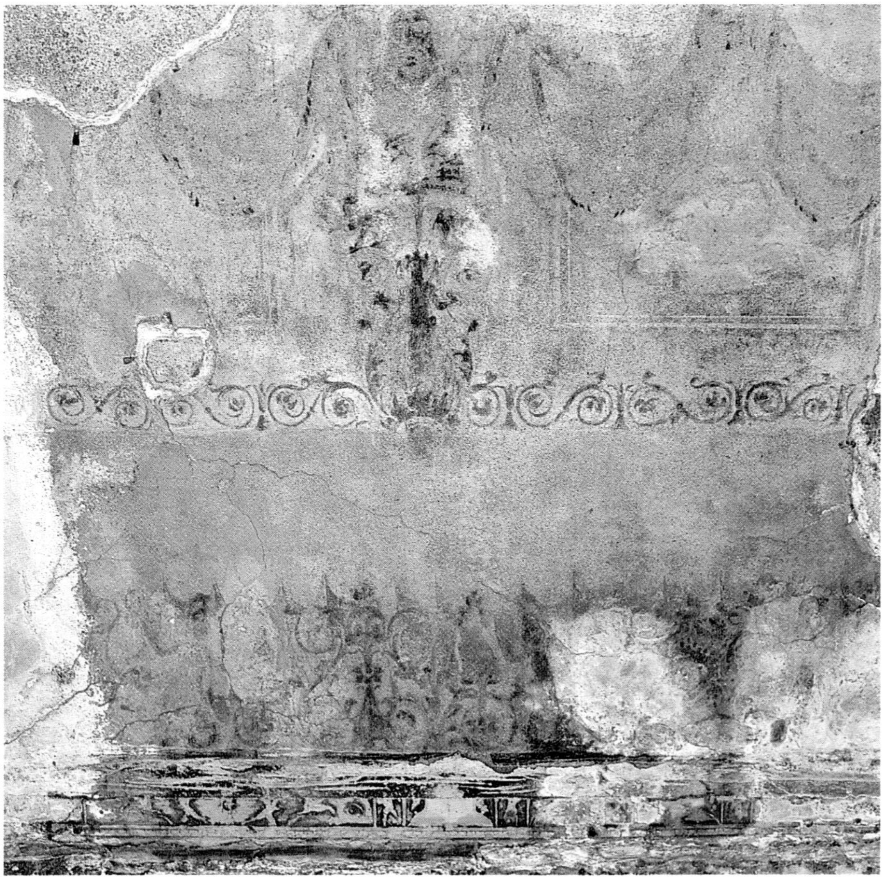

132. 'Vault of the owls', detail of the medallion with figures on a candelabrum motif

133. 'Vault of the owls', series of ornamental friezes, detail

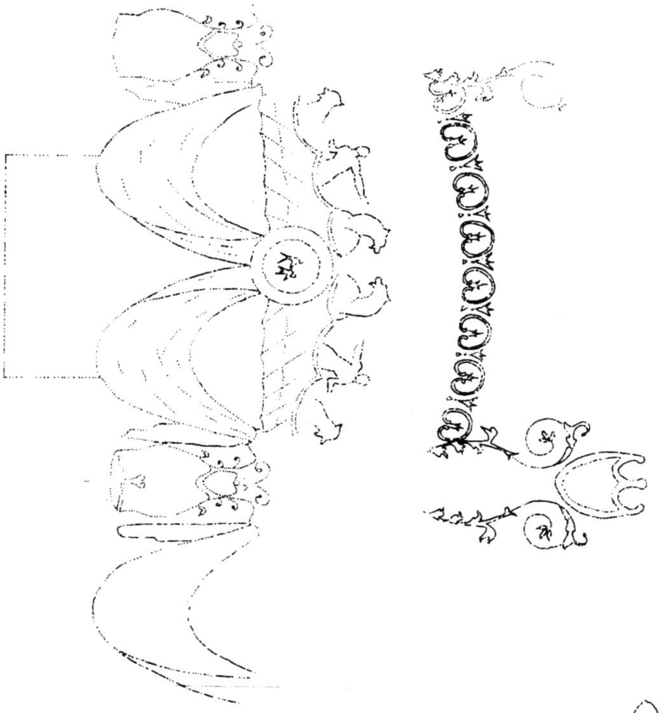

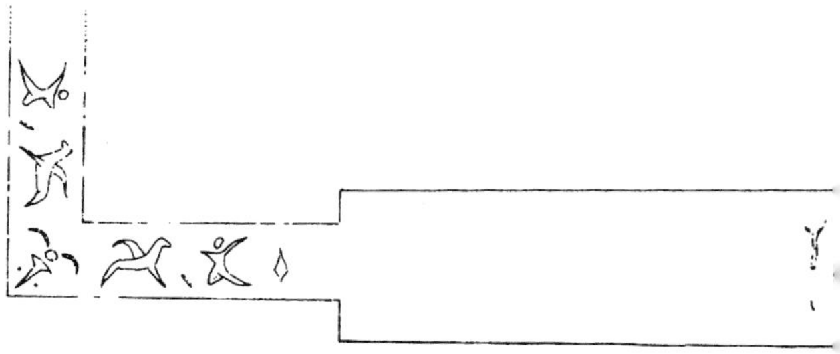

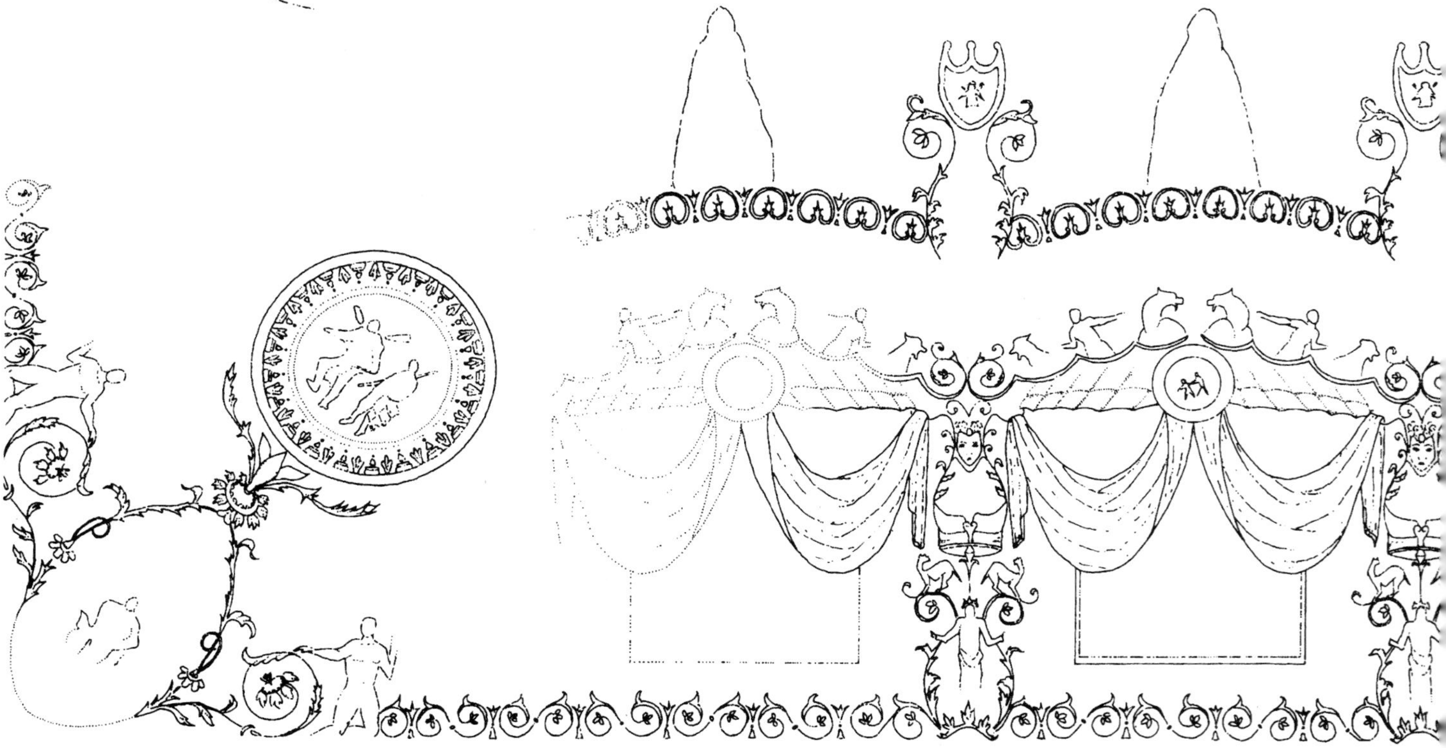

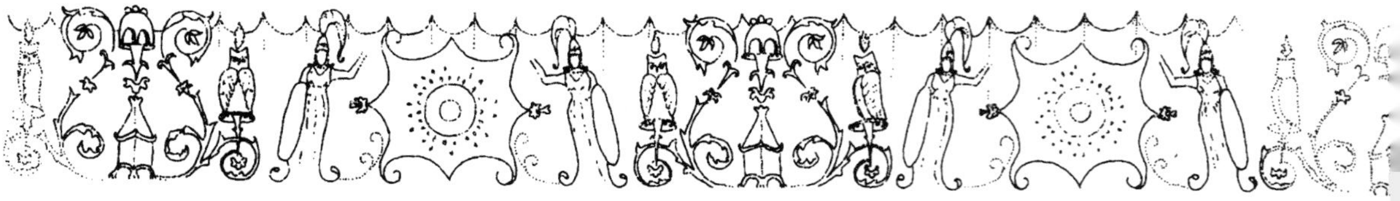

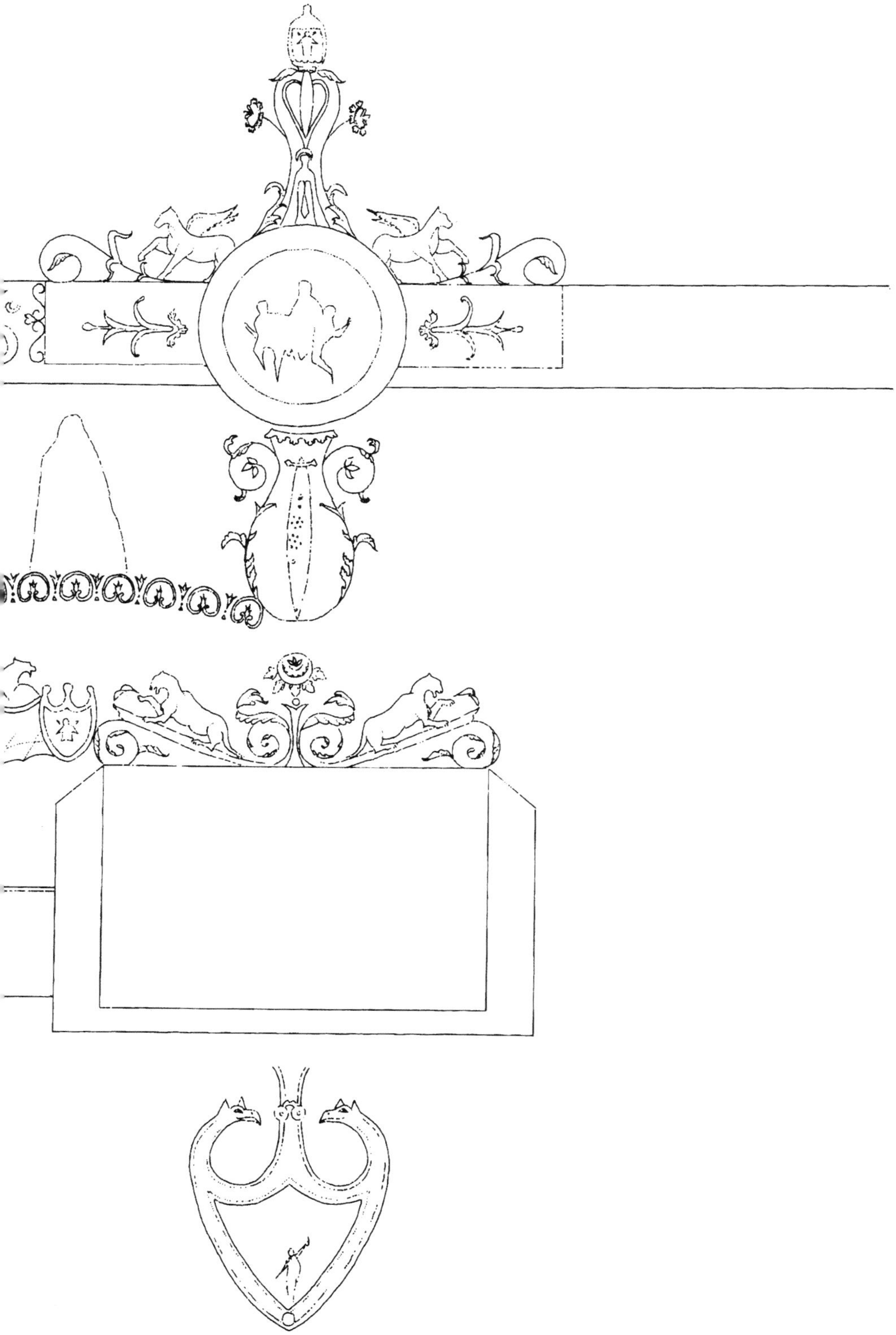

134. 'Vault of the owls', outline reconstruction of the vault decoration in its current condition

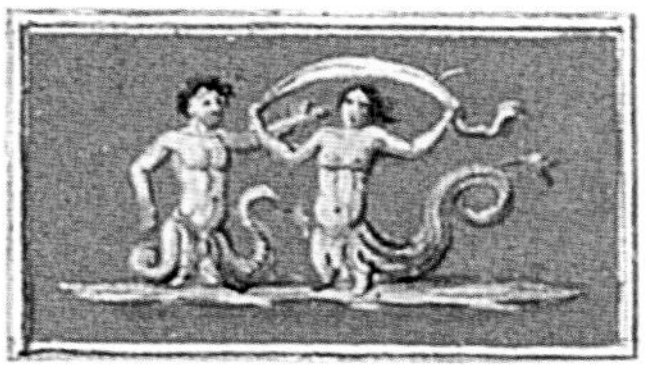

The yellow vault (31)

The decorative concept of the yellow vault also alludes to the marquees of the Hellenistic period which were decked out lavishly with festoons, hides and drapery for formal processions.

The yellow-gold background is divided up by bands of red which form multiple rectangular panels. Within these panels, arranged ingeniously in a particularly striking ornamental composition, are satyrs' heads, gorgon masks, winged griffons, horse-like sea creatures, genies and winged human figures emerging from stalks and floral calyces, tendrils and vine-shoots. These decorative elements relate to an artistic taste which for the most part derived from the middle east. In some places the motifs are set in isolation, in others they are connected with one another. The most diverse combinations of motifs did not escape the notice of artists like Ghirlandaio, Filippo Lippi, Pinturicchio, Amerigo Aspertini, Giovanni da Udine, who copied them in their painted works. Amidst the variety of motifs, the group consisting of a trophy of arms depicted with two satyrs sitting back to back on its base was a subject of particular interest. This was reproduced many times in drawings and sketches of the sixteenth century (*Codex Escurialensis*, fol. 14; Anonymous, Uffizi, Orn. 130).

In Mirri's interpretative rendering of the whole composition (which corresponds reasonably well to a drawing made recently), the centre is occupied by an *emblema* with a winged genie figure hovering in the air. This is set in a circular motif made up of miniature gorgon masks and winged female figures, emerging from elegant volutes, placed on a delicate embroidery-like arabesque.

Motifs of delicate candelabra combined with female figures, set on satyr heads or fantasy animals, emerge from the corners and run along the axes of the central

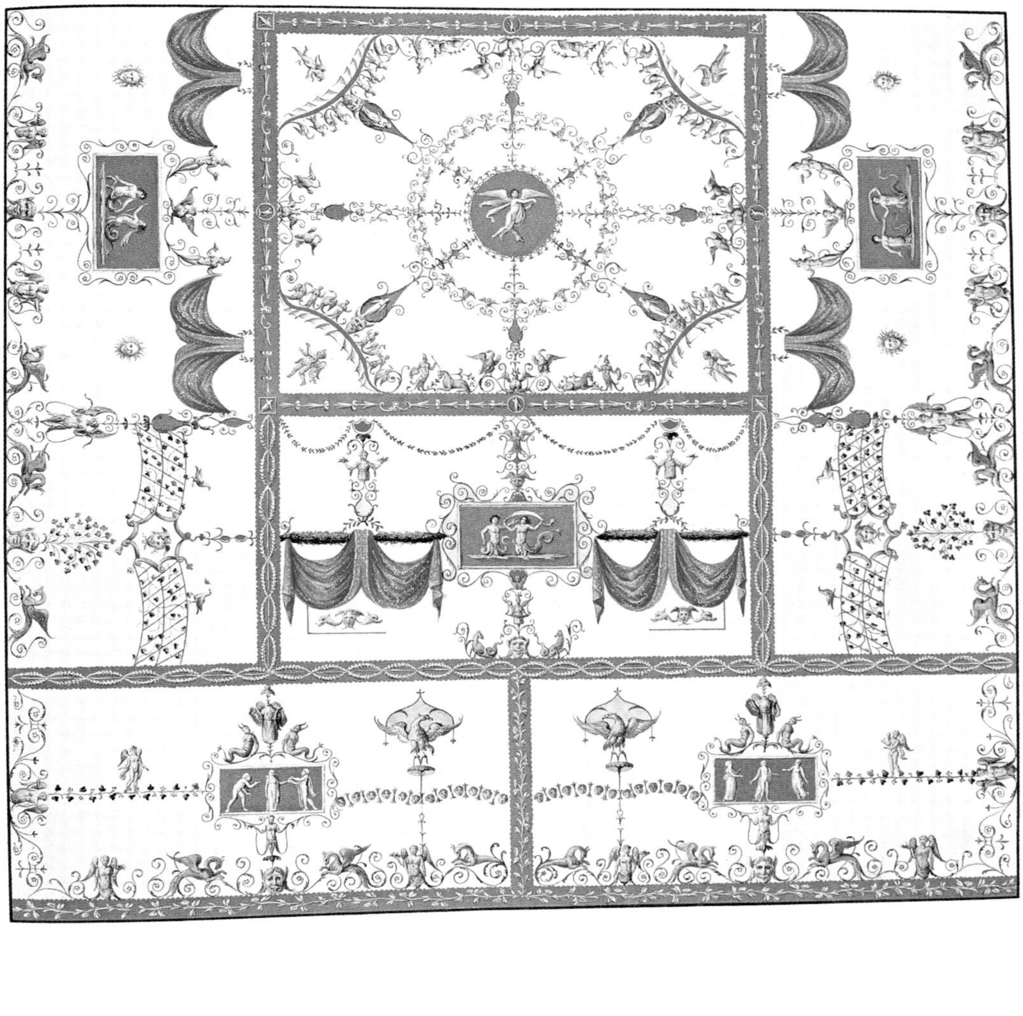

135. 'Yellow vault', decoration of the vault (Mirri 1776)

136. 'Yellow vault', outline reconstruction of the vault decoration in its current condition

137. 'Yellow vault', detail of the decoration, with reconstruction of the original colours

138–139. 'Yellow vault', details of the decoration in its current condition

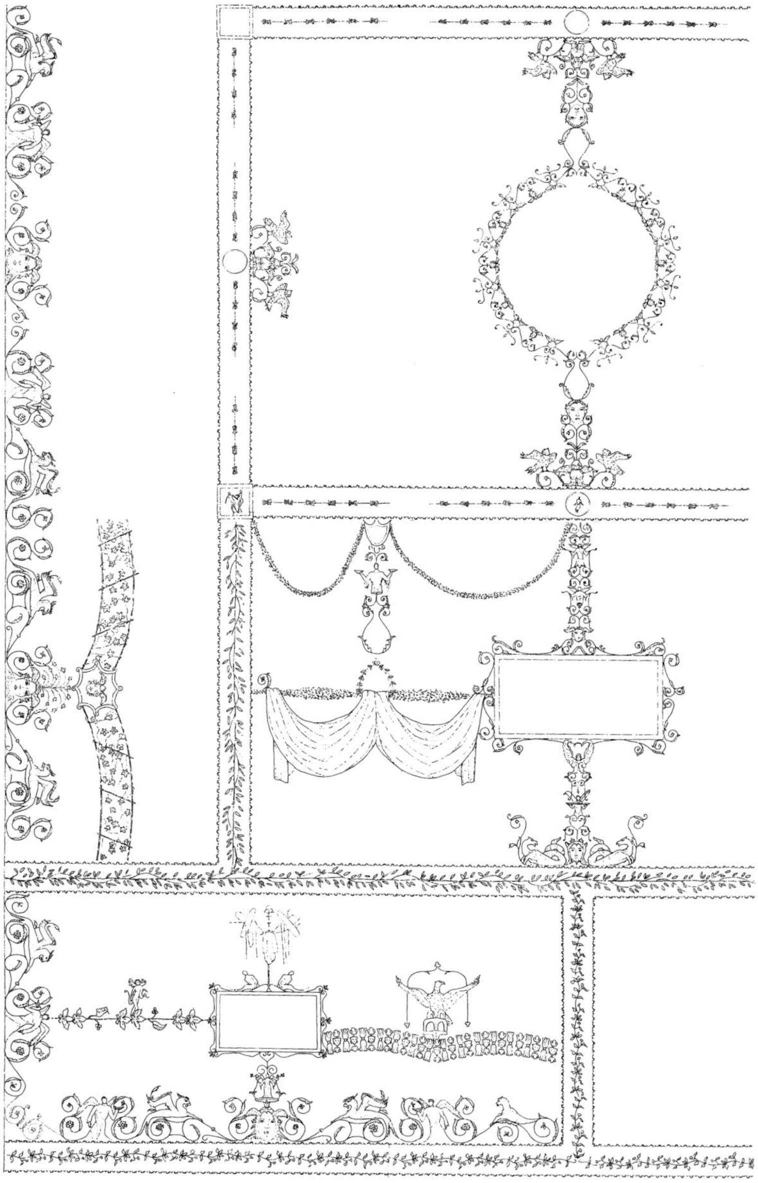

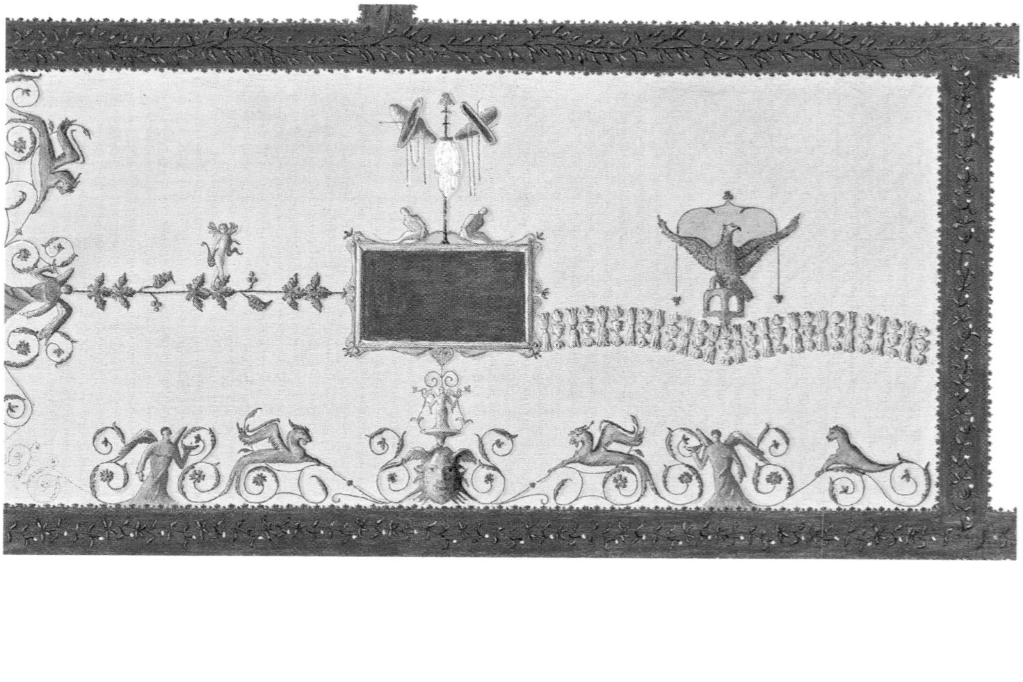

panel. The intersection of these motifs also forms the centre of attention for the viewer.
The arrangement of the candelabra to correspond with the form of the vault, which produces an optical illusion of depth, is analogous to that seen in the adjacent 'vault of the owls'.
This significant similarity of detail in the layout of the decorative scheme, its strikingly baroque character and its emphasis on the fantastic, designed with purely decorative intent, all suggest that the same artistic personality was responsible for the decoration of both ceilings.
In the myriad of decorative devices and fantastic filling motifs, particularly striking are the blue drapery and the *pinakes*, rectangular panels of cinnabar red, set in the centre of the remaining panels. They contain scenes with pairs of Tritons and other figures, most of which cannot be identified. In some cases they may have portrayed cult scenes, as is suggested by the traces which survive *in situ* (confirmed by the *Codex Escurialensis*); a sacrificial group is visible in a *pinax* which acts as a base for the group with the trophy of arms.
The same decorative freedom seems to lighten the decoration of the lunette, which is still partially visible in drawings (Windsor 194, fol. 22, n. 11051) of the school of Ghirlandaio and in frescoes (Aspertini, the Oratory of Saint Cecilia in Bologna) of the sixteenth century, when they were still partly buried, and subsequently by Mirri, who depicted the whole decorative scheme after the exposure of the buried parts.
Along with the drapery and the hanging festoons small *pinakes* of window form recur, as do winged griffons in rampant forms, and small winged figures supporting floral candelabra, above which are winged creatures perched on vine branches. All the motifs are set as acroterial decorations on the upper levels of a series of *aediculae* which open onto a enclosed monochrome background.

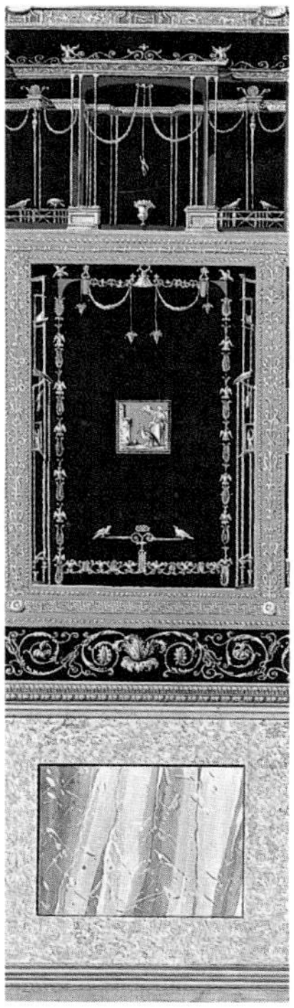

The black vault (32)

Only a few parts of the vault and some wall panels in an extremely poor state of conservation and legibility survive of the painted black background decoration of the alcoved room in the private imperial apartment. However, the appearance of its refined *ductus* painted ornamentation can be seen in the details of the vault preserved in the *Codex Escurialensis* (Fol. 13. 14). The reconstruction by Ponce offers a complete image of the decoration of the walls and of the vault, and that by Mirri adds to it its original polychrome character.
A black background is delineated by a network of slender, calligraphic candle sticks with plant-like motifs set vertically. According to Mirri's reconstruction these intersect with horizontal friezes containing grotesques in shades of red, blue and white. Rectangular panels and round and almond-shaped medallions contain, respectively, small figured scenes and single stucco figures, and are woven into a network, further animating the surface along with hanging garlands and small *pinakes*. These emerge from a background highlighted by a red or white outline, although their location is not always correct in the 18th century engravings,.
The whole scheme emulates an elegant and refined work of jewellery in which the artist, as noted by De Romanis in the 19th century, 'seems to have had in mind a depiction of a number of necklaces inter-

140. 'Black vault', decoration of the vault (Mirri 1776)

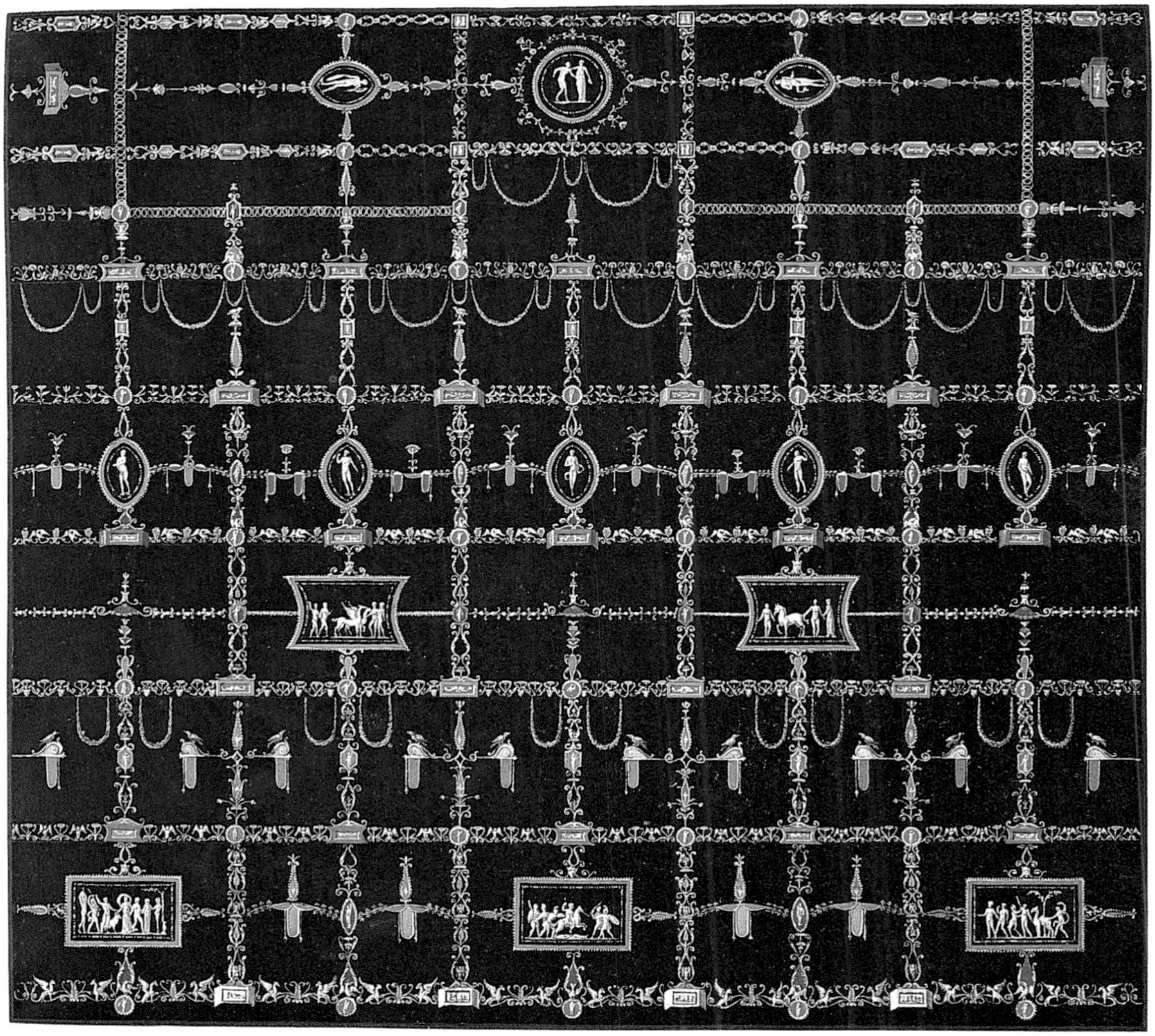

141. 'Black vault', decorated part of the wall in its current condition

142. Hall 'of the black vault', decorative division of the wall in its current condition

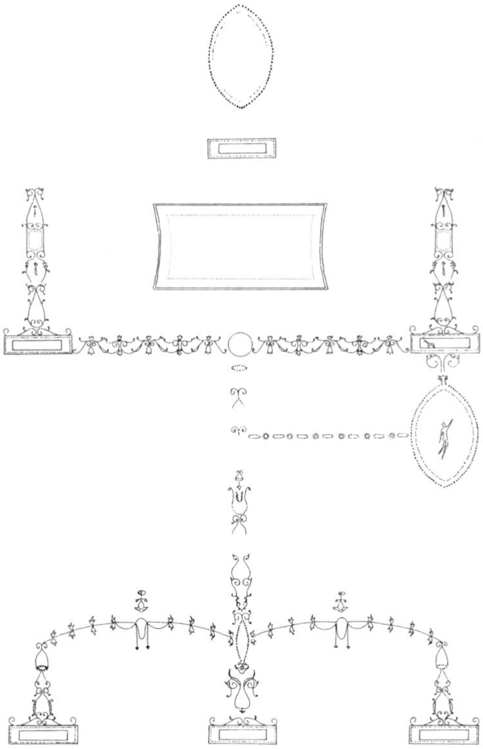

posed by small panels and cameos of different form.' The elegant medallion motif which characterises the decoration of the 'black grotto' particularly interested Giovanni da Udine who adapted it to enliven the pilasters of the Loggia of Raphael in the Vatican. This motif is combined with others derived from the decoration of other rooms of the west wing such as the 'vault of the owls'.

Above a marble socle about two metres high, the painted decoration of the walls is framed by elegant plant-like spirals topped by menander motifs which subdivide the walls into panels. These panels are surrounded by ovolo moulded cornices and candlesticks. They contain small panels at the centre and double-branched floral candelabra at the bottom upon which sit two birds facing each other. Above all this, depictions of porticoes with perspective architecture open the walls in the manner of the so-called third style with decorative details such as hanging figures, vases and garlands.

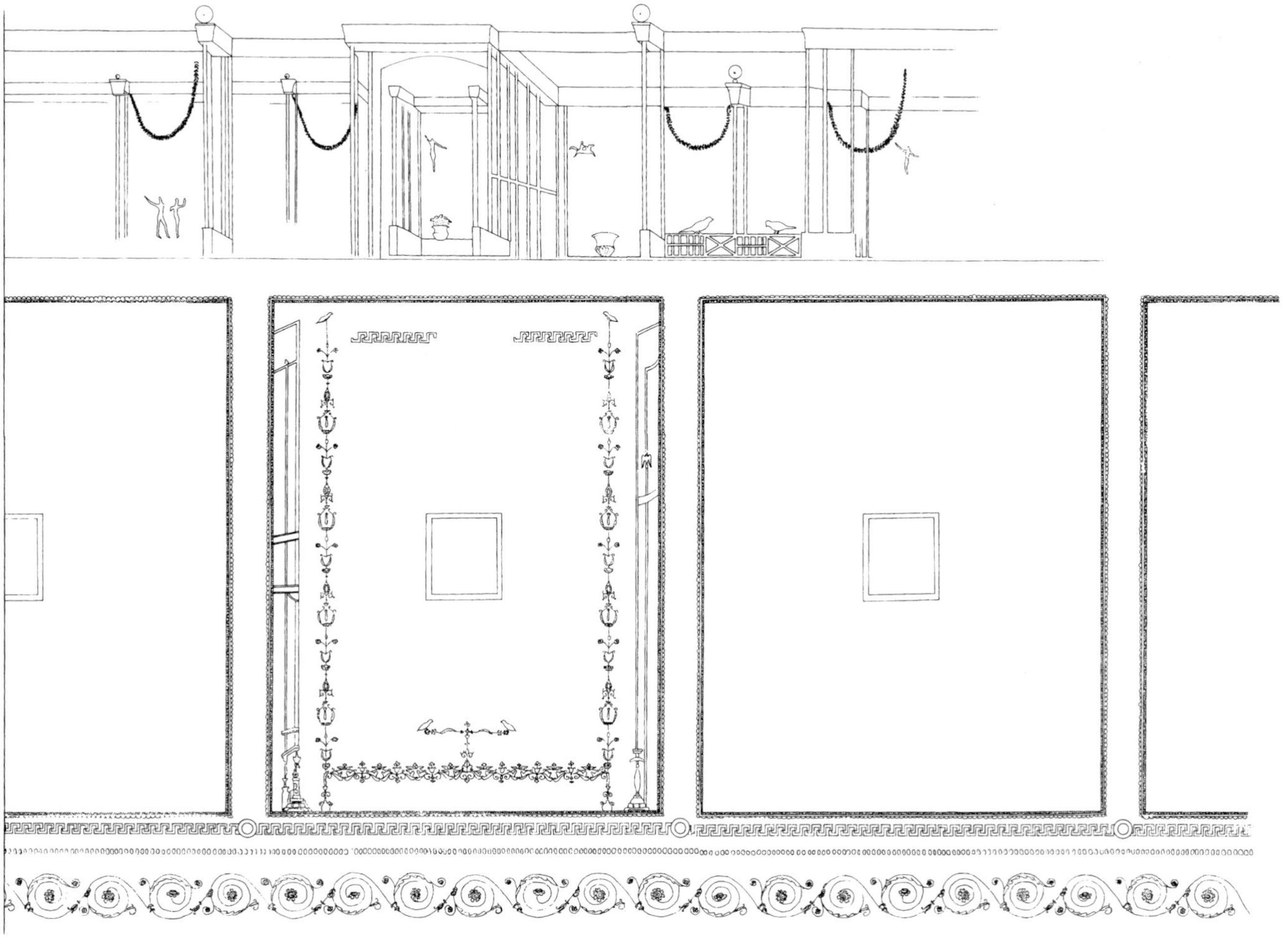

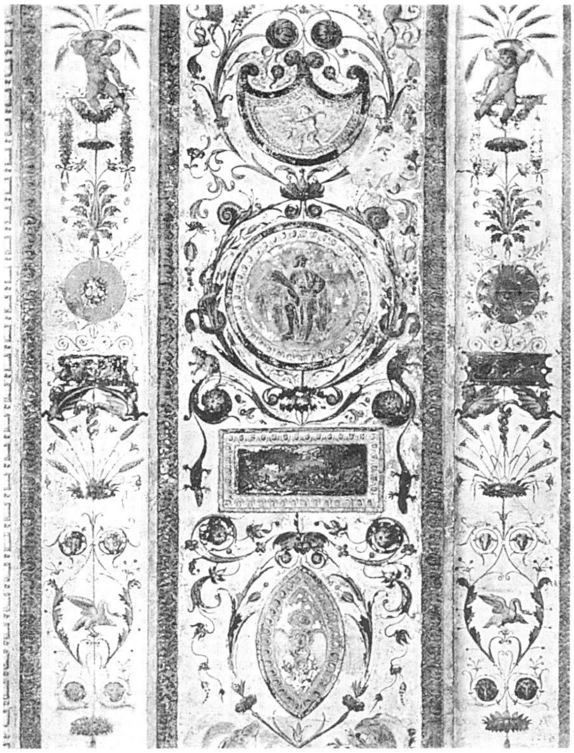

143. Loggia of Raphael, pilaster decorated by Giovanni da Udine with an ornamental motif derived from the 'black vault'

144. Hall 'of the black vault', decorative division of the wall into panels, depicting the wings of buildings and architecture with slender columns of metallic appearance (Mirri 1776)

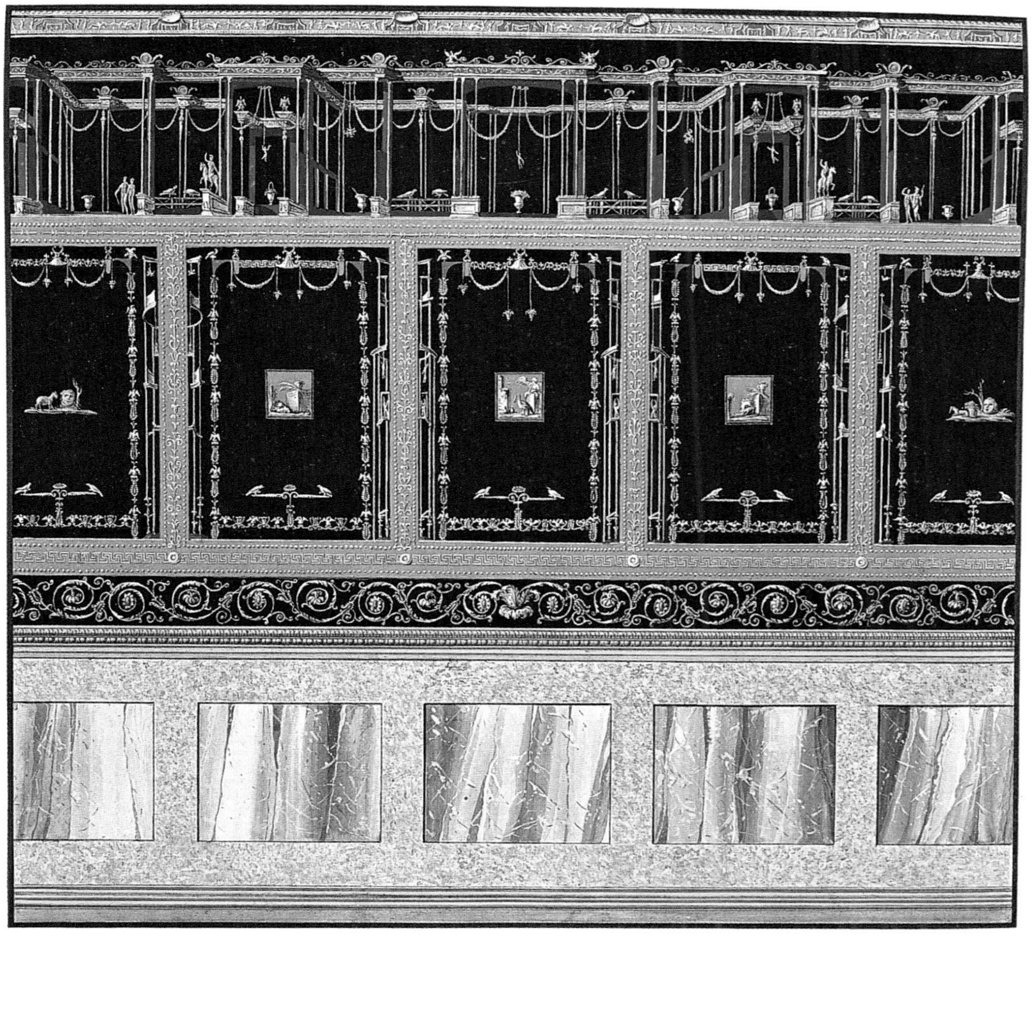

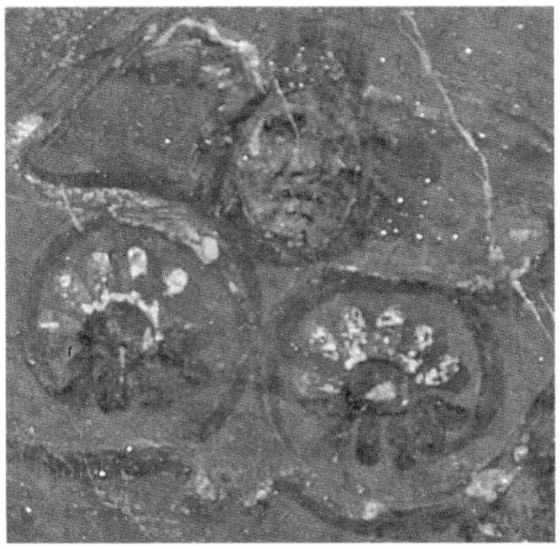

Room no. 33

From the existing remains and by comparison to the 18th century etchings it is clear that this room is amongst the most richly ornate of the west wing. A new level of splendour is achieved with its red background, extensive use of gold leaf and high marble socle (which in the work of Mirri is inferior to the original).

Within it we find numerous ornamental elements already seen in the decoration of the 'yellow vault' and the 'vault of the owls'. The motif of the tent or of drapery even recurs to provide a background to scenes within panels and to continuous friezes. Analogous is the exuberant variety of the decorative 'grotesques' and of plant-like candelabra which subdivide the space framing the panels and the figured *pinakes*. Also present is the motif of the anthropomorphic *tropaeum* and elements arched in simple plant shoots or shaped by bands covered by animal-like figures amongst plant-like spirals.

As in the 'vault of the owls', the complex arrangement is dominated by a figured scene at the centre of the vault and framed by depictions of winged figures heraldically arranged at the sides of a plant motif and separated by gorgons' heads. Within this frame friezes are used to create the sides of two wide concentric panels. The outer panel is shaped by winged figures terminating in volutes and serpent-footed sea beings silhouetted against a continuous curtain.

A series of griffons ending in spirals and flanking *gorgoneia* defines the four sides of the inner panel. From the mid-points and corners of the frame of the central scene complex candle-stick motifs are directed outwards. These are composed of, alternately, masks with winged beings combining animal and plant-like features and eagles with masks set between plant-like elements.

The panels formed by these contain (in the inner squares) pairs of goats and (in the corner squares) Erotes hovering and dancing.

Further candle-stick motifs are formed by closely-woven 'grotesques' with gorgon heads and peacocks facing one another between volutes and plant-like motifs. These candle-sticks clearly articulate the space between the two large panels into rectangles and squares. Within these are figured scenes and pairs of curtains loosely suspended from a plant-like stalk. The hem of the curtains is wrapped around an arched double band, a motif often appropriated by artists of the Renaissance such as Giovanni da Udine and Peruzzi to decorate vaults and walls.

Between the pairs of curtain motifs, emerging from *peltae*, are candelabra with plant-like devices which spread out from masks, alternating with pairs of winged figures ending in tendrils. These support small frames with stucco figured friezes. Above these frames are placed trophies which emphasise the axes of the entire decorative scheme. The trophies are flanked by two winged figures, perhaps in the act of adorning them, according to the scheme well known from reliefs and sarcophagi. In Mirri's engraving only one of these pairs has two winged figures. In the others, one of the figures is depicted as wingless. Depiction of trophies more frequently appears as a decorative device in the ensemble of the west wing. However, it may also have programmatic significance, designed to recall the military victories of the *princeps*.

Both the reconstructions of Mirri and Ponce, even though they differ in some details, suggest that the central panel depicted a bacchic scene. Dionysus is seated on a throne in front of a shrine of *tholos* (round) form, holding a *patera* and *pedum* (?) and surrounded by four female figures, perhaps the Seasons, while a young boy offers him a *rython* or drinking horn. The remaining figured scenes are probably connected with the mythology of this god, although they are not completely clear or easy to interpret. A depiction of the birth of the god (of which numerous fragments remain in situ) and his delivery by Hermes to the nymphs of Mount Nissa are recognisable.

From the other surviving remains, one cannot recognise the other attributes of the god, such as the crown of vine leaves, which are clearly depicted in the 18th century reconstructions. Furthermore, interpretations of the scene vary, despite the male figure with the crown of vine leaves in Mirri's engraving (which is our only source of evidence) and the *paredroi* scenes which bear testimony to the Dionysiac character of the entire decorative cycle of the vault. Some who consider the *Domus* to be the seat of the sun-god identify the deity depicted as Helios in the act of hearing the youthful Phaeton's request to drive the chariot of the Sun. But if a symbolic character can be attributed to the scenes depicted, then Dionysus might represent the exaltation of artistic values and of nature, elements fundamental to Neronian ideology. From the remains it is impossible not to notice the

145. Room no. 33, outline restoration of the vault decoration in its current condition

146. Room no. 33, outline restoration of the chain decoration of the apse, in its current condition

147. Room no. 33, decoration of the vault (Mirri 1776)

close connection existing between the *tholos* which characterises the scene (some faded indications of this *tholos* still remain) and Dionysus. The Dionysiac theme which decorated the cubiculum (20) overlooking the peristyle adapts itself well to the adjacent complex made up of the large *oecus* (44), the winter triclinium, and the grotto of the nymphaeum of Polyphemus (45) decorated with mosaic emblems in glass paste, shells and stalactites, a type of 'bacchic cave' (which, later in the history of the Neronian palace became, as it were, a real dark cave).

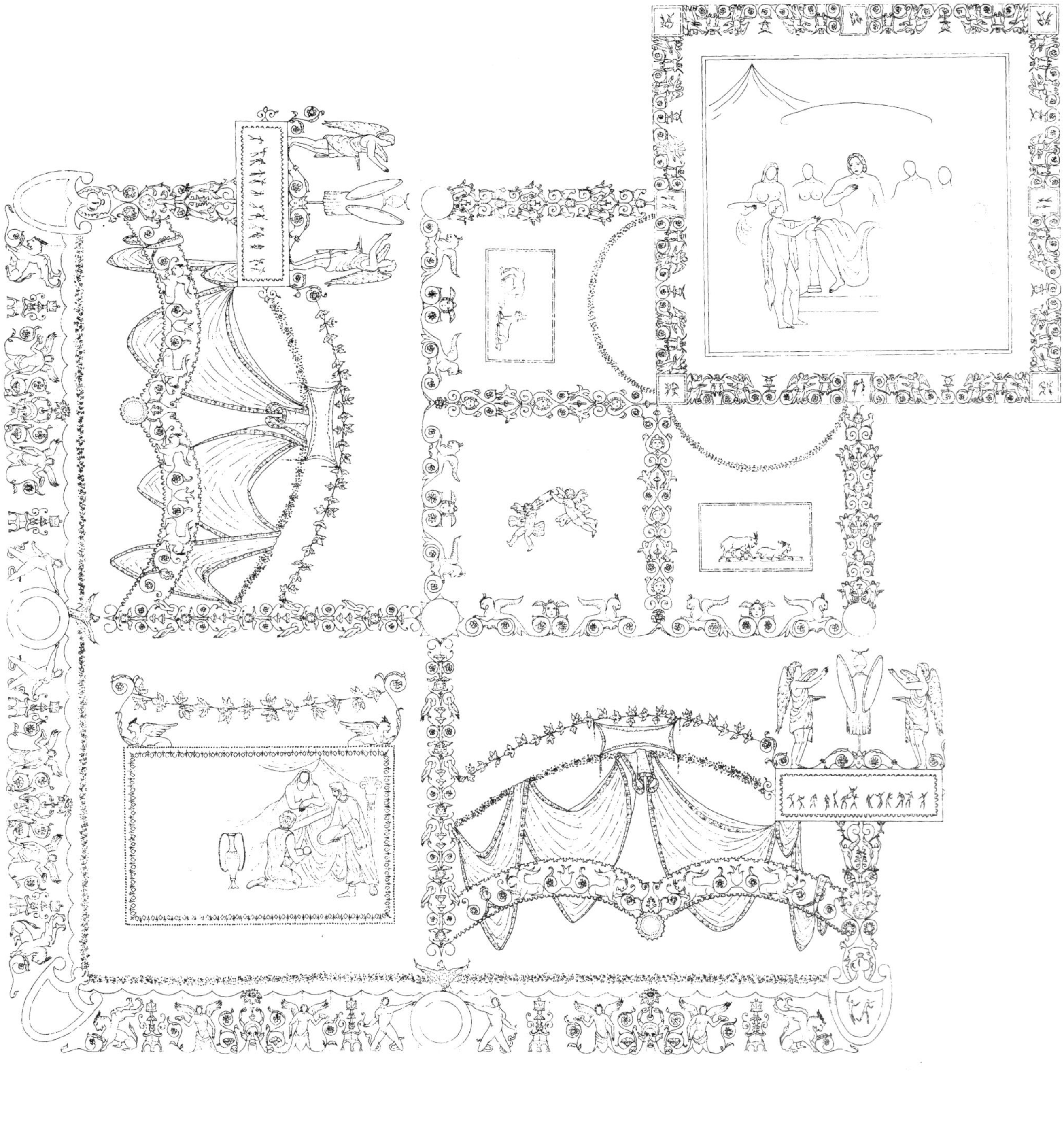

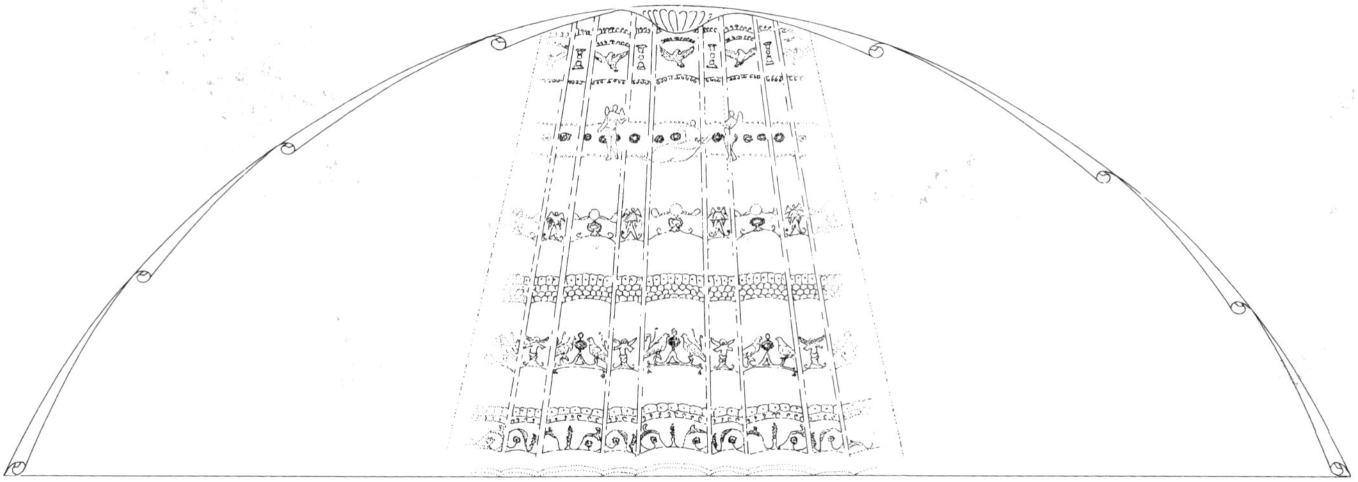

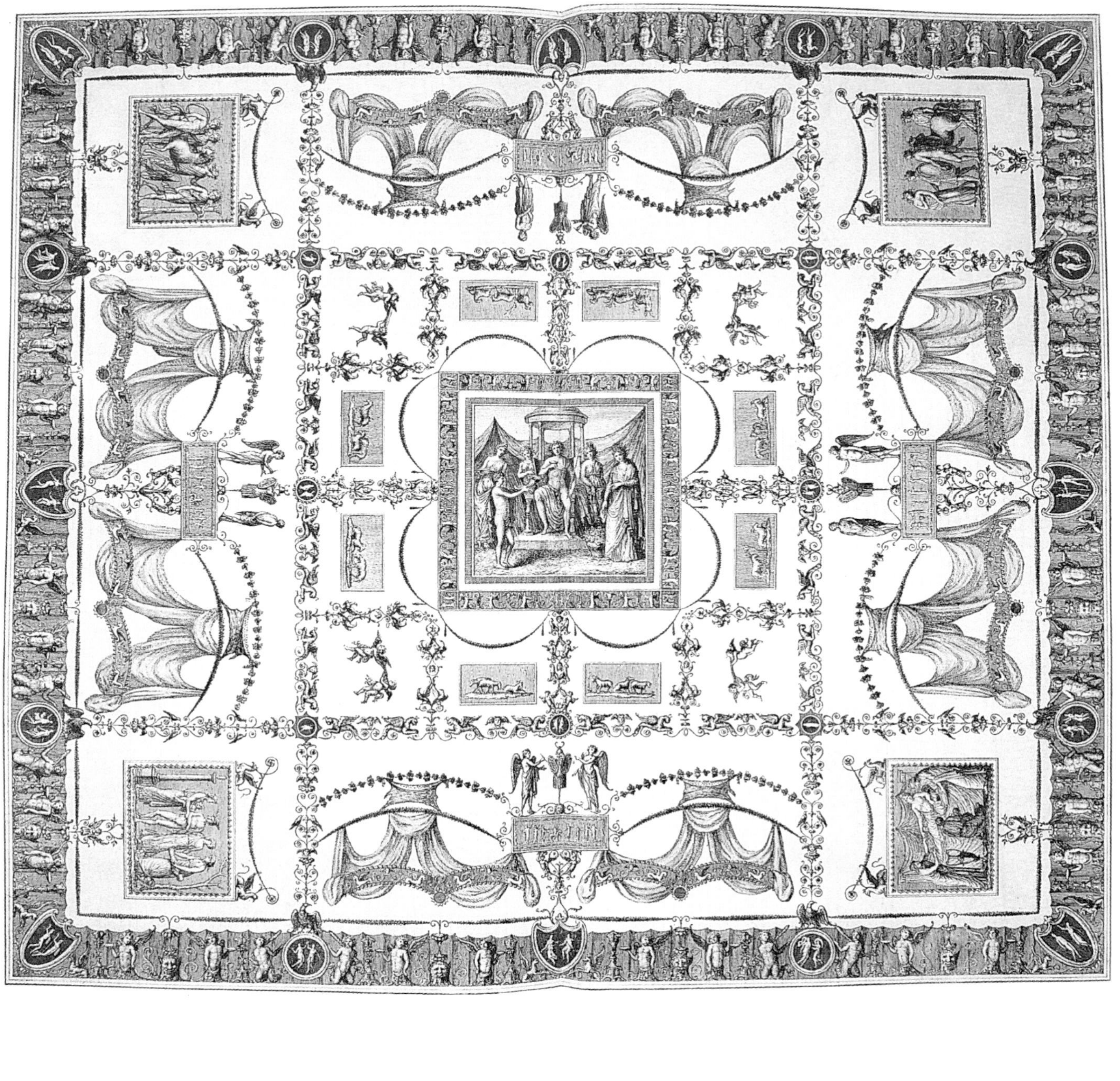

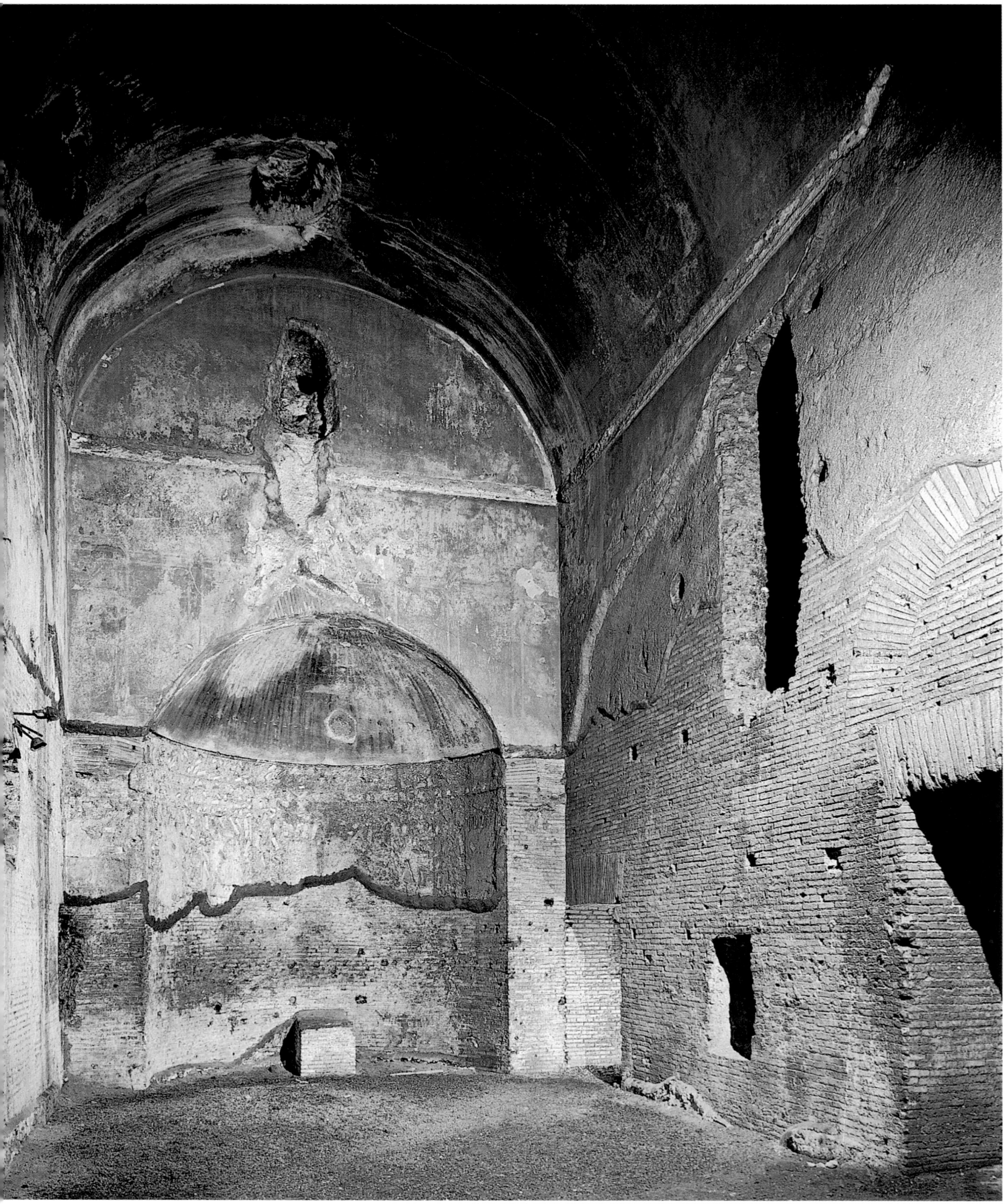

148. Room no. 33, red-ground decoration of the room

149. Room no.33, vault, frieze with gorgon's head and griffon between floral scrolls, detail

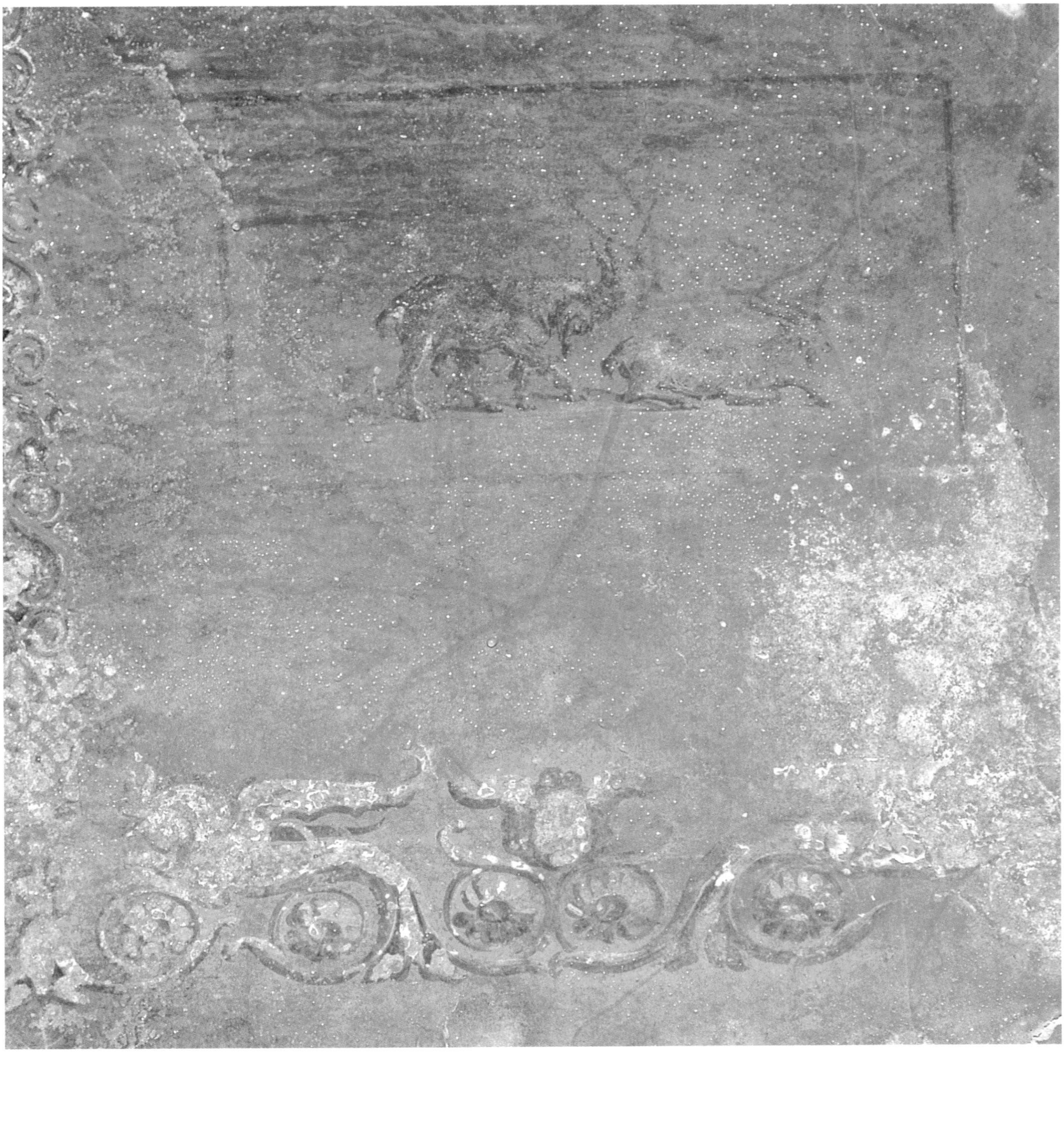

150–151. Room no. 33, vault, Victories decorating a trophy

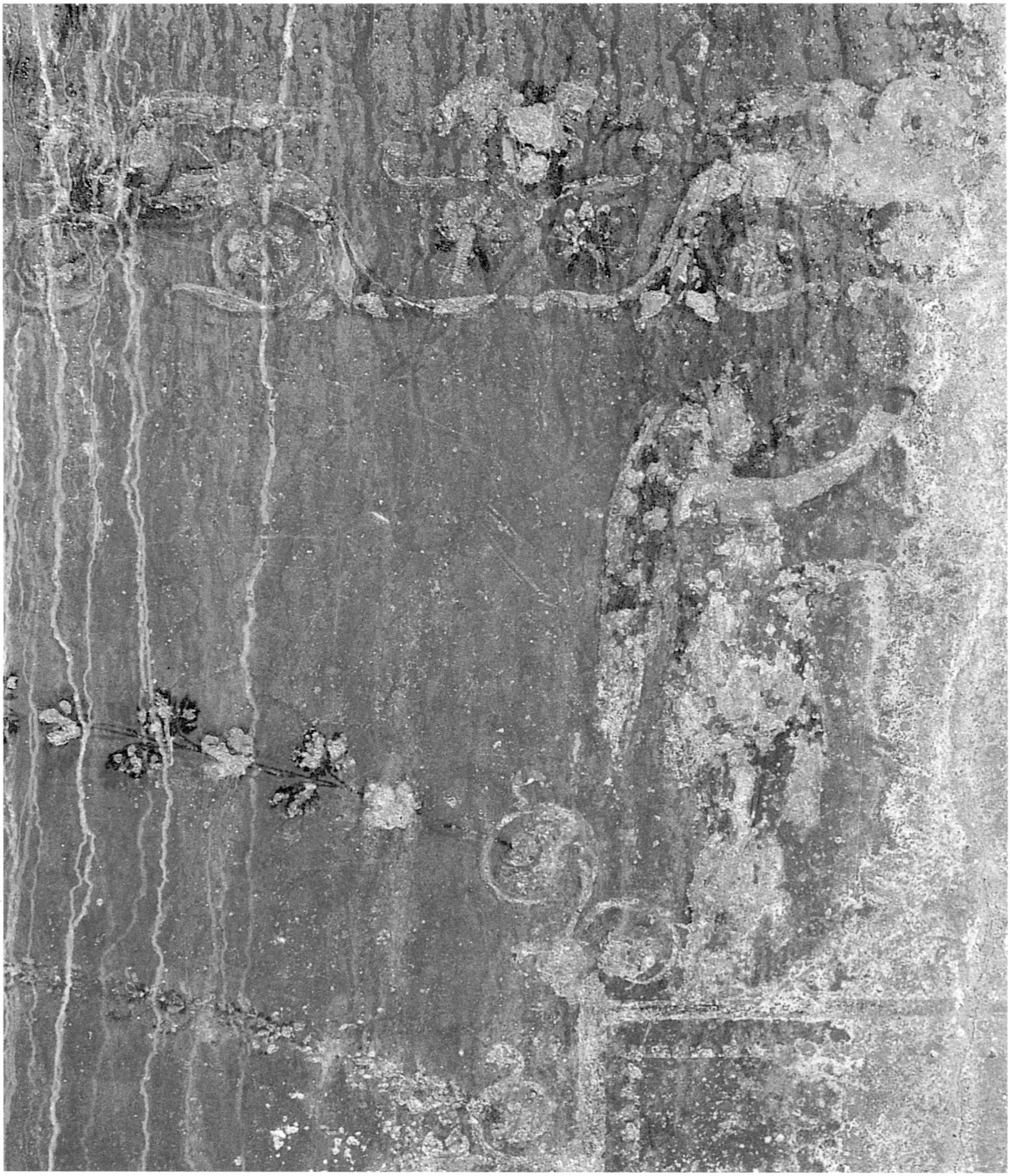

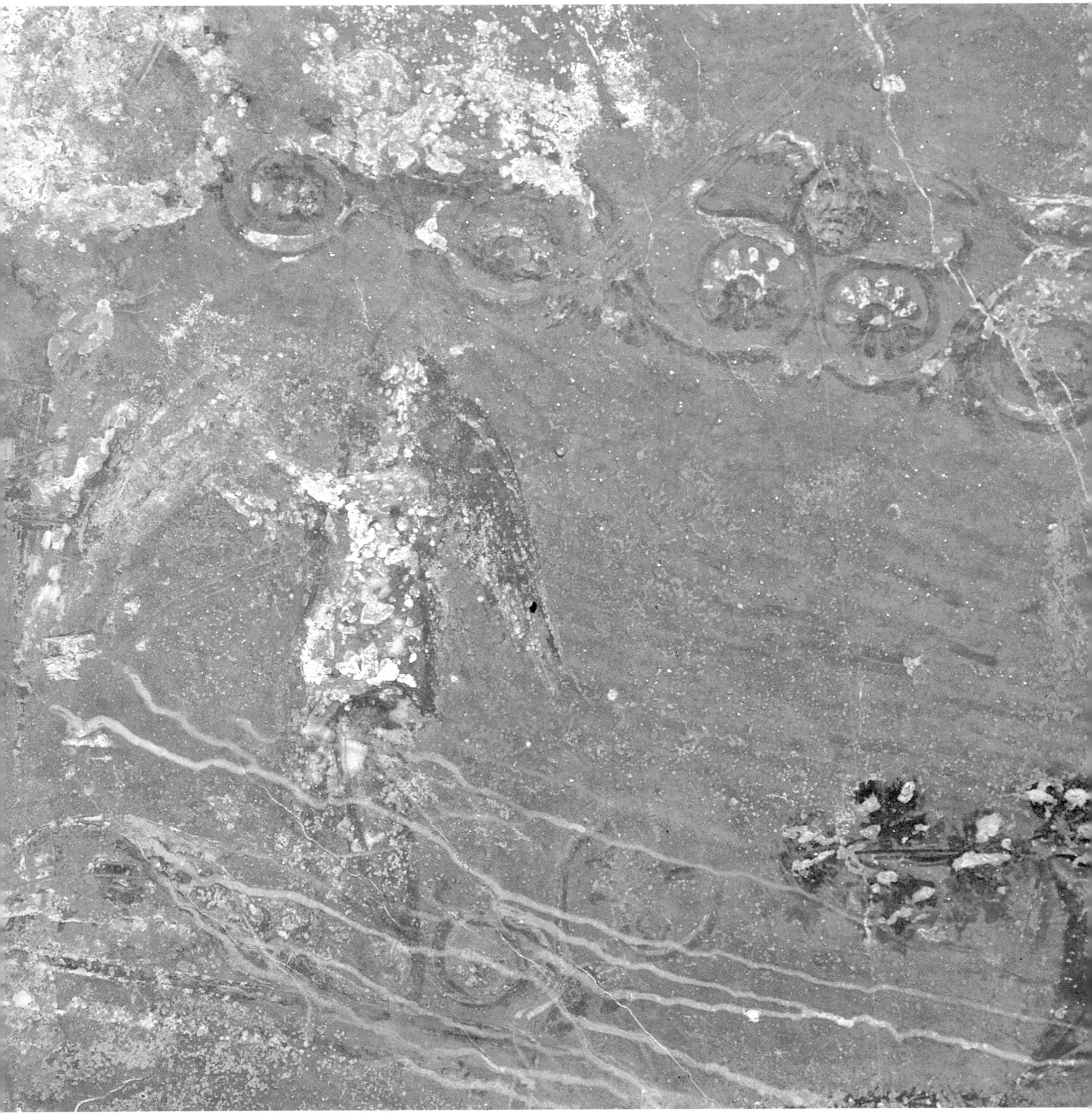

152. Room no. 33, vault, detail, pinax with the remains of figures moulded in stucco

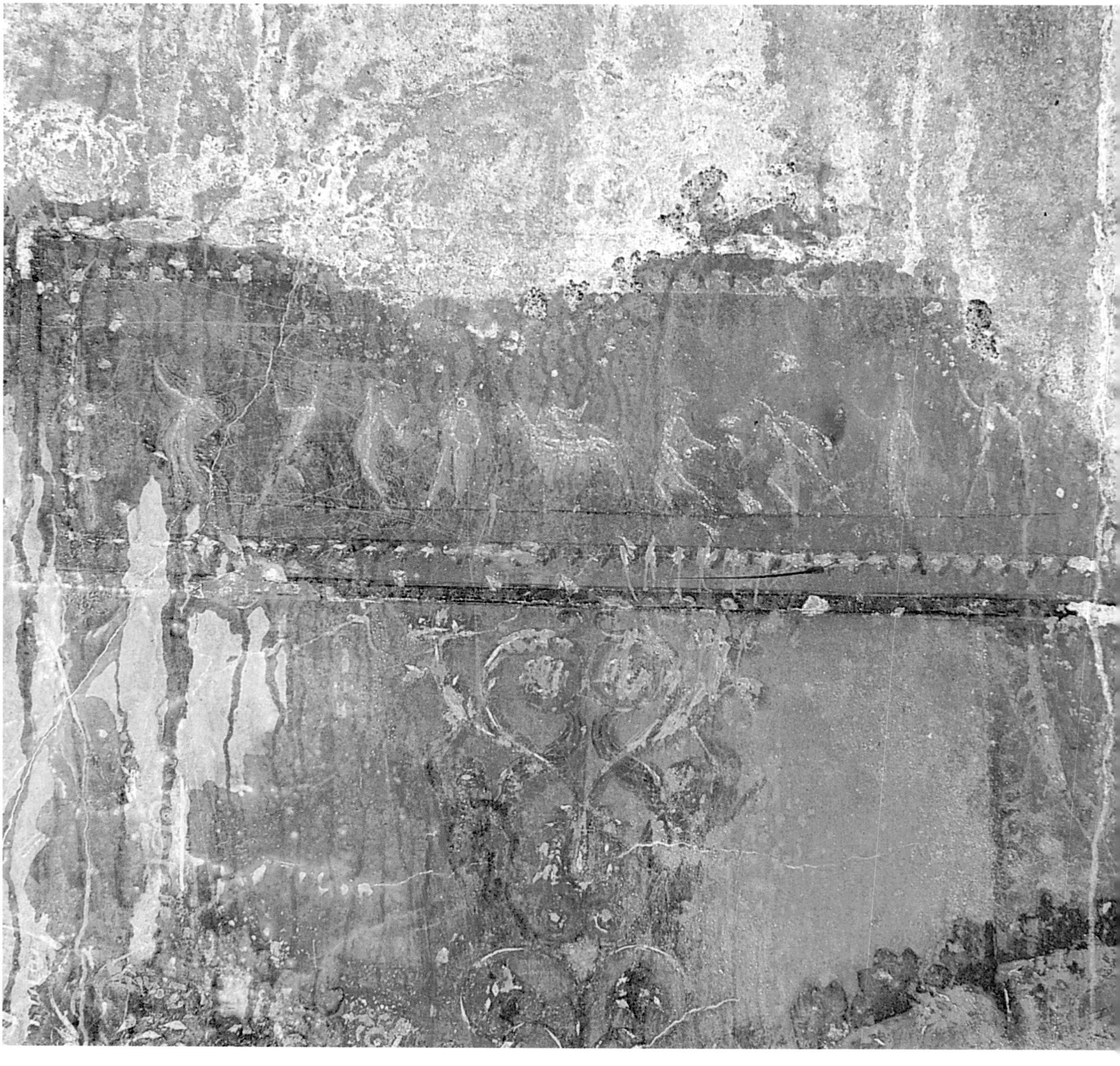

153. Room no. 33, vault, detail of the decoration with motif of pelta (lunate shield) with stucco figures

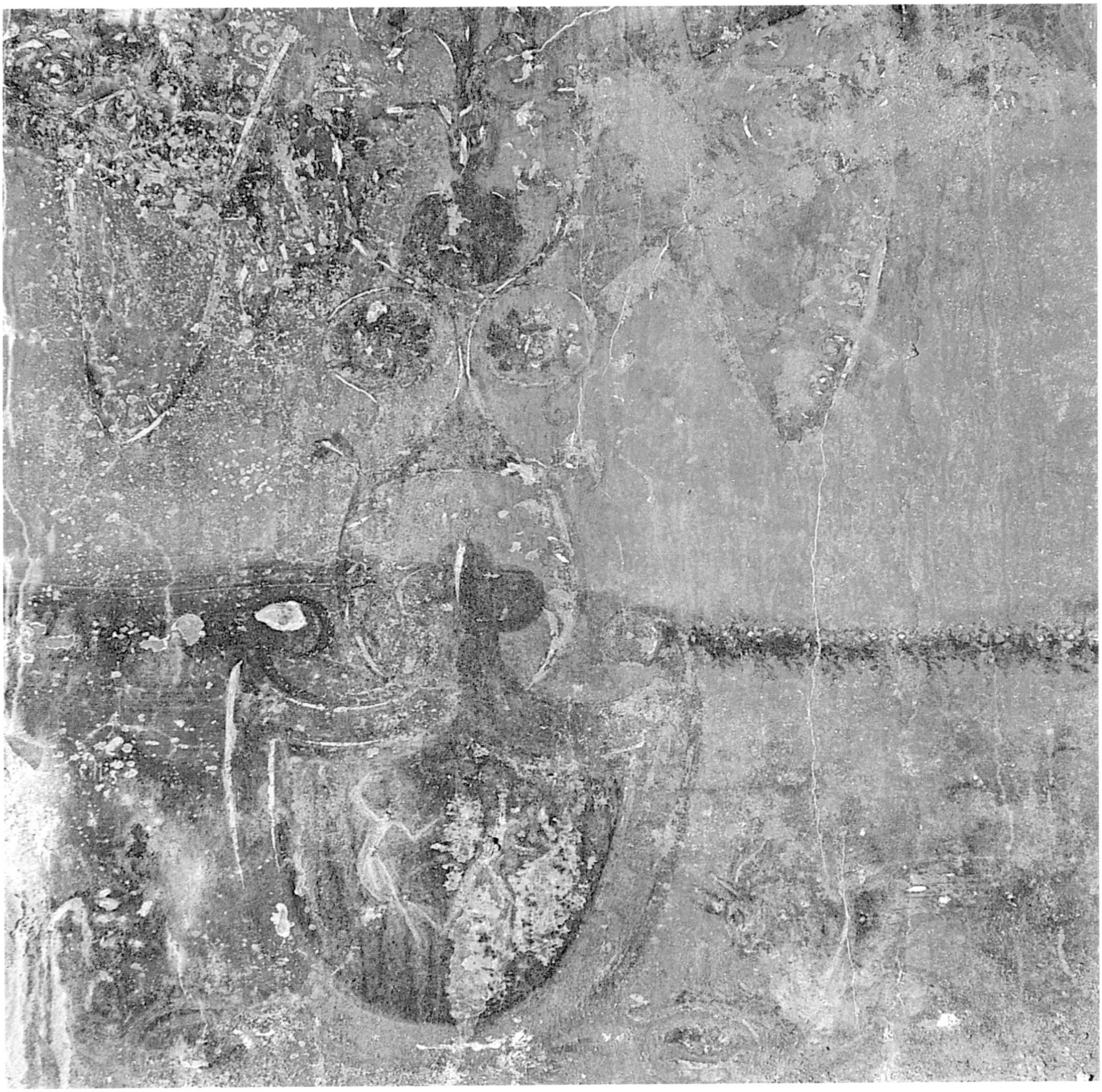

154. Room no. 33, vault, detail with scene depicting the birth of Dionysus

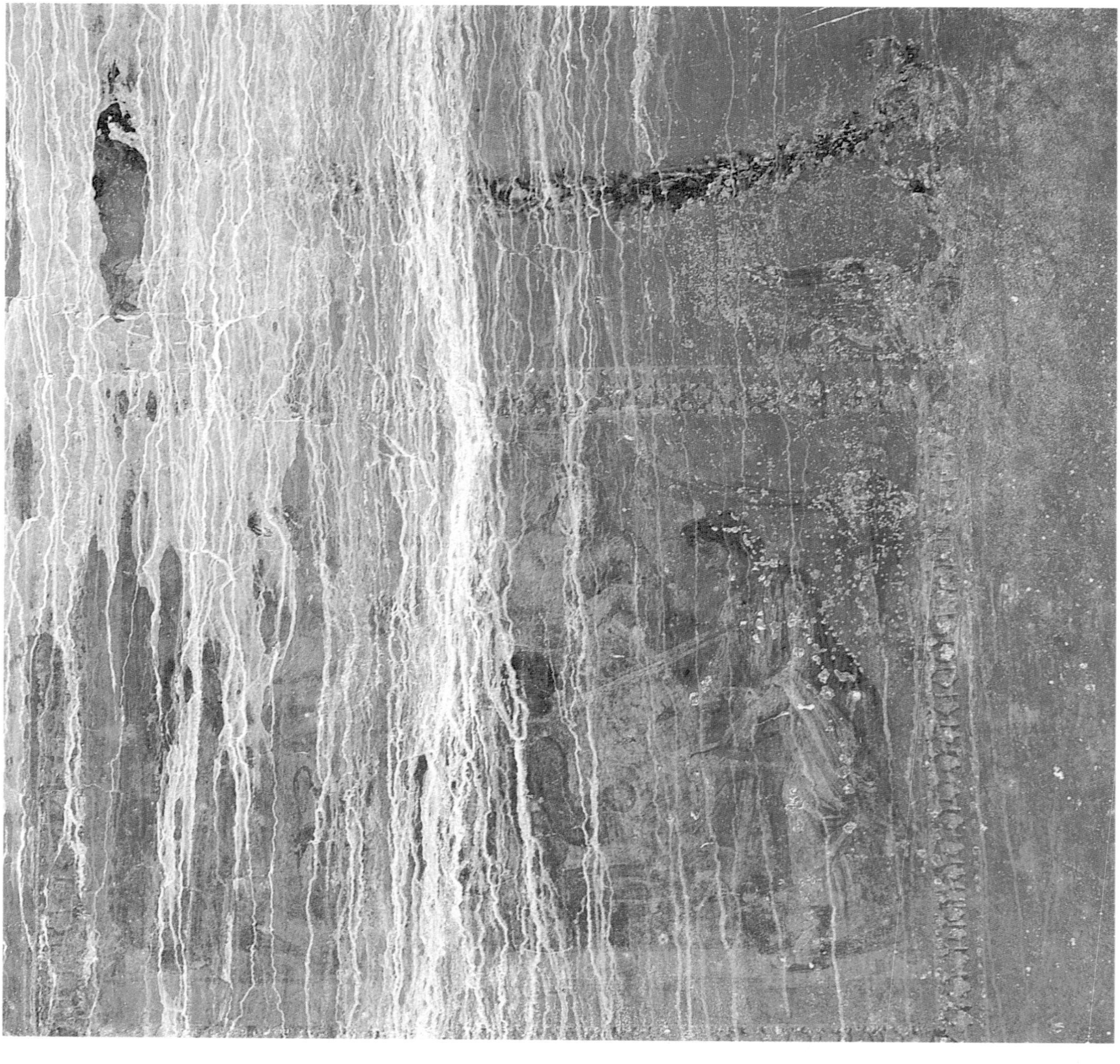

155. Room no. 33, vault, central panel depicting Dionysus and the Seasons (Mirri 1776)

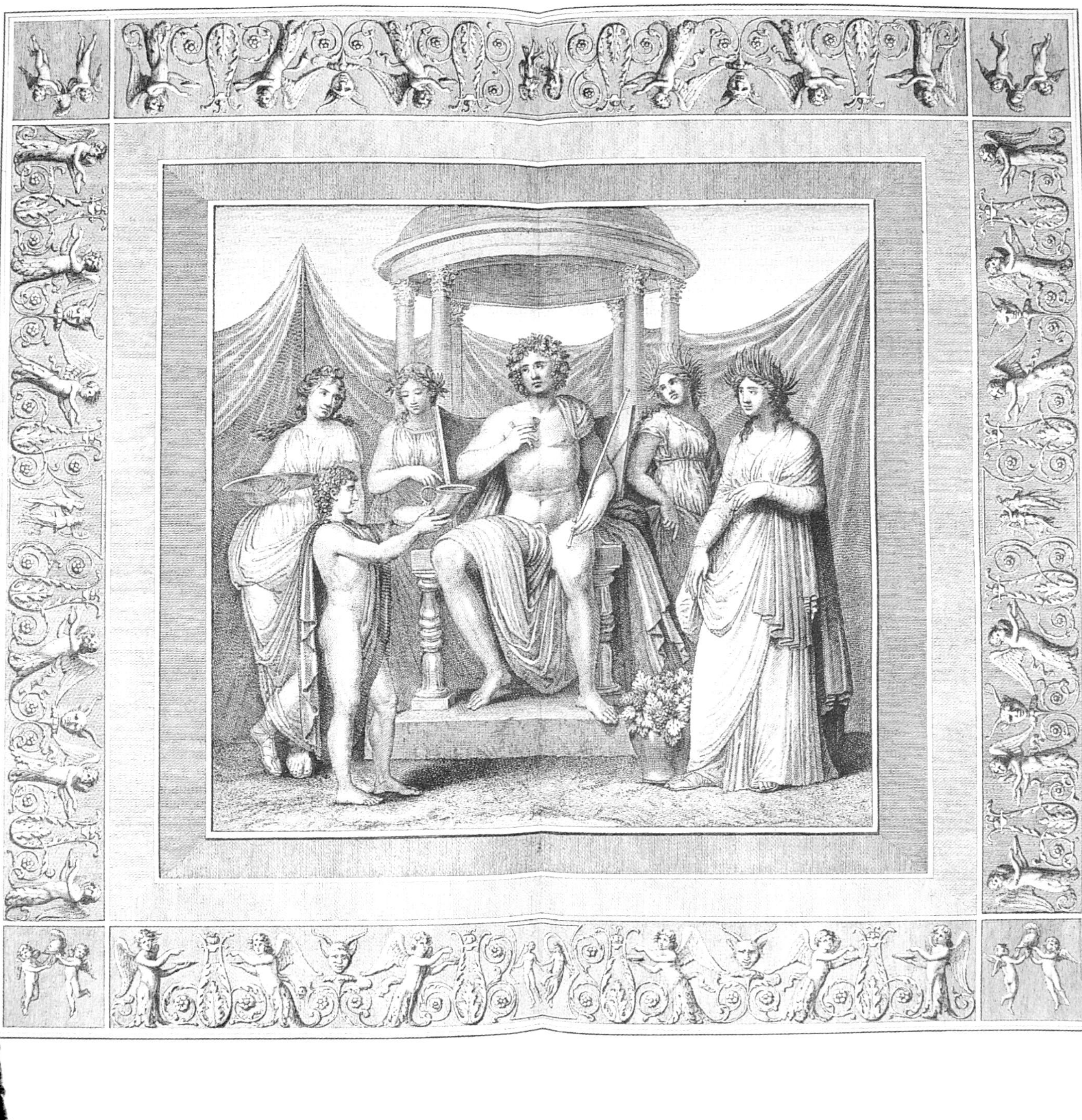

The abbreviations used for journals follow those of the Archäologische Bibliographie.

P.S. Bartoli, G.P. Bellori, *Le pitture antiche delle grotte di Roma e del sepolcro dei Nasoni*, Rome 1706.

L. Mirri, G. Carletti, *Le antiche camere delle Terme di Tito e le loro pitture*, Rome 1776.

N. Ponce, *Description des bains de Titus*, Paris 1786.

A. De Romanis, *Le antiche camere esquiline, dette comunemente delle Terme di Tito disegnate e illustrate*, Rome 1822, figs. I-IX.

F. Weege, *Bemalte und vergoldete Stuckdecke der Domus Aurea*, in *Antike Denkmäler*, III, 1912-1913, p.1 ff., figs. XIII-XVIII.

F. Weege, *Das goldene Haus des Nero*, JdI 28, 1913, pp. 1-118.

H.P. L'Orange, Domus Aurea, *der Sonnenpalast*, SymbOslo, suppl. 11, 1942, pp. 68-100.

C.L. Ragghianti, *Pitturi di Pompei*, Milan 1963.

N. Dacos, *Per la storia delle Grottesche. La riscoperta della Domus Aurea*, BdA, 51, 1966, pp. 43-49.

N. Dacos, *Fabullus et l'autre peintre de la Domus Aurea*, DialA, 2, 1968, pp. 210-226.

N. Dacos, *La découverte de la Domus Aurea et la formation des Grotesques à la Renaissance*, London – Leiden 1969.

A. Guiliano, *Pitture della Domus Aurea in disegni rinascimentali*, Xenia 11, 1981, pp. 78-82.

Y. Perrin, *Nicolas Ponce et la Domus Aurea de Neron: une documentation inédite*, MEFRA, 94, 1982, pp. 833-891.

W.J.T. Peters, *Die Landeschaftsbilder in den Wand- und Deckenmalereien der Domus Aurea*, BABesch, 57, 1982, pp. 52-62.

W.J.T. Peters, P.G.P. Meyboom, *The roots of provincial Roman painting: results of current research in Nero's Domus Aurea*, in *Roman Provincial Wall Painting of the Western Empire*, Oxford 1982, pp. 33-74.

P.G.P. Meyboom, *Fabullus démasqué*, in *Om de tuin geleid. Feestbundel Prof. W.J.T. Peters*, Nijmegen 1984, pp. 31-39.

M. de Vos, *Nerone, Seneca, Fabullo e la Domus Transitoria al Palatino*, in *Gli orti Farnesiani sul Palatino*, (International conference, Rome, 28 – 30 November 1985), Rome 1990, pp. 167-186.

W.J.T. Peters, P.G.P. Meyboom, *Decorazione ed ambiente nella Domus Aurea di Nerone*, in *Functional and spatial analysis of wall painting*, (Proceedings of the Fifth International Congress on Ancient Wall Painting, Amsterdam, 8-12 September 1992), Leiden 1993, pp. 59-63.

M. Royo, *Le palais dans la ville: formes et structures topographiques du pouvoir impérial d'Auguste à Néron*, MEFRA, 106, 1, 1994, pp. 219-245.

Lexicon Topographicum Urbis Romae, a cura di E.M. Steinby, I, Rome 1993, s.v. *Colossus: Nero* (C. Lega); II, Rome 1995, s.v. *Domus Aurea* (A. Cassatella); *Domus Aurea: vestibulum* (A. Cassatella, S. Panella); *Domus Aurea: area dello stagnum* (C. Panella); *Domus Aurea: porticus triplices miliariae* (E. Papi); *Domus Aurea: il palazzo sull' Esquilino* (L. Fabbrini); *Domus Aurea: complesso del Palatino* (A. Cassatella); *Domus Transitoria* (M. de Vos).

M. Medri, *Suet. Nero, 31. 1. Elementi e proposte per la ricostruzione della Domus Aurea*, in *Meta Sudans, 1. Un' area sacra 'in Palatio' e la valle del Colosseo prima e dopo Nerone*, Rome 1996, pp. 165-180.

S. Santoro Bianchi, *I passi plautini sulla pittura*, MEFRA, 109, 2, 1997, pp. 765-812.

E.M. Moorman, *La pitture romana fra costruzione architettonica e arte figurativa*, in *Romana Pictura: la pittura romana dalle origini all' età bizantina*, edited by A. Donati, (Catalogue of an exhibition, Rimini, 28 March – 30 August 1998), Milan 1998, pp. 14-32.

E.M. Moorman, *'Vivere come un uomo': l'uso dello spazio nella Domus Aurea,* in *Horti Romani,* (Acts of an International conference, Rome, 4-6 May 1995), edited by M. Cima, E. La Rocca, Rome 1998, pp. 345-361.

E. Champlin, *God and man in the Golden House,* in *Horti Romani* (cit. sop.), pp. 333-334.

SOURCES OF ILLUSTRATIONS AND PHOTOGRAPHS

134, 136, 137, 141, 142, 145, 146: Studio Pragma (Massimo Sabatini, Giuseppe Ruffo, Marco Fulgenzi)

28: Studio MCM (Marta Carusi, Monica Cola, Raffaella Cola, Franco Trasatti)

Photographic documentation edited by Eugenio Monti of the Soprintendenza Archeologica di Roma.
Photographs taken by Eugenio Monti with the Studio Cozzi-Scribani.

This volume has been published
on behalf of Elemond spa
by Tipografica La Piramide
(Rome) in 2001